D1259825

*Henry Fielding
and the
Language of Irony*

HENRY FIELDING
and the
LANGUAGE OF IRONY

Glenn W. Hatfield

CHICAGO & LONDON
The University of Chicago Press

Library of Congress Catalog Card Number: 68–16693
THE UNIVERSITY OF CHICAGO PRESS, CHICAGO 60637
The University of Chicago Press Ltd., London W.C.1
© *1968 by The University of Chicago*
All rights reserved
Published 1968
Printed in the United States of America

FOR LICIA
IN
MEMORY

ACKNOWLEDGMENTS

Much of the research on which this study is based was made possible by a United States Government (Fulbright) Grant, for which I should like to express my gratitude to the International Educational Exchange Program of the United States Government and to the United States Educational Commission in the United Kingdom. I should like to thank the University of Washington Graduate School and the Agnes H. Anderson Fund for financial aid, and *Modern Philology* (University of Chicago Press), *Philological Quarterly* (University of Iowa Press), and *Texas Studies in Literature and Language* (University of Texas Press) for permission to reprint material which appeared, in somewhat different form, in their pages.

I owe thanks also to Robert C. Elliott, who has seen the project through all its diverse phases and has offered invaluable counsel and encouragement at every stage; to James Sutherland, who read some of the early chapters, and Andrew Wright, who read an entire early draft; to my colleagues Elizabeth Dipple, Jocelyn Gilbertson Harvey, and Donald Taylor, who read all or parts of the manuscript at different stages; to Marie Farr, who typed the final draft; and to Anne Gilkey, who helped with the proofreading.

My deepest and saddest obligation is to my wife, Licia E. Hatfield, who did not live to see this book in print which now, so inadequately, honors her memory—"one whose image never can depart from my breast."

A NOTE ON TEXTS

At the time the present book goes to press, only one volume has appeared in print of the new Wesleyan Edition of *The Works of Henry Fielding*, which promises, on the strength of Mr. Battestin's excellent first volume, to be the authoritative edition that Fielding scholars have so long wanted. But in the meantime we must still make do with the so-called "Henley Edition" (*The Complete Works of Henry Fielding*, ed. William Ernest Henley, 16 vols. [New York: Croscup & Sterling, 1902], which, despite textual inaccuracies, remains the most comprehensive and generally accessible collected edition. For purposes of uniformity and convenience, therefore, all references to Fielding in my text will be to this edition. Wherever possible, however, I have taken the precaution of collating quotations with the original editions or with more reliable modern editions such as the Wesleyan *Joseph Andrews*, ed. Martin C. Battestin (Middletown, Conn.: Wesleyan University Press, 1967), the Regents Restoration Drama Series edition of *The Author's Farce*, ed. Charles B. Woods (Lincoln, Neb.: University of Nebraska Press, 1966), *The Tragedy of Tragedies*, ed. James T. Hillhouse (New Haven: Yale University Press, 1918), and *The Journal of a Voyage to Lisbon*, ed. Harold E. Pagliaro (New York: Nardon Press, 1963). Occasionally, as indicated in the footnotes, I have preferred readings from one of these texts. Unless otherwise noted, citations of the *Champion* are to the two-volume 1741 reprint edition. For the *Covent-Garden Journal* I have used the edition of Gerard Edward Jensen, 2 vols. (New Haven: Yale University Press, 1915); and for the *True Patriot*, that of Miriam Austen Locke (University, Ala: University of Alabama Press, 1964). References to the *Jacobite's Journal* are to the original paper, which has never been reprinted in full. Any other textual deviations or preferences are identified in the footnotes.

CONTENTS

INTRODUCTION

The eighteenth century, like the twentieth, was a language-conscious age. Everyone in the period, as S. A. Leonard says, "appears to have noted the imperfection of the language and the necessity for remedial measures."[1] The importance of this pre-occupation with language has been brought home to students of seventeenth- and eighteenth-century literature by the pioneering studies of R. F. Jones and George Williamson.[2] Martin Price, Aubrey Williams, and John Traugott, in their respective studies of Swift, Pope, and Sterne,[3] have shown how deeply it was felt in some of the major Augustan writers, and Dr. Johnson's well-known involvement with the subject has been freshly illuminated for our time by the work of W. K. Wimsatt.[4] But Henry Fielding, who in the words of Leslie Stephen, "more than anyone, gives the essential—the very form and pressure of the time,"[5] has never

[1] *The Doctrine of Correctness in English Usage, 1700–1800* (Madison, Wis.: University of Wisconsin Press, 1929), p. 11.
[2] Richard Foster Jones, "Science and English Prose Style in the Third Quarter of the Seventeenth Century," *The Seventeenth Century* (Stanford, Calif., Stanford University Press, 1951), pp. 75–110; "The Attack on Pulpit Eloquence in the Restoration: An Episode in the Development of the Neo-Classical Standard for Prose," *ibid.*, pp. 111–42; "Science and Language in England of the Mid-Seventeenth Century," *ibid.*, pp. 143–60; *The Triumph of the English Language: A Survey of Opinions Concerning the Vernacular from the Introduction of Printing to the Restoration* (Stanford, Calif., Stanford University Press, 1953). George Williamson, "The Restoration Revolt against Enthusiasm," *Studies in Philology*, 30 (1933): 571–603; *The Senecan Amble: A Study in Prose from Bacon to Collier* (London and Chicago, 1951; reissued 1966).
[3] Martin Price, *Swift's Rhetorical Art: A Study in Structure and Meaning* (New Haven: Yale University Press, 1953); Aubrey Williams, *Pope's Dunciad: A Study of Its Meaning* (Baton Rouge: Louisiana State University Press, 1955); John Traugott, *Tristam Shandy's World: Sterne's Philosophical Rhetoric* (Berkeley and Los Angeles: University of California Press, 1954).
[4] *The Prose Style of Samuel Johnson* (New Haven: Yale University Press, 1941); *Philosophic Words: A Study of Style and Meaning in the "Rambler" and "Dictionary" of Samuel Johnson* (New Haven: Yale University Press, 1948).
[5] Leslie Stephen, *History of English Thought in the Eighteenth Century* (London, 1876), 2: 380.

been accorded the serious attention he deserves as an author whose attitude toward language not only places him firmly within this tradition of linguistic criticism and reform but also, since the writer is involved with language above all men, is crucially relevant to his art.

Fielding has not, indeed, in the traditional view, been credited with much sophistication at all in matters of language. As a stylist he has been both praised and damned, but it is open to question whether the negative or positive opinions have misrepresented him most. One can dismiss as mere slander such contemporary criticisms as the one in *Old England* for September 5, 1748, attacking Fielding's "Ignorance in Grammar, his false English and his Meanness of Language."[6] William Godwin's charge that the style of *Tom Jones* is "feeble, costive and slow" and that it is marked by a "hide-bound sportiveness" which is "hard, pedantic and unnatural" is surely perverse.[7] Taine's judgment that Fielding was a "careless," slapdash stylist, an "amiable buffalo" who lacked "even literary vanity," only betrays the Frenchman's lack of sympathy for Fielding's English temperament.[8] And William Mudford's editorial opinion that his style was careless, ungrammatical, and full of "inelegancies" and that Fielding must "have studied the art of writing with very little attention" can be relegated to the unattended grave of minor criticism from which it was exhumed.[9]

But the praise of Fielding's admirers, well-intentioned as it doubtless is, is not so handily dealt with. Its dominant effect, placing the emphasis on Fielding's stylistic vigor and "ease" to the exclusion, almost, of everything else, has been to represent him as a writer gifted in his loquacity but without subtlety, sophistication, or verbal sensitivity. George Eliot, in a famous passage in *Middlemarch*, expressed delight in "the lusty ease of his fine English."[10] John Stuart Mill declared that Fielding's style combines "in a remarkable degree ease with

---

[6]Cited by Frederick T. Blanchard, *Fielding the Novelist* (New Haven: Yale University Press, 1926), p. 32.

[7]"Of English Style," *The Enquirer* (London, 1797). Cited by Blanchard, p. 241.

[8]*History of English Literature*, trans. Van Laun (London, 1871), 2: 176. Cited by Blanchard, pp. 444–45.

[9]Preface, *British Novelists* (London, 1811). Cited by Wilbur L. Cross, *The History of Henry Fielding* (New Haven: Yale University Press, 1918), 3: 202–3.

[10](London, 1871), 1: 250–51. Cited by Blanchard, p. 453.

force."[11] Andrew Lang wrote of its "delightful ease."[12] Henry Craik noted its "massive carelessness" but praised its "consummate ease," which is entirely free, he added, of "constraint of subtlety."[13] J. H. Lobban commended Fielding's "vigorous easy style."[14] However valid such criticism may be impressionistically, it fails to take into account the expense of conscious art with which the effect of "ease" was achieved, and it misses entirely the awareness of medium, the consciousness of the process of communication between character and character and between author and reader, the sheer sensitivity to language, which are the marks of Fielding's writing at least as much as the surface effects of stylistic "ease" and "vigor."

Even Andrew Wright, whose recent analysis of the rhetoric of the novels eloquently illuminates the richness and complexity of Fielding's linguistic consciousness, emphasizes the "festive" role of his stylistic mannerisms somewhat at the expense, it seems to me, of the serious concern with language that underlies this verbal "play." For though it is true that "Fielding means not simply to criticize [the abuses of speech that he mimics] but also to delight," it is a misleading oversimplification to argue that these mannerisms have "the purpose of rejoicing in the follies which language is capable of, *rather than* of condemning the impure or inaccurate use of language" (my italics),[15] when "*as well as*" would surely state the case more fairly. As Henry Knight Miller explains in another recent study of Fielding's rhetoric, the effect is not just verbal exuberance for its own sake but also "a deepened consciousness that the language (and the actions) of a society customarily assume an ideal world of values, where motives are clear, things are really what they seem, and words mean exactly what they are supposed to mean—but that *in fact* there is a comic gulf between this pleasing assumption and the, one may say, existential reality."[16]

[11]*Autobiography* (New York, 1874), p. 117. Cited by Blanchard, p. 364.
[12]*Letters in Literature* (London & New York, 1889), p. 38. Cited by Blanchard, p. 491.
[13]Introduction, *English Prose Selections* (New York, 1895), 4: 10. Cited by Blanchard, pp. 499–500.
[14]*English Essays* (London, 1896). Cited by Blanchard, p. 500.
[15]*Henry Fielding: Mask and Feast* (Berkeley and Los Angeles: University of California Press, 1965), p. 180.
[16]"Some Functions of Rhetoric in *Tom Jones*," *Philological Quarterly*, 45 (1966): 230–31.

Nor is Miller the first of his critics to recognize the seriousness of Fielding's concern with language. Leslie Stephen noticed how pointedly he distinguished between the moral codes by which men actually lived and those "by which they affected to be governed in language," and how, like Dr. Johnson, he "refused to be imposed upon by phrases."[17] Winfield H. Rogers has pointed out that Fielding's "use of words as satiric or ethical symbols is at once a part of his predilection for symbolism and of his desire for exact expression. . . . It was ethically, and frequently satirically, effective to show what terms had, might, or should stand for."[18] Sheridan Baker has found the chief virtue of Fielding's style to lie not in its ease or vigor but in Fielding's "alert attention to the meanings of words."[19] Middleton Murry has noted how this works to clear "our minds . . . of cant."[20] Morris Golden has written of Fielding's "distrust" and "suspicion" of language,[21] and William B. Coley has called attention to his "attitude toward the corrupting word."[22]

Fielding's attitude toward the corrupting word is the subject of the present study. Or rather, it is about Fielding's attitude toward the word as both corrupting and corruptible. For corruption, as Fielding saw it, worked both ways. "There is a strict Analogy," he wrote, "between the Taste and Morals of an Age; and Depravity in one always induces Depravity in the other."[23] Debased language contributed to the undermining of society, but a debased society also contributed to the undermining of language, and to a man who was both moralist and man of letters, as Fielding eminently was, the alternatives seemed equally bad.

"It is possible," he observed in *Tom Jones*, "for a man to convey a lie in the words of truth."[24] The passage, in context, has

---

[17]*History of English Thought in the Eighteenth Century*, 2: 377.

[18]"Fielding's Early Aesthetic and Technique," *Studies in Philology*, 40 (1943): 541–42.

[19]"Henry Fielding and the Cliché," *Criticism*, 1 (1959): 357.

[20]"In Defence of Fielding," *Unprofessional Essays* (London: Cape, 1956), p. 49.

[21]*Fielding's Moral Psychology* (Amherst: University of Massachusetts Press, 1966), p. 150.

[22]"Fielding's Comic: A Study of the Relations between Wit and Seriousness in a Comic Augustan" (Ph.D. diss., Yale University, 1954), p. 220.

[23]Letter XL, in Sarah Fielding's *Familiar Letters between the Principal Characters in David Simple* (London, 1747), 2: 298.

[24]*The Complete Works of Henry Fielding*, ed. William Ernest Henley (New York: Croscup & Sterling, 1903), 5: 334. All volume and page references in my text will be to this edition.

to do with the unmasking of a hypocrite, Blifil's confederate Mr. Dowling. But it is also typical of Fielding's pervasive awareness that the medium in which he worked and the motives which moved him were both subject to the grim possibility of corruption, of perversion, of prostitution. The problem, then, on the one hand, was to gauge the effects of the abuse of language on the society in which it was practiced. But equally a matter for concern was the question of what happens to the "words of truth," the common stock of language available alike to the hypocrite and the honest man, to the hired hack and the serious writer, when these words are regularly perverted to the service of lies. Do the words escape unsoiled, or do they bear the taint of the lie? May the honest man speak them or the serious author write them with the assurance that his own sincerity will scrub them clean and restore their pristine values, or will they remain suspect and spread their rot to the thoughts and sentiments they convey? Is the communication of truth, indeed, in the form of the direct profession, possible at all? The problem was a real one for Fielding, and he was not alone in the eighteenth century in his concern about it. Thomas Jefferson, in a letter to George Washington, complained that he was unable to express his gratitude for Washington's services to his country, "for such is become the prostitution of language that sincerity has no longer distinct terms in which to express her own truths."[25]

Fielding's sensitivity to the linguistic prostitutions of his age and his lifetime search for a means, in the absence of "distinct terms," of expressing the truths of sincerity, are the concerns of this book. For everywhere one turns in his works, from the earliest plays through the great novels, one comes upon expressions of the theme and sees evidence of Fielding's personal struggle with a corrupt and intractable medium. An understanding of his attitude toward language and communication helps account not only for his hatred of hypocrisy, but also for his contempt for Grub Street, his suspicion of politics, his distrust of the learned professions, and his aversion to polite society. Even more important, perhaps, Fielding's preoccupation with language and communication suggests an underlying rationale for some of his

[25]Jan. 22, 1783, *The Papers of Thomas Jefferson*, ed. Julian P. Boyd *et al.*, (Princeton, N.J.: Princeton University Press, 1952), 6: 222.

most characteristic methods as a writer—for his self-conscious manipulation of style, for his use of the notorious "interpolated tales," for his elaborate apparatus of authorial self-dramatization (including those favorite cruxes of the critics, the prefatory chapters, the digressions, and the "intrusive" commentary), and finally (as my title tries to suggest) for his commitment to the mode of irony as a kind of sublimation of the very corruptions of speech which that irony mocks and exploits—a special language, almost like poetic diction, in which the truths of sincerity might be reunited at last with the words of truth. For "the language of irony," as I hope to be able to show in the succeeding chapters, is for Fielding a way of at once exposing the corruption of words and rescuing them from the debased condition into which they have fallen. It is a way of speaking truth in a corrupt medium.

Chapter I
THE CORRUPTION OF LANGUAGE

"Several Words, in all Languages," Fielding wrote in the *Champion* for January 12, 1739/40, "have, with great Injustice been wrested and perverted . . ., and, by long Use and Corruption, been brought to convey Ideas foreign to their original Signification." The statement, like so many of Fielding's observations on language, occurs in an ironic context: his subject is turncoats, whom he has undertaken to defend on the ground "that no Man is so good a Judge of the true Merits of a Cause, as he who hath been on both Sides of it." Typically, however, Fielding is conscious of the key term of his discussion *as a word*. That is, he feels compelled to call attention to it, to isolate it for a moment from its context, and to scrutinize it as a phenomenon in its own right.

The word "turncoat," he solemnly assures his readers, "is an Instance of this Injustice" done to certain words. Originally, he says, it was "intended to express what we generally call good Housewifery," and turncoats were simply men who, "as soon as their Coat was sufficiently soiled on one Side, were wont to order it to the right about, and make a very handsome and decent Figure with the other Side." Later, however, the term was "metaphorically applied to those Gentlemen, who, perhaps, from much the same Reasons, turned from one Party to the other; changing their Opinions, as the other did their Coats, to the very Reverse of what they formerly were." It takes its place, then—like "the *Greek* Word for Tyrant, which originally signified no more than King; and in our Language the Words Knave, Villain, etc."—among those "Words which have been once used in a much better Sense than they at present enjoy." But as the apologist for "those Gentlemen" to whom it is now applied, Fielding argues that the term has still "a very strong

7

Title to those frugal Honours which it originally received," and he hopes that "these my Labours may again restore it" to that original honorific sense.

The passage is interesting for several reasons. No one is likely to misunderstand that Fielding's real purpose in focusing attention on the word and its meanings is not to extenuate the shame of the turncoat but to expose it all the more nakedly. If "turncoat" in its original literal sense meant what Fielding says it did, then it expressed not "good Housewifery," but just the opposite —the kind of grubby attention to appearances typified by sweeping dirt under the carpet or changing one's collar instead of taking a bath. Thus the metaphorical turncoat, the trader in political allegiances, is twice condemned by analysis of the word which describes him: his defection is not only "wrong" in some abstract moral sense, it is also sordid and petty and ridiculous. We should not, then (as readers of Augustan literature should scarcely need to be reminded), be put off by irony when judging the "seriousness" of such a passage. Fielding is not *really* trying to rescue the word "turncoat" from its pejorative associations, but in a very real and serious sense he *is* laboring to "restore it" to its "original meaning," or rather, he is trying to revive in the word the vivid metaphorical implications which he feels have been worn away by thoughtless usage. If it is not actually, as he pretends to think, one of those words brought "by long Use and Corruption . . . to convey Ideas foreign to their original Signification," it yet has in common with such words the fact of "corruption": it has undergone a diminution of power and immediacy, and the writer who wants it to convey its full potential force to his reader is obliged to pause, as Fielding does, and labor at restoring its "original" sense. Without such reinforcement the word fails to communicate the "idea" the writer assigns it. The corruption of usage has rendered it unfit to carry its rightful burden of meaning.

Despite the ironic tone of the passage, therefore, there is every reason to believe that Fielding's complaint of the "great Injustice" done to words by the wrestings and perversions of usage was seriously meant, and that the doctrine of linguistic corruption it records was for him a valid one. Still, if this were his only statement of the idea one would be justified in taking it as a mere satiric device of the moment, a handy expedient for getting at the turncoats who are the objects of attack, and one would probably be right in not attaching any importance to it as evidence of Fielding's genuine attitude toward language and communication. But it is *not* an isolated phenomenon in his work. As with Swift and Pope and Sterne, Fielding's view of language must be pieced out largely from his scattered references and remarks and inferred from various aspects of his practice. None of the major writers of the eighteenth century—not even Swift in his *Proposal for Correcting, Improving, and Ascertaining the English Tongue* or Johnson in his Preface to the *Dictionary*—left anything resembling a fully developed theory of language, and Fielding was no exception. But on at least three occasions—once near the beginning of his most productive period, once near the middle of it, and once near the end—he put his views down in a form explicit and extensive enough to suggest that the corruption of language was a serious matter to him throughout his career and that it had implications far beyond the immediate applications he makes in any one of these instances. None of these statements is entirely free of the complicating ambiguities of irony, but neither can any of them be lightly dismissed for that reason. The subject, in every case, emerges as a serious one, and Fielding's brand of irony is itself, as we shall see, very often as much an instrument for the critique of language as a weapon against the other vices and follies of mankind.

The first of Fielding's principal statements on the corruption of language appeared in the next issue but one of the *Champion* after the paper on turncoats. Apparently feeling that the idea deserved an essay to itself, Fielding begins (as was traditional in discourses on language) with the question of whether or not the gift of speech is exclusively human and one of the factors which distinguish men from animals. He decides that "tho' the Use of Speech be not peculiar to Man, I believe the Abuse of it is." The emphasis, however, is not on the semantic distortion which had been his pretended subject in the earlier *Champion* essay, or on the weakening of metaphorical force which had been his real concern in that paper, but on the utter meaninglessness of many words and phrases currently in use in polite speech, professional discourse, and the parlance of tradesmen. "I am inclined to believe," he declares, "that if we could, by a kind of Chemical Operation, separate those Parts of our ordinary Conversation, which either leave any Idea in the Mind of the Speaker, or convey any to that of the Hearer, from those which do not, the former would be found scarce to bear the Proportion of a tenth Part to the latter."

Here again the generally facetious tone of the piece and the satiric exaggeration of certain parts of it are warnings that it must not be taken literally as a statement of Fielding's views on language. Plainly his case against the persons under attack was not limited to their abuse of words, and it is clear that to some extent the account of their linguistic corruptions is as much a means of exposing these other failings as it is an end in itself. But the basic seriousness of Fielding's position may be sought not merely in his satiric exploitation of the theme but also in what is surely a genuine concern over the linguistic effects of the "Word-squandering" which he sees going on at all levels of society, a concern, as always, for what happens to the "words of truth" when they are perverted to unworthy ends. "What a Number of Words," he cries at one point, "hath . . . Custom stripp'd of their Ideas, and in a Manner annihilated?"

Whether Fielding really believed that 90 per cent of the words spoken in ordinary discourse contributed nothing to the communication of ideas, we have no way of knowing. But even the certain knowledge that this was an exaggeration for effect and a device for getting on with his attack on various elements of society would not invalidate the linguistic criticism which follows it. Fielding plainly believed that such thoughtlessly squandered phrases as "obedient humble Servant," "upon my Honour," and "very cheap" *were* lowered in value, *were*, in fact, in some cases, rendered all but worthless as sincere expressions of truth, and that the words out of which they were composed did not escape contamination even when removed to some other context. If "obedient humble Servant" is a meaningless pleasantry, and as often as not an insincere one, then what becomes of the word "humble" and the word "obedient"? Emptied of meaning in one phrase, can they regain it in another? Will they not always be diminished in strength and redolent of insincerity as a consequence of this "corruption"? If the oath "upon my Honour" has become a mere expletive sworn by villains and good men alike, then does not "Honour," a word traditionally supposed to carry a heavy load of dignity, suffer as well? Can the honest writer or speaker trust such corrupted words to convey his meanings, and, if not, how is one to express the mighty idea for which "Honour" once stood?

Titles are corruptive for the same reason, for though "Honourable" and "Right Honourable" may serve in communication as *labels*, Fielding's charge that they are "stript of all Ideas whatever" is, like his examination of the word "turncoat" in the earlier *Champion* essay, a complaint against the use of words without thought of their "original" (or literal) meanings. This, he felt, compounds corruption by leading men to acquiesce in the application of titles to those whose lives and principles are a mockery of the titles' original meanings and so to contribute still further to the debasement of the grand abstractions from which they originally derived. "Doctor," he wants his readers to remember, meant a learned man, and he believed that this knowledge alone was enough to give the lie to the quacks who had appropriated the word as a cover for their own ignorance. Thoughtless usage, in Fielding's view, had a lot to answer for, and he believed that the restoration of words to their rightful values would expose the deceits which masked themselves in meaningless language. A knowledge of the meanings of words was a protection against the impostures of society.

But if singling out as meaningless such phrases as "learned in the Law" and "fair Trader" is an oblique way of saying that lawyers are not so wise as they pretend to be nor tradesmen so honest as they claim, it is also a form of protest against the removal of these phrases from the language of sincerity. Having been pressed into the service of the lie, they are forever contaminated with the suspicion of untruth, and the man who wants to describe a *truly* learned lawyer or a *truly* honest merchant is put to the trouble of finding other means of expressing these ideas. But even more disturbing to the man who desires to express a simple truth in the most simple and direct language is the fact that the pretense and the claim themselves, insofar as they are conveyed in words, are corruptive of language—not just of particular phrases but of the process of verbal communication itself.

Fielding, we may be sure, understood why the Houyhnhnms in *Gulliver's Travels*, shocked at the human predilection for saying *the Thing which was not*, should have reminded Gulliver that "the Use of Speech was to make us understand one another, and to receive Information of Facts."[1] If "learned in the Law" and "fair Trader" are suspect because they serve other masters than truth, then in a sense *all* pretenses and claims in language are suspect, and a man whose livelihood and mission in life involved him intimately in the values of language—"what if Nature hath granted to us, we have . . . barbarously and scandalously abused"[2] —could not be expected to accept such a dilemma lightly.

How Fielding's refusal to accept this situation was reflected in other aspects of his work will be the subject of later chapters. For the present we are concerned merely with examining his explicit treatments of the theme. The next of these, of any length or consequence, was his *Essay on Conversation*, which was published in the *Miscellanies* of 1743. Fielding's topic was broader than a modern understanding of the title might suggest, subsuming the verbal aspects of conversation within its larger social sense. For to Fielding and his age the word "conversation" had a much more general meaning than it possesses today: it meant social intercourse in general and therefore included actions (social behavior) as well as words. The "art of conversation" becomes, then, for Fielding, "the art of pleasing or doing good to one another," and is founded on "good-breeding." For this reason his attitude toward some of the same linguistic "abuses" he habitually attacks elsewhere is here softened by the spirit of toleration. Conventional compliments, forms, and titles, empty as they are, yet serve a useful purpose in society because "the business of the whole is no more than to convey to others an idea of your esteem of them, which is, indeed the substance of all the compliments, ceremonies, presents, and whatever passes between well-bred people." Philosophers may point to their lack of meaning and consequence, but "The truth is, we live in a world of common men, and not of philosophers."

Yet Fielding's personal contempt for such hollow forms,

---

[1]*The Prose Works of Jonathan Swift*, ed. Herbert Davis (Oxford: Shakespeare Head Press, 1941), 11: 224.
[2]*Champion*, Jan. 17, 1739/40.

despite his official recognition of their social value, is apparent too: "These ceremonies, poor as they are, are of more consequence than they at first appear, and, in reality, constitute the only external difference between man and man. Thus, His grace, Right honourable, My lord, Right reverend, Reverend, Honourable, Sir, Esquire, Mr., etc., have in a philosophical sense no meaning, yet are perhaps politically essential, and must be preserved by good-breeding." And once this contempt is awakened, he finds it impossible to restrain the ironic virulence which such abuse of noble and once meaningful words everywhere arouses in him.

If men were to be rightly estimated, and divided into subordinate classes, according to the superior excellence of their several natures, perhaps the lowest class of either sex would be properly assigned to those two disgraces of the human species, *commonly called a beau, and a fine lady.* . . . I have myself seen a little female thing *which they have called My Lady*, of no greater dignity in the order of beings than a cat, and of no more use in society than a butterfly; whose mien would not give even the idea of a gentlewoman, and whose face would cool the loosest libertine; with a mind as empty of ideas as an opera, and a body fuller of diseases than an hospital—I have seen this thing express contempt to a woman who was an honour to her sex, and an ornament to the creation. (XIV, 248, 252, 265–66; my italics)

It would be a mistake, though, on the basis of even such a fine outburst as this, to attempt to read the whole of *An Essay on Conversation* as ironic. The spirit in which it is written is dominantly permissive, and its purpose, as Fielding himself specified in the Preface to the *Miscellanies*, was "to show, that true good-breeding consists in contributing . . . to the satisfaction and happiness of all" (XII, 238). Fielding is ever the realist, fully at home in a world populated by "common men, and not . . . philosophers," and a willingness to compromise with the ideal is one of the hallmarks of his moral realism. Yet he never, let it be said, loses sight of the ideal, and the significance of the ambivalent linguistic attitude one finds in *An Essay on Conversation* is that even in the act of compromise he cannot resist calling attention to the corruption of language which this compromise entails.

Terms like "beau" and "fine lady" may serve a useful function in society as tags attached to certain types and classes of persons, without any normative connotations, but, even while acknowledging this, Fielding is not willing to let the matter rest. He is compelled to let his readers know that these terms had—and for him still have—primary meanings as well, and that judged by these the persons "commonly called a beau and a fine lady" stand condemned for their unworthiness to the titles they bear. For him the so-called "fine lady" is "a little female thing" and "this thing"—more accurate terms, it is suggested, than her conventional title, and implicit definitions (precise in their very lack of qualification) of the popular sense of the term. But at the same time, the inescapable fact that such persons *are* "commonly" so called has corrupted the titles themselves beyond redemption, and to attempt to employ them in their original senses, without special precautions, would be insulting to the persons so described. One is forced, then, to search for substitutes. "Gentlewoman" (unlike its companion term "gentleman") has apparently escaped corruption by virtue of its comparative rarity, and, preserving the ideas of "gentleness" and "gentility" among its connotations,[3] serves Fielding as a synonym for "fine lady" without sharing in the obloquy of its indiscriminate popular application. And though we do not know the station in life of the person Fielding sets in opposition to the "little female thing" (one is tempted, from the sheer emotional force of the passage, to suppose it was a real person, and some one close to him), it is surely significant that he refers to her simply as "a woman," allowing the qualifying clause which follows to do the job of implying that it is she who has the juster claim to the title which "this thing" and others of her type have corrupted. There is no doubt that Fielding recognized the inevitability of the linguistic corruptions he recorded and was even able to appreciate their social necessity, and it is true that he was perfectly capable of using the idea, facetiously or with ironic bitterness, as a means to other ends. But it is also true that he was deeply conscious of the fact of corruption in the words which were his own medium of expression and that he was everywhere involved in a personal decontamination of the English language.

[3]See below, pp. 120–21.

Neither the *Champion* papers nor the *Essay on Conversation*, however, really seems to support the implication of the "turn-coat" piece that Fielding was concerned with words brought "by long Use and Corruption . . . to convey Ideas foreign to their original Signification." In each of these essays he seems more occupied with the absence of meaning than with its perversions. In one sense, of course, the reduction of words to meaningless-ness is itself a perversion, but it does not fit the examples of "tyrant," "knave," and "villain" which Fielding cites in the "turncoat" paper and would seem to constitute another kind of corruption. Or more accurately perhaps, meaninglessness is the final stage of corruption, the condition of pure verbalism apo-theosized in Pope's vision in *The Dunciad* of the "uncreating word."[4] But surely there are intermediate stages in the corruptive process. A word does not become meaningless overnight, and if "Honour" no longer carried any sense of its "original idea" in the oath "upon my Honour" or in the title "Right Honourable," it yet must have meant *something*, however diminished by these associations, when used in other contexts. This kind of inter-mediate corruptions of words—in some ways more dangerous than utter meaninglessness because conveying perverse ideas rather than no ideas at all—was the subject of Fielding's third and final major treatment of the corruption of language theme in a satiric essay in the *Covent-Garden Journal* for January 14, 1752.

The method, once again, is ironic. Ostensibly the object of attack is "that Privilege which Divines and moral Writers have assumed to themselves of doing Violence to certain Words, in Favour of their own Hypotheses, and of using them in a Sense often directly contrary to that which Custom (the absolute Lord and Master, according to Horace, of all the Modes of Speech) hath allotted them." The consequence of "this Abuse of Words," says Fielding, is very grave: "For whilst the Author and the World receive different Ideas from the same Words, it will be pretty difficult for them to comprehend each other's Meaning; and hence, perhaps, it is that so many Gentlemen and Ladies have contracted a general Odium to all Works of Religion or Morality; and that many others have been Readers in this Way

[4] *The Works of Alexander Pope*, Twickenham ed., vol. 5, ed. James Sutherland (London: Methuen, 1943), p. 409.

all their Lives without understanding what they read, consequently without drawing from it any practical Use." But the most
striking feature of the paper is the "Modern Glossary" Fielding
appends to the essay. This list, he explains, of terms "at present
greatly in Use," is intended as an aid not to the readers but to the
writers of moral treatises, for it is the latter, after all, who are out
of touch with current usage. The glossary will supply this deficiency by fixing to the words "those exact Ideas which are annexed
to every of them in the World," and thus make fruitful communication once again possible between "the learned in
Colleges" and "the polite Part of Mankind."

It would be possible, up to this point, to read the *Covent-
Garden Journal* essay as straightforward criticism, in the tradition, perhaps, of John Eachard's critique of pulpit oratory in
Grounds and Occasions of the Contempt of the Clergy (1670), upon
the linguistic abuses of moralists and theologians. Only our
knowledge that Fielding would not have seriously deprecated
"the Works of Barrow, Tillotson, Clark, and others of this
Kind," whom he here sets up as representative moralists and
divines whose language needs "the Labour of a good Commentator,"[5] and our sense that he seldom uses terms like "the
World" and "the polite Part of Mankind" as other than ironic
corruptions, make us wary. But we have only to look at the
Glossary itself to confirm our suspicions that the linguistic abuse
Fielding is attacking is not that of the learned moralists but that
of the "Gentlemen and Ladies" whose usage he pretends to
admire. The first word, ANGEL, is "The Name of a Woman,
commonly of a very bad one." Further on, DAMNATION is
"A Term appropriate to the Theatre; though sometimes more
largely applied to all Works of Invention." DEATH is defined as
"The final End of Man; as well of the *thinking Part of the Body*,
as of all the other Parts." RELIGION is dismissed as "A Word of
no Meaning; but which serves as a Bugbear to frighten Children
with." TEMPERANCE becomes "Want of Spirit"; and VIRTUE

---

[5] For Fielding's debt to and high regard for these moral and religious writers, see James
A. Work, "Henry Fielding, Moral Censor," *The Age of Johnson* (New Haven: Yale
University Press, 1949), pp. 139–48; and Martin C. Battestin, *The Moral Basis of
Fielding's Art: A Study of "Joseph Andrews"* (Middletown, Conn.: Wesleyan University
Press, 1959).

and VICE are bracketed together merely as "Subjects of Discourse."

The "words of truth" are suffering here not at the hands of pedantry, nor are they necessarily the victims of hypocrisy. They are simply the verbal products of a corrupt society, measuring by their semantic distortions the widening distance between the ideal (represented in the "proper" senses of the great ethical and spiritual abstractions) and the reality (reflected in the actual usage of these words, as defined by Fielding, in society). As in the cases of "turncoat," the conventional forms of compliment, and titles, Fielding's objection is to a usage that reduces words to mere arbitrary labels and so loses sight of their "original" meanings. But here he recognizes that these labels sometimes still do retain significations of a sort. They still have "Ideas" annexed to them, even if these are only shrunken peas of sense rattling about inside the husks of terms once great with meaning. "Captain," one of the titles cited in the *Champion* essay as meaningless, meant to Fielding a headman, or leader—a sense evident in the etymology of the word and hence, so Fielding reasoned, its proper and original meaning.[6] But in the Glossary he defines it as "Any Stick of Wood with a Head to it, and a Piece of black Ribband upon that Head"—a sense that (with allowances for satiric depersonalization) was probably an accurate reflection of popular usage in an age in which army officers bought their commissions, and, if they had any political influence, often spent their entire careers swaggering and hectoring in London on unlimited leaves of absence from their regiments. Again the implication is that exposure of the semantic corruption of the word will lay bare also the social corruption which is its cause but which the lingering, vacant dignity of the word itself still masks from view.

But what is most interesting about this Glossary of abused terms is that it is a virtual compendium of Fielding's own characteristic ironic vocabulary, with the ironic values of the words made explicit and specifically identified with "corrupt"

---

[6]In *The Journal of a Voyage to Lisbon* Fielding observes that the "tyrant" of a ship "is called the captain; a word of such various use and uncertain signification, that it seems very difficult to fix any positive idea to it: if indeed there be any general meaning which may comprehend all its different uses, that of the head, or chief, of any body of men, seems to be most capable of this comprehension." Henley ed., 16: 206.

popular usage. Despite the satiric fiction that the Glossary is for the benefit of moral and religious writers, relatively few of the terms are strictly moral or religious. Most of them, in fact, are merely representative terms from the language of *manners*, words of diverse meanings in the language in general but having in polite society special senses which reflect the narrowness and triviality of that society's values. They are the technical terminology of high society, its special jargon, its cant. GALLANTRY, for example, is seen as a splendid euphemism masking sordid immorality; it is defined as "Fornication and Adultery." GREAT, "applied to a Thing, signifies Bigness; when to a Man, often Littleness, or Meanness." HONOUR is narrowed to "Duelling." LOVE is glossed as "A Word properly applied to our Delight in particular Kinds of Food; sometimes metaphorically spoken of the favourite Objects of all our *Appetites*." WORTH is "Power. Rank. Wealth." And WISDOM, "The Art of acquiring all Three."

No reader of Fielding will have to be told that there are familiar faces here. Most striking, perhaps, is the word GREAT, in the definition of which, as Austin Dobson observed many years ago, lies "a distinction which has the very ring of Jonathan Wild."[7] But one is reminded also of Tom Thumb, who is "Tom Thumb the Great" in *The Tragedy of Tragedies*, and who is great in the perverse sense of "littleness" just as Jonathan is in the sense of "meanness":

> han't you heard
> (What ev'ry Corner of the Court resounds)
> That little *Thumb* will be a great Man made.[8]

Rarely, in fact, does the word appear in Fielding, especially in the epithet "great man," in any but these reverse senses. As early as 1732, he has Captain Bravemore, in the comedy *The Modern Husband*, account for a porter's demand for a bribe by explaining, "Sir, the servants of a great man are all great men" (X, 20). Fanny, in *Joseph Andrews*, asks Joseph, "Are all the great folks

[7]*Sidewalk Studies* (London: Oxford University Press, 1903), p. 83.
[8]*The Tragedy of Tragedies, or The Life and Death of Tom Thumb the Great, with the Annotations of H. Scriblerus Secundus*, ed. James T. Hillhouse (New Haven: Yale University Press, 1918), p. 102.

wicked?" (I, 266) and Amelia wonders at the inhumanity of "our great men" (VII, 236). Fanny, of course, is innocent of any ironic intent, and Amelia just as certainly is too grave to indulge in sarcasm. But we may be sure that the ironic distinction implied by the Glossary definition, between the "proper and original" sense of the word and the corrupt popular usage which applies it indiscriminately to any person in high place, is never far from Fielding's mind, whether he puts the word in the mouth of a character or pronounces it in his own voice.

The Glossary definition of "great" thus merely makes explicit the ironic meaning that Fielding habitually assigns the word throughout his works, but the important thing is that it does so in the context of a discourse, however ironic in its own right, on the corruption of language. The implications of this with regard to Fielding's general employment of the ironic method will be considered more fully in a later chapter. Our present purpose in going outside the scope of the *Covent-Garden Journal* essay is simply to show that Fielding's earlier ironic use of many of the same terms which appear in his Glossary of corrupted words was something more than coincidental. The pervasiveness of such ironic usage would itself, perhaps, prove little. But when the ironic occurrence of these words is repeatedly accompanied by implicit or explicit reference to the corruption of language theme, it is impossible not to see this as representative of a definite pattern in Fielding's thought and practice—a pattern which, once we have learned to look for it, we shall be the better equipped to recognize in its other less clearly defined manifestations in his work.

It would be tedious, in pursuing this point, to try to trace through Fielding's works the ironic careers of each of the other Glossary entries, but perhaps a few further examples are necessary. "Honour" is for Fielding almost as inevitably an ironic word as "great," and though the Glossary definition ("Duelling") is not the only ironic sense in which he uses it, it typifies the kind of absurd reduction to which he apparently felt the word had been subjected by popular usage. In the play *The Temple Beau* (1730), however, this particular sense is not only preserved intact, but is set in exactly the same kind of contrasting relationship to the proper sense of the word (the usage of moral and religious writers) as that implied in the Glossary. The cynical Valentine, questioned by his friend Veromil about the "honour" of his fortune-hunting activities, replies, "Ha, ha, ha! you and I had strange notions of that word when we read the moralists at Oxford; but our honour here is as different from that as our dress. In short, it forbids us to receive injuries, but not to do them" (VIII, 131). In *A Journey from this World to the Next* (published in the *Miscellanies* of 1743), the narrator meets a departed spirit who announces that the "distemper" he died of was "honour, for I was killed in a duel" (II, 219). More familiar, perhaps, to most readers, will be the episodes in *Tom Jones* in which Jones, fallen in with a company of soldiers, is urged to fight a duel with the cowardly Ensign Northerton but ingenuously argues, in protest, that the military "code of honor" seems to him inconsistent with the doctrine of Christian forgiveness. Later, however, when Jones does meet Northerton again, it is the ensign who demands "satisfaction," and Jones is shocked that such a proven villain should dare "to *contaminate* the name of honor by assuming it" (IV, 162–63; my italics). Major Bath, in *Amelia*, is a sort of "humours" character whose ruling passion, as his blustering never lets us forget, is "honor" in this same reductionist sense: "A man of honor wears his law by his side." Even Amelia herself is affected by the corruption of the term. Begging Dr. Harrison to prevent an impending duel between Booth and Colonel James, she urges that he take care, however, not to compromise Booth's "honor." Dr. Harrison, whose concept of honor, like Jones's, reflects the grand abstraction of the moralists, cries, "Again honor! . . . indeed I will not suffer that noble word to be so basely and barbarously *prostituted*" (VII, 132, 304–5; my italics).

For Fielding, however, the word not only *was* "contaminated" and "prostituted," but this circumstance would seem to have been, as in the case of "great," the source of its ironic potential. His awareness, pointedly shared with the reader, that it is also, in its "original" sense, a "noble word," provides the built-in standard of judgment whereby the irony is given moral significance. But if GREAT and HONOUR, in the Glossary and in Fielding's ironic usage, have been narrowed in meaning from grandness to triviality, RELIGION ("A Word of no Meaning") and VIRTUE (among "Subjects of Discourse") are emptied of meaning altogether. As early as 1728, moreover, in *The Masquerade*, Calliope assured the poet that "that thing, which we in English,/Do virtue call," is nothing but "a perfect shadow" and "a masque";[9] in 1732, Mr. Modern, in *The Modern Husband*, defined it as "nothing more than a sound" (X, 17); in 1741, Mammon, in *The Vernoniad*, added coarsely that it was only "a name a bubble or a fart" (XV, 53), and in 1751, in *Amelia*, Mrs. Matthews was still dismissing both terms on the authority of "that charming fellow Mandevil, . . . [who] proves religion and virtue to be only mere names" (VI, 127–28).[10] But again the most memorable instances of Fielding's ironic exploitation of the meaninglessness of "virtue" and "religion" will for most readers be those in *Tom Jones*, particularly in the disputes of Thwackum and Square, where these words become, along with "honor," quite literally nothing more than "mere names" and "Subjects of Discourse." "I have asserted," Square sums up at one point, "that true honor and true virtue are almost synonymous terms, and they are both founded on the unalterable rule of right, and the eternal fitness of things; . . . but that this honor can be said to be founded on religion, . . . if by religion be meant any positive law," he rejects as heatedly as though Thwackum's argument to the contrary were not conducted on a plane of empty verbalism equally remote from the real world (III, 116). And if here the linguistic corruption seems to be laid at the door of the very "Divines and moral Writers" who in the *Covent-Garden Journal* essay stand for the proper usage of words, the divine Thwackum and the moralist Square are plainly not of the same school as Barrow, Tillotson, and Clarke.

Of the other words defined in the Glossary, one might also single out LOVE, which Fielding nearly always, as in the Glossary, ironically identifies with appetite (that "indecent passion";[11]

---

[9]Reprinted in *The Female Husband and Other Writings*, ed. Claude E. Jones (Liverpool: Liverpool University Press, 1960), p. 11.

[10]It seems unlikely that Fielding had any specific reference to Mandeville's works in mind; at any rate, neither I nor a recent annotator of *Amelia* have been able to find any such statement in Mandeville, though the sentiment, to be sure, is thoroughly characteristic of him. See A. R. Towers, Jr., "An Introduction and Annotations for a Critical Edition of *Amelia*" (Ph.D. diss., Princeton University, 1952), p. 197, n. 37.

[11]*Love in Several Masques* (1728), Henley ed., 8: 35.

"that passion . . . which the gentlemen of this our age agreed to call LOVE";[12] ". . . according to the present universally received sense of that phrase, by which love is applied indiscriminately to the desirable objects of all our passions, appetites, and senses, and is understood to be that preference which we give to one kind of food rather than to another."[13]); and WISDOM, which he repeatedly treats as the debased word it has become in the Glossary ("Artful men sometimes miscarry by fancying others wiser, or, in other words, greater knaves, than they really are";[14] "You insinuated slyly that I was wise, which, as the world understands the phrase, I should be ashamed of";[15] "By Wisdom here, I mean that Wisdom of this World, . . . [for] I am extremely doubtful whether by a *Wise Man* is generally meant any other than a Man who is pursuing the direct Road to Power or Wealth, however dirty or thorny it may be.")[16]

Fielding's peculiar ironic usage of many of the "abused" words which appear in the *Covent-Garden Journal* "Modern Glossary" indicates, then, that his preoccupation with language and its abuses was deeply ingrained in his thought and practice. The discourse on the corruption of language which introduces the Glossary is, however, as we have noted earlier, itself ironic. Fielding pretends to identify his sympathies with the loose usage of polite society, which is actually the target of his attack, and to condemn the strict usage of the "Divines and moral Writers" who provide the standard from which the attack is made. But the essay is significant because it throws light, albeit indirectly, on the serious rationale underlying Fielding's position on linguistic corruption and exposes its principal and immediate source. The paper begins with a reference to Locke's *Essay Concerning Human Understanding*:

"One may observe," says Mr. Locke, "in all Languages, certain Words, that, if they be examined, will be found, in their first Original, and their appropriated Use, not to stand for any clear and distinct Ideas." Mr. Locke gives us the Instances "of Wisdom, Glory, Grace.

---

[12]*Jonathan Wild* (1743), Henley ed., 2: 81.
[13]*Tom Jones* (1749), Henley ed., 4: 178.
[14]*Tom Jones*, Henley ed., 3: 282.
[15]*Amelia*, Henley ed., 7: 140. Dr. Harrison is the speaker.
[16]*Covent-Garden Journal*, Nov. 4, 1752.

Words which are frequent enough (says he) in every Man's Mouth; but if a great many of those who use them should be asked what they mean by them, they would be at a Stand, and not know what to answer: A plain Proof, that tho' they have learned those Sounds, and have them ready at their Tongue's End; yet there are no determin'd Ideas laid up in their Minds, which are to be expressed to others by them."

Fielding goes on then, in discussing the several causes which Locke assigned for such abuse of words, to turn Locke's critique to his own satiric purposes by asserting that the philosopher had overlooked the abuses perpetrated by moralists and theologians. The quotation, however, is interesting in its own right. Bringing together two separate sections from Chapter 10 of the treatise on language in Book III of Locke's *Essay*, Fielding blurs an important distinction which Locke makes in the original. The first sentence, from Locke's Section 2, has to do with words which, in their *original* usage, had no distinct referents—deliberately vague terms such as those coined by the schoolmen. The rest of the quotation, including the examples (Wisdom, Glory, Grace) is from Locke's Section 3, and concerns words which, though originally meaningful, are carelessly used by most men "without any distinct meaning at all." It is actually only this second kind of abuse that Fielding is concerned with in the *Covent-Garden Journal* essay, but his telescoping of the quotation can be put down to something more than mere carelessness. For, like the rest of the argument, the quotation is adjusted to an ironic context: it must *seem* to be directed against moral and religious writers guilty of a pedantic abuse of language while at the same time enlisting Locke's authority against the popular abuse that is Fielding's real subject. Thus his appeal to Locke as the sanction of the satiric attack must be given an importance beyond the essay's surface facetiousness of tone. He apparently expected his readers to be familiar enough with Locke's critique to recognize its double-edged appropriateness to the matter at hand, and he presumably intended his own critique to be understood as a serious extension of the Lockean position.

These impressions are strengthened by the fact that Fielding had also appealed to Locke in the *Champion* essay on the meaninglessness of phrases worn out by conventional and professional usage:

Mr. *Lock*, in his Chapter of the Remedies of the Abuse of Words, says, "That whoever shall consider the Errors and Obscurity, the Mistakes and Confusion, that are spread in the World by an ill Use of Words, will find some Reason to doubt whether Language, as it has been employed, has contributed more to the Improvement or Hindrance of Knowledge amongst Mankind."[17]

A later *Champion* paper, moreover, makes a very similar appeal in a different connection. The essay in question is the famous one in which Fielding sets out his considered definition of the term "good-nature." It is not true, he begins, that this concept, as some have asserted, can be expressed in no other language than English, but he does allow that the term has, in general usage, a wide and sometimes contradictory variety of meanings.

I am apt to suspect when I see sensible Men totally differ in Opinion concerning any general Word, that the complex Idea in their several Minds which this Word represents is compounded of very different Simples. "Those gross and confused Conceptions (says Mr. *Lock*) which Men ordinarily have, and to which they apply the common Words of their Language may serve them well enough in their ordinary Discourses and Affairs; but this is not sufficient for philosophical Enquires."[18]

The Lockean distinction which Fielding here observes—presumably in order to dignify his own definition of "good-nature" —between the language of "ordinary Discourses and Affairs," in which a certain amount of carelessness and confusion is allowable, and the language of philosophical inquiries, in which precision and consistency of meaning are required, is one which he more characteristically chose to ignore. More so than Locke, he recognized that the two levels of language were ultimately one, sharing a basically common vocabulary, and that "corruption" or "abuse" on one level could not fail to affect the other. This, surely, is the point of the "Modern Glossary," as it is of the earlier *Champion* paper, where the abuses of polite conversation (the empty compliments, etc.) are condemned equally with the learned jargon of doctors and lawyers. But the logical

---

[17]*Champion*, Jan. 17, 1739/40. The Locke quotation is from the *Essay Concerning Human Understanding*, Book III, Ch. xi, Sec. 4.

[18]Mar. 27, 1740. The reference is to Locke's *Essay*, Book III, Ch. x, Sec. 22, slightly misquoted.

possibility of such a distinction, which Fielding could assume, when it suited his purposes, on the authority of Locke, helps further to account for the internal ambivalence of his *Essay on Conversation* as well as for its inconsistency with his other utterances on language. Looseness and even meaninglessness could be tolerated in conversational usage when the immediate end of discourse was not the communication of ideas but the conveyance of esteem and pleasure, though as we have seen, Fielding could not finally conceal his disapproval of such license even in the "world of common men, and not of philosophers."

He does not, however, in the *Essay on Conversation*, invoke the authority of Locke, perhaps for the very reason that here, for a change, he was more concerned with excusing the abuse of language than with exposing it. But apart from the Lockean distinction between levels of language that it assumes, there exists also an interesting parallel between one passage of Fielding's *Essay* and another in an earlier work which suggests that Locke's theory of language could not have been far from his mind even in this case when he chose not to refer to it. Casting about in the *Essay* for a word expressive of the foundations of conversation, Fielding settles on "good-breeding," but cautions, typically, that this word itself needs definition, "being so horribly and barbarously corrupted, that it contains at present scarce a single ingredient of what it seems originally to have been designed to express." His own sense of the word, which he identifies with its "original" meaning, is opposed to the current "corrupt" sense:

> The word . . . good-breeding . . . [was], I apprehend, not at first confined to externals, much less to any particular dress or attitude of the body; nor were the qualifications expressed by it to be furnished by a milliner, a tailor, or a periwig-maker; no, nor even by a dancing-master himself. . . . In short, by good-breeding (notwithstanding the corrupt use of the word in a very different sense), I mean the art of pleasing, or contributing as much as possible to the ease and happiness of those with whom you converse. (XIV, 248–49)

But this passage, significant in its own right as another direct statement by Fielding of the doctrine of the corruption of language, becomes doubly interesting when one compares it with a very similar statement which occurs in a note in *Plutus*, the translation of Aristophanes' comedy which Fielding had brought out, in collaboration with the Rev. William Young, the year before the publication of the *Miscellanies*. The term in question here is not "good-breeding" but "good-manners," a close synonym surely, which occurs in Act II, Scene 5, of the text. Poverty argues that she is a better patron of mankind than Plutus, the God of Riches, because, among other reasons, "Good-Manners dwell entirely with me; for all Abuse belongs to Riches." The gloss on "Good-Manners" follows:

The Deficiency and Corruption of our Language, by the Confusion introduced into it from our applying improper and incorrect Ideas to Words, of which Mr. *Locke* so justly complains, makes [*sic*] it exceeding difficult to render adequately so copious and exact a Language as the *Greek*; especially in what regards their Philosophy and Morals. The Greek Word here is κοσμιώτης, which properly signifies the good Order of the Mind. . . . Hence κοσμιώτης is used more at large to signify the Behaviour arising from such a Disposition of Mind. When we translate this *Good-Manners*, we must be understood in the true and genuine, and not in the corrupted Use of the Word.[19]

The importance of this note is twofold. Not only does it state Fielding's belief in the corruption of language in a context for once completely free of the ambiguities of irony and facetiousness of tone, but it also makes it unequivocally clear that his authority for this belief was the linguistic theory of John Locke. If the appeal to Locke is missing from the *Essay on Conversation*, its appearance in this parallel passage in the *Plutus* notes (which must have been written at about the same time) indicates that Locke's influence was at work in the *Essay* as well. In each of the other extended statements of the corruption theme, in the *Champion* papers of 1739 and 1740 and in the *Covent-Garden Journal* essay of 1752, spanning Fielding's greatest productive years, this influence is made fully explicit, and a still earlier reference in the Preface to the second edition of *Tom Thumb* (1730) suggests that Locke was standing behind Fielding's attitude toward language from the very outset of his career.

---

[19]*Plutus* (London, 1742), p. 56. The note, which is unsigned, might, of course, be Young's. But its enunciation of a theme so characteristic of Fielding makes the latter the likelier author.

Noting that "Mr. *Lock* complains of confused Ideas in Words," Fielding ironically recommends as a way of avoiding this confusion the method of the modern preface, as typified by Colley Cibber, of emptying words of meaning altogether through gross misuse.[20] Moreover, Fielding frequently echoes Lockean terminology in even his more offhanded remarks on language. Kenneth MacLean, in his study of Locke's influence on eighteenth-century literature, cites, for example, the passage in *Tom Jones* in which Square employs the phrase "abuse of words" (III, 211) and the one in which Fielding himself, as narrator, observes that Mrs. Waters uses words "without any fixed ideas" (IV, 199).[21]

Such instances might easily be multiplied, and several will be considered in later chapters where the relationship of Locke's theory to some of the specific areas of Fielding's linguistic preoccupation will be more fully explored. But surely the references cited in the present chapter are sufficient to establish that Fielding's concern with language and its corruptions was an earnest and a longstanding one and that it had a serious philosophical basis in the linguistic theory of John Locke. Fielding's own statements, not least because they are so often ironically oblique, are not themselves satisfactory expositions of the linguistic attitudes they assume. In what sense was language seriously thought to be "corruptible"? On what kind of conception of language did such a view depend? Fielding does not himself ever pause to answer such questions with any degree of completeness. Clearly he expected his readers, as his many citations attest, to be familiar with the idea as it occurs in Locke, whose statement was the crowning synthesis of nearly a century of linguistic theorizing and has become the classic document of the seventeenth- and eighteenth-century critique of language. The next chapter, accordingly, will deal with the philosophical assumptions underlying Fielding's position, as these found expression in the linguistic theories of Locke and others of the period, and in the not always explicit attitudes toward language and its abuses which these theories presupposed.

[20]Reprinted in the Hillhouse ed. of *The Tragedy of Tragedies*, 1 : 49.
[21]Cited by MacLean in *John Locke and English Literature of the Eighteenth Century* (New Haven: Yale University Press, 1936), pp. 112–13. MacLean also cites, of course, most of Fielding's more explicit references to Locke's theory of language which I have quoted above, as well as many passages illustrative of Locke's general influence on Fielding.

Chapter II

"WORDS AND IDEAS": FIELDING AND THE AUGUSTAN CRITIQUE OF LANGUAGE

The idea of the "corruption of language" is as old, perhaps, as the study of language itself. It takes cognizance of an obvious fact—the phenomenon of linguistic change—and it was in this sense that the phrase was most often used in the seventeenth and eighteenth centuries. For Fielding, however, it meant this and something more. He was not interested, so far as we know, in linguistic change as such, and there is little evidence that he was worried, in the manner of Pope,[1] over the possibility that such as Chaucer is would Fielding be. The kind of corruption he was concerned about was that which had already infected and rendered suspect the language of the day, the language which he, as a writer, had no choice but to use.

He was not, then, a reformer of the tongue in the sense that Dryden and Swift would have liked to be, with their visions of an English Language Academy for the purpose of "settling" usage and arresting change,[2] and he was probably more skeptical than Dr. Johnson himself of the aspirations of eighteenth-century lexicographers to "fix" the English language. He did not live to see the publication of Johnson's *Dictionary* (1755), but he was familiar with Nathan Bailey's *Universal Etymological English Dictionary* (1721) and, though the evidence is slim, seemed little impressed with its pretensions of settling the proper meanings of words. A witness for Colley Cibber, on trial in the *Champion* "for the Murder of the English Language," testifies before the Court of Censorial Enquiry that she saw the defendant "often

---

[1] Our sons their fathers' failing language see, / And such as Chaucer is, shall Dryden be. *An Essay in Criticism*, lines 482–83.
[2] Dryden proposed a language academy in the dedicatory epistle of his *Rival Ladies* (1664), Swift in his *Proposal for Correcting, Improving, and Ascertaining the English Tongue* (1712).

. . . look in a Book [called] *Bailey's Dictionary. At which there was a great Laugh*"[3]—though whether at the expense of Cibber or Bailey (or both) it is not clear. In an earlier *Champion* paper about the "arcana" of politics he quotes with apparent approval Bailey's definition of the word "Mystery," but refers to the lexicographer himself as "the learned Mr. *Bailey*,"[4] the kind of "corrupt" epithet which in Fielding is always suspect of irony.[5] And in *Tom Jones*, Sophia's blunt statement of her objection to Blifil as a suitor—"I hate him"—elicits from Aunt Western the recommendation that if she is ever to "learn a proper use of words," she "should consult Bailey's Dictionary" and learn that "it is impossible you should hate a man from whom you have received no injury" (III, 339–40). Mrs. Western, of course, is the most dubious of advocates, but it is interesting, both as evidence of Fielding's concern for detail and as an indication of why he may have distrusted the lexicographer's claims to authority, that Bailey's definition of the word in question supports her quibble. "To hate," according to Bailey (in the original version of his *Dictionary* which Fielding must have had in mind), meant "To bear an ill-Will to"—a sense which would indeed make the word inappropriate to describe the feelings of the determined but generous-spirited Sophia. And though Bailey's addition of a second meaning in a later (1730) expanded edition of the *Dictionary* would accommodate Sophia's sense of the word ("To have an Aversion to"), the limitations of the lexicographer's methods are clear, particularly in the case of a word such as "hate" which could not be referred back to a respectable Latin or Greek "original" and which had therefore to be defined according to the compiler's own knowledge of current usage. Even Dr. Johnson, the first dictionary-maker who tried systematically to register all the various senses of words, would probably not have satisfied Fielding's apparent objections to a method which so conspicuously failed to reflect the subtlety and variety of living speech. Fielding would have agreed, no doubt, with Johnson's own self-deprecating caveat in his Preface to the *Dictionary* that "to enchain syllables, and to lash the wind, are

[3]May 17, 1740.
[4]Feb. 14, 1739/40.
[5]See below, p. 77.

equally the undertakings of pride, unwilling to measure its desires by its strength."

Nor is it likely that the man who sometimes called himself Scriblerus Secundus approved any more than did the original Scriblerians of the program of the Royal Society for "improving the English tongue" by bringing it, in Bishop Sprat's famous words, "as near the Mathematical plainness" as possible so as to enable scientific and philosophical writers to state "so many *things* almost in an equal number of *words*."[6] The special liability of abstract words to perversion and multiplicity of meaning was recognized by nearly all of the seventeenth- and eighteenth-century critics of the tongue. But the orthodox assumption that language was (or ought to be) the exact mirror of objective nature gave more comfort in a materialistic age to those reformers who wished to banish abstractions from the language altogether on the grounds that they could not be assigned concrete referents[7] than to the humanists who saw in the shifting meanings of such words a threat to traditional immaterial values which must be resisted, they believed, not by substituting the mechanistic vocabulary of a Hobbesian materialism in which the great ethical and spiritual truths of man and nature would be inexpressible, but rather by shoring up the abstract words themselves. There is no such direct attack in Fielding on the Royal Society's supposed wish to purge the language of abstractions as Swift's description in Part III of *Gulliver's Travels* of the School of Languages at the Grand Academy of Lagado, whose professors manage to dispense with words altogether and to discourse entirely by means of "things" which they clumsily carry about with them for that purpose. But, like Pope in Book IV of *The Dunciad*, Fielding ridiculed the preoccupation of the Royal Society *virtuosi* with meaningless trivia like the polyp which is the overt subject of *Some Papers To Be Read before the Royal Society* (1743) and curious anomalies like the pullet in *Tom Jones* "with a letter in its maw," which "would have delighted the Royal Society" (V, 210)—at the expense, it is always implied, of universal principles of nature and intangible human values; and in the *Champion* for April 27, 1740, he refers in passing to "such

[6]Thomas Sprat, *History of the Royal Society* (London, 1667), Part II, Sec. 20.
[7]See A. C. Howell, *"Res et Verba:* Words and Things," *ELH*, 13 (1946): 131–42.

as we generally say can hardly write and read, or, in other Words, a Man qualified to be a Member of the R——— S———y."[8]

Of grammarians, the most flourishing breed of language reformers in his own time, Fielding was perhaps more tolerant, though again the evidence of his views is rather slight. Against the legal "Art of Tautology" in the *Champion* essay on the abuse of words he cites the authority of William Lily, whose Latin grammar was the standard work on that subject throughout the seventeenth and eighteenth centuries and the probable source of many of the rules which English grammarians sought (as Fielding does here) to import into English.[9] The examples in the turncoat essay of "corrupted" words (tyrant, villain, knave) were apparently borrowed by Fielding from Michael Maittaire's *English Grammar* (1712), a work which avowedly set out to "draw a Parallel between [the English] Language and the Learned ones" and which offered the same three words as instances of "how powerful and arbitrary is Use and Custom in abusing . . . the true and original signification of words."[10] The grammarian James Harris was a friend of Fielding and may have been an occasional contributor to the *Covent-Garden Journal*. His *Hermes* (1751), the classic eighteenth-century statement of the theory of universal grammar, was in Fielding's library at the time of his death.[11]

At most, then, we can conclude that Fielding was acquainted

[8]See also *The Mock Doctor*, scene xvii; *Champion*, Apr. 29, 1740; *True Patriot* Nos. 5 and 22; *Covent-Garden Journal* Nos. 2 and 70; and *An Attempt toward a Natural History of the Hanover Rat*, attributed to Fielding by Jensen in "Two Discoveries," *Yale University Library Gazette*, 10 (1935); 23–32.

[9]"I need not mention that Custom so notorious among Gentlemen of the Law, of taking away from Substantives, the Power given them by Mr. *Lilly* of standing by themselves, and joining two or three more Substantives to shew their Signification." *Champion*, Jan. 17, 1739/40. Lily's rule is "A Noun Substantive is that standeth by himself, and requireth not another Word to be joined with him to shew his Signification." Lily's grammar appeared in numerous editions from the time of its publication in 1527 until well into the nineteenth century, and under various titles. The edition I have used is *A Short Introduction to Grammar* (London, 1742). The noun substantive rule appears on p. 1.

[10]*The English Grammar, or An Essay on the Art of Grammar Applied to and Exemplified in the English Tongue*, pp. vii, 213.

[11]See Cross, 1: 247, 374, 379; and "A Catalogue of the . . . Library of the Late Henry Fielding," reprinted in Appendix to Ethel M. Thornbury's *Henry Fielding's Theory of the Comic Prose Epic* (Madison: University of Wisconsin Press, 1931). Fielding inserted an abstract of *Hermes* in *Covent-Garden Journal*, Mar. 14, 1752.

with the grammatical reformers of his time and may have sympathized with some of their aims. He associated himself, in another *Champion* paper, with Quintilian's pronouncement "that Grammar is the Foundation of all Science"[12] and included in the indictment against Colley Cibber the charge "that you, not having the Fear of Grammar before your Eyes, . . . in and upon the *English* Language an Assault did make." But Fielding's actual assessment of the relative importance of grammar is probably reflected in the testimony of the critic who, in support of Cibber's claim "that other *Literati* have used the said Language more barbarously than I have," produces enough examples of sheer meaninglessness in the works of a certain "very great and Eminent Physician" that the hapless Cibber's share in the crime seems small by comparison. For "it may be more properly called the Murder of the Language to bring Sentences together without any Meaning, than to make their Meaning obscure by any Slip in Grammar or Orthography."[13]

The grammarians, like the advocates of a Language Academy, the Royal Society theorists, and the other would-be reformers of the age, believed that the rule of language could be imposed from above. "Corruption" for them was mere change, whether in morphology, pronunciation, spelling, or meaning, and so long as this process could be either arrested or directed by some external authority, the language, they believed, was safe. It could be fixed; it could even be improved. But there is no evidence that Fielding shared this assumption. For all his concern about the condition of the language he was not a reformer in this sense because he was too conscious of the fact that language is, above all else, the words which men *use*, whether they are responsible citizens of the Republic of Letters like himself, ignorant hacks like Cibber, or obfuscating pedants like the "very great and Eminent Physician" who shares Cibber's responsibility for the murder of the English language. Corruption was change, to be sure, but not merely the historical process which distinguished the modern Dryden from the archaic Chaucer and which threatened, by the same token, the immortality of all writers.

[12]Apr. 29, 1740.
[13]*Champion*, May 17, 1740.

Corruption for Fielding was more significantly the change which was going on in his own time—the change from meaning to meaninglessness, the change from grandness of import to triviality, the change which was contaminating the vocabulary of sincerity with the suspicion of hypocrisy, the change which rendered "very great" and "eminent" into ironic words not simply by means of a conscious understanding with the reader that their senses should be reversed, but by virtue of the current irresponsible use in society which had already made this reversal implicit in the words themselves.

In a passage already quoted from the *Covent-Garden Journal*, Fielding declares that the moralists and theologians "offend" by using words "in a Sense often directly contrary to that which Custom (the absolute Lord and Master, according to Horace, of all the Modes of Speech) hath allotted them." The deferential tone, of course, is ironic, and "Custom" is the real object of attack. But the effectiveness of the Modern Glossary depends on our recognizing that the definitions of the terms in question *are* an accurate reflection (allowing, as always, for satiric distortion) of popular usage—not what the words *used* to mean, or *ought* to mean, but what they actually *do* mean in common use. The serious point of the essay, then (as of Fielding's other statements of the corruption theme and of much of his irony of "corrupted" words), lies in the juxtaposition of two kinds or levels of usage. One level (represented here by the "Divines and moral Writers") is traditional and responsible; the other (represented in this instance by the "polite Part of Mankind") is popular, current, and irresponsible. But even more basically, perhaps, the point of the essay lies in an unresolved tension between a recognition of the power of popular usage and a denial of its right to that power, a belief on the one hand that the meaning of words is inviolable, and a recognition on the other that in practice meaning is arbitrary, inconstant, and frequently nonexistent, the product not of inherited culture and wisdom but only of social whim and chance, the mirror not of the permanent ideals of religion, morality, and civilization, but only of the shabby and shifting values of the moment.

The idea that usage (or "Custom") was the ruler of language was by no means new. There was classical authority for it in

Horace and Quintilian, and the former's dictum on

usus

Quem penes arbitrium est et jus et norma loquendi,[14]

which Fielding cites, was a special favorite of English writers on
language. The biblical accounts of the origin and evolution of
language, to which most of the language theorists paid lip service
at least, tended to the same conclusion. Language was the gift of
God to Man, the special power given Adam to "name" all the
creatures of the earth. These names were at first, by the grace
of God, constant and universal, mirroring exactly the things
which they described. But at Babel, God's wrath brought down
upon Man the curse of dispersal and multiplicity of tongues, and
thereafter His blessing on the marriage of words and things was
withdrawn. The arbitration of language was left to Man alone,
and the result was the mutability and confusion of all modern
tongues.

The corruption of language was the inevitable result of its
government by a corrupt humanity, and English theorists of
language from the early seventeenth century on were well aware
of it. "Words are formed at the will of the generality," wrote
Bacon, "and there arises from a bad and inapt formation of
words a wonderful obstruction to the mind."[15] Bacon himself
offered no remedies for this situation, but the implications were
clear: if learning is ever to advance beyond the vague and
cumbersome formulations of the present, steps must be taken
either to remove the existing language from the control of "the
generality" or else to devise a new medium of discourse altogether free (like poetic diction) of their influence. John Wilkins'
Essay towards a Real Character and a Philosophical Language
(1668), for example, was predicated on the assumption that
human reason could construct a "universal" tongue close to, if
not identical with, the original language invented by the divinely
inspired Adam. The belief of such eighteenth-century grammarians as James Harris and Robert Lowth in a "universal
grammar" rested on a similar faith but with less reliance on the

---

[14]*Ars Poetica*, lines 71–72.
[15]*Novum Organum* (London, 1620), Aphorism 43.

biblical underpinnings. Even Sprat conceived of the ideal scientific medium as a kind of reconstruction of a perfect original: a "return back to the primitive purity and shortness" of language.[16]

But whether the ideal was regarded as a past perfection to be recovered or as a pattern of future excellence to be reached by a gradual process of "refinement," the appeal was always to an authority above current usage—reason, "the nature of things," universal grammar, etymology.[17] Even Dr. Johnson, who endeavored in the *Dictionary*, so he said, merely "to discover and promulgate the decrees of custom," could not suppress his doubts as to whether "the sovereignty of words" belonged to custom "by right or by usurpation,"[18] and in his actual definitions he decided, as often as not, in favor of the latter by utterly excluding current meanings which he felt were "incorrect." He defined the word "journal," for example, as D. Nichol Smith has pointed out, as "any paper published daily," even though at the time he wrote and for a considerable period before nearly all of the English newspapers so entitled were weeklies.[19] "Every dictionary," observed Anselm Bayly in *An Introduction to Languages* (1758), "is more or less formed upon the principle, that names were imposed from some reason, and that language is ideal."[20] In the eighteenth century, at least, this was probably true, and not only of dictionaries but of any approach to the problems of language which appealed to some "original" standard of purity or to some "universal" principle of language. The doctrine of usage as the arbiter of language was everywhere acknowledged, but the whole effort of the reform movement was bent on repudiating its final implications: that authoritative control was impossible for any medium which took its life from the active principle of use. It was perhaps the needs of the new science for a more precise medium, as R. F. Jones has maintained,[21] or the

---

[16]*History of the Royal Society*, Part II, Sec. 20.
[17]See S. A. Leonard, *The Doctrine of Correctness in English Usage*, p. 14 and *passim*.
[18]*Plan of an English Dictionary, The Works of Samuel Johnson*, ed. Arthur Murphy (London, 1792), 2: 23.
[19]D. Nichol Smith, "The Newspaper," *Johnson's England* (Oxford: Clarendon Press, 1933), 2: 339.
[20]P. 76.
[21]See especially "Science and English Prose Style in the Third Quarter of the Seventeenth Century," *The Seventeenth Century*, pp. 75–110.

reaction against the rhetorical excesses of Puritan and "meta-physical" "enthusiasts," as George Williamson has argued,[22] which first gave impetus to the campaign to reform the English language. But it was the common struggle to wrest control away from "the generality" which gave it its real unity of purpose.

Fielding, in his appeals to etymology and in his ironic invocations of the "original" meanings of words, was at one with his age in denying the *right* of current usage to the rule of language. But he was too much of a realist to underestimate its power and too conscious of the ground the enemy had already won to have much faith in the more sanguine plans of reform. The campaigns to reform the tongue, however successful they may have been by Fielding's time in the formalization of spelling, pronunciation, and grammar, had failed dismally in their attempts to arrest semantic change, or to "settle the significations of words." The vocabulary of the eighteenth century, says Joan Platt, a modern historian of the language, was "remarkable for having adopted a great number of new senses for words already existing, rather than in having acquired many completely new words." The process of "degradation," whereby a word passes out of standard "good English" and is relegated to use by lower, ignorant classes only, was much more common in this period, she notes, than "amelioration," or the process of a word's rising in respectability, and one aspect of this degradation was an inevitable "deterioration" in meaning. In the course of decline, a word once powerful and serious often became weak and facetious as semi-educated middle-class speakers, trying to imitate their "betters," succeeded only in dragging the word in question down from the level of respectability. Another cause she isolates for this "deterioration" is the "rise of journalese" in the early eighteenth century. But the most prevalent kind of semantic change Miss Platt discovers in the period is the process of "specialization," the change of a word's meaning (as in the classic case of "wit") from a general or abstract primary sense to a more concrete, specific, or particular one. The process, of course, could work the other way too, and "generalization" was also a factor in the changing meanings of the time. But "the eighteenth century was

[22]See especially "The Restoration Revolt against Enthusiasm," *Studies in Philology*, 30 (1933): 571–603.

peculiarly the period in which the restrictive tendency worked in preparation for modern colloquial English."[23] Lord Chesterfield, always a shrewd observer of his times, noticed the same tendencies, though he was inclined to place the blame particularly on the ladies: "Not content with enriching our language by words absolutely new, my fair countrywomen have gone still further, and improved it by the application and extension of old ones to various and very different significations. They take a word and change it, like a guinea into shillings for pocket money, to be employed on the several occasional purposes of the day."[24]

These are the kinds of "corruptions," it is clear, with which Fielding was concerned, and there was good reason for fearing that the forces of popular usage were getting the upper hand. "Great" and "eminent," for all their original power and seriousness, seemed to have been reduced not only in social status but also, as a consequence, in meaning as well, and insofar as they still conveyed any "ideas," these were as likely as not to have a facetious edge, or at least to lend themselves readily to facetiously ironic usage. "Honor," narrowed in popular application to such senses as "dueling," was a great abstraction broken down into the small change of specialized meanings; and "virtue" and "religion," the victims of similar forces, had been reduced, according to Fielding, to the condition of sheer meaninglessness.

Nor was Fielding alone in singling out such words as the

---

[23]"The Development of English Colloquial Idiom during the Eighteenth Century," *Review of English Studies*, 2 (1926): 70, 194. On the changing meaning of "wit," see Stuart M. Tave: "The word was sinking [from the mid-seventeenth century] into common, trifling, and narrow usages—mere quickness and sharpness in the making of similitudes, the odd metaphor, the lucky simile, the wild fetch, epigrammatic turns and points, quibble, conceit." By the early eighteenth century, it had "become so degraded by its association with the unimportant and even the profane that it was more and more difficult to use it with grave connotation." *The Amiable Humorist* (Chicago: University of Chicago Press, 1960), pp. 58, 63. See also J. E. Spingarn, ed., *Critical Essays of the Seventeenth Century* (Oxford: Clarendon Press, 1908–9), 1: lviii–lxiii; and Edward Niles Hooker, "Pope on Wit," *The Seventeenth Century*, p. 23. Fielding's contributions to the traditional discussion of the meaning of "true wit" may be seen in the *Covent-Garden Journal* Nos. 18 and 19.

[24]*World* No. 101, 1754. Cited by William Matthews, "Polite Speech in the Eighteenth Century," *English*, 1 (1937): 500. Cf. Boswell's statement that Dr. Johnson "was very much offended at the general licence, by no means 'modestly taken' in his time, not only to coin new words, but to use many words in senses quite different from their established meaning, and those frequently very fantastical." *Life of Johnson*, ed. G. B. Hill, rev. L. F. Powell (Oxford: Clarendon Press, 1934), 1: 221.

products of debilitating semantic change. "No one in the eighteenth century," remarks Ian Watt, "seems to have spoken about great men . . . without irony."[25] Gay's use of the term, in *The Beggar's Opera* (1728), as a noble word fallen among thieves, is almost identical with Fielding's in *Jonathan Wild*; and Steele, in the *Spectator*, strikes off a parenthetical qualification which is pure Fielding in its identification of the ironic word with its corrupt usage: Louis of France and Peter of Russia, he says, are "the two greatest Men now in *Europe* (according to the common acceptation of the Word Great)."[26] Again, in the *Tatler*, Steele lists among his achievements as the "Censor of Great Britain" the separation he has made of "Duellists from Men of Honour," referring, apparently, to the *Tatler* No. 25, in which, anticipating Fielding's formulation of the same point in *The Temple Beau*, he declares that "as the matter now stands, it is not to do handsome actions denominates a man of honour, it is enough if he dares to defend ill ones."[27] Similarly, Robert South (whose *Sermons* Fielding owned and much admired[28] and who is doubtlessly among those "Divines and moral Writers" whom he regularly takes as the standard of proper usage) complained in one of his series of sermons on "The Fatal Imposture and Force of Words" of the "outrageous, ungoverned violence and revenge, . . . passing by the name of *sense of honour*, . . . which is as much the natural result, as it is the legal reward of virtue. And yet, in spite of nature and reason, and the judgment of all mankind, this high and generous thing must be that in whose pretended quarrel almost all the duels of the world are fought." South is aware, too, of the corruptive influence on the word of so-called titles of honor: "Princes, indeed, may confer honours, or rather titles and names of honour; but they are a man's or woman's own actions which make him or her truly honourable, . . . Honour

---

[25]"The Ironic Tradition in Augustan Prose from Swift to Johnson," *Restoration and Augustan Prose: Papers Delivered by James R. Sutherland and Ian Watt at the Third Clark Library Seminar, 14 July, 1956* (Los Angeles: University of California Press, 1957), p. 38.

[26]No. 139, Aug. 9, 1711, Everyman ed. (London: Dent, 1958), 1: 418–19.

[27]*Tatler*, Everyman ed. (London: Dent, 1953), pp. 33, 186. This is also one of the themes, of course, of Steele's *The Conscious Lovers* 1722). For *The Temple Beau* passage, see above, pp. 19–20.

[28]"A Catalogue of the . . . Library of the Late Henry Fielding." For Fielding's knowledge of South's sermons, see Martin C. Battestin, *The Moral Basis of Fielding's Art*.

being but the reflection of a man's own actions."[29] Pope, in his Scriblerian role of the mock rhetorician who recommends "to our Authors the Study of the *Abuse of Speech*" as the surest means to literary success, is another witness to the corrupting title when, in *The Art of Sinking in Poetry* (1728), he ironically reminds would-be authors that "Every Man is honourable who is so by *Law, Custom,* or *Title*."[30]

Fielding was conscious also of the "generalizing" process in language, which works not to shrink the grand old abstract words but to inflate formerly restricted and trivial terms into false new abstractions, reflecting once again the shabbiness of modern values. In "A Dissertation Concerning High People and Low People" in *Joseph Andrews*, he defines the former as "people of fashion," thus distinguishing them from low people, who are "those of no fashion." But, as so often, he pauses to examine the key word of his definition: "Now, this word of fashion hath by long use lost its original meaning, from which at present it gives us a very different idea." Formerly, he says, it referred only to "dress," but now it has come to mean birth, accomplishment, social status, and a whole complex of superficial aristocratic values. Yet "the word really and truly signifies no more [than dress] at this day" (I, 180). Again, in the *Covent-Garden Journal* for May 9, 1752, he returns to the same phrase and speculates ironically about how the "Term, PEOPLE OF FASHION . . . first acquired its present Meaning, and became a Title of Honour and Distinction," defending his mock derivations against "those who have not much considered the barbarous Corruption of Language." But plainly it was the process of specialization which Fielding was most seriously alarmed about, particularly when it threatened to narrow words to the point of meaninglessness or to splinter their meanings so finely that the same word would mean radically different things, covering the whole range, perhaps, from greatness to pettiness, to different speakers and writers and, more seriously yet, to speakers and their hearers or to writers and their readers.

Fielding's interest in language, then, was characterized by his

[29] *Sermons Preached upon Several Occasions* (Philadelphia, 1844), 3: 3–4.
[30] *The Art of Sinking in Poetry*, ed. Edna Leake Steeves (New York: Columbia University Press, 1952), p. 77.

preoccupation with semantic instability in the language of the
present, particularly as it affected the great ethical and spiritual
abstractions, by his sensitivity to the power of popular usage,
and by his distrust of authoritative programs of reform. It was
for these reasons, probably, that he was attracted by the linguistic
theory of John Locke. For Locke was pre-eminently in the
eighteenth century the philosopher of semantics as well as the
first of the major theorists of language really to deal adequately
with the idea of usage as the matrix and arbiter of speech. An
effective use of language, he taught, depended not on rules and
methods of control but on an understanding of the psychology of
communication. He recognized the desirability of a dictionary
compiled on scientific principles, but he thought such a project
not feasible and emphasized instead the *personal responsibility* of
each serious *user* of the language to purify, as it were, his own
language. But Locke was also, for all his affinities to the Royal
Society and for all his distrust of metaphysics, no enemy of
abstractions, and he gave their defenders a philosophy of abstract
words which was at once true to the modern experience and
expectations of language and loyal to the traditional values which
such words were believed to represent.

The main thesis of the *Essay Concerning Human Understanding*
(1690), it will be remembered, is that the human understanding
is imperfect and our knowledge limited. Book I develops the
basic proposition that ideas are not innate in the mind. Book II
establishes that all ideas have their source in either sensation or
reflection (the mind's perceptions of its own operations on the
ideas received from sensation), and are either simple (proceeding
directly from sensation), complex (produced by reflection), or
relations (comparisons of two or more ideas). Book IV exposes
the weaknesses and limitations of the human mind, especially
the "disease" of the association of ideas. There are no certain
truths available to man, but only probability and faith—except
in morality, which is "amongst the sciences [along with mathe-
matics, etc.] capable of demonstration" (IV, iii, 18)[31] and therefore certain. Thus man's understanding and knowledge, though

[31] All references to Locke are to *An Essay Concerning Human Understanding*, ed. Alexander
Campbell Fraser (Oxford: Clarendon Press, 1894). Citations are to book, chapter, and
section.

limited by his dependence on sensation and the imperfect work-
ings of the mind, are adequate for his conduct in this world and
sufficient for the duties of life.

This, so Locke informs us, was his original plan, and it was not
until he had already written the first two books of the *Essay* that
he was struck with the realization that words "interpose themselves so much between our understandings, and the truth which
it [*sic*] would contemplate and apprehend, that, like the medium
through which visible objects pass, the obscurity and disorder
do not seldom cast a mist before our eyes, and impose upon our
understandings" (III, ix, 21). The result of this afterthought was
Book III, "Of Words."

A consideration of the nature and function of language was
particularly essential to Locke's design because one of his basic
assumptions was the reality in objective nature of "particulars"
only and the unreality of "universals." Such concepts as
"essence" and "species" have no counterparts in nature. They
exist only in the minds of men and are built up out of their perceptions of "particulars" in the outer world. But this situation
is not, according to Locke, grounds for despair or cynicism, nor
is it a reason for spurning abstractions. It is merely one of the
conditions of human understanding—the peculiarly human (but
not therefore contemptible) way of looking at the world. Far
from despising abstract universals, in fact, Locke values them as
the highest reaches of human thought, and language occupies
a crucial place in his system because it supplies the agency
whereby the process of abstraction is carried out: "In mixed
modes [i.e., abstract ideas] it is the name that seems to preserve
essences, and give them their lasting duration. For, the connexion between the loose parts of those complex ideas being
made by the mind, this union, which has no particular foundation
in nature, would cease again, were there not something that did,
as it were, hold it together, and keep the parts from scattering"
(III, v, 10).

We do not know whether Fielding subscribed to Locke's view
that abstract ideas have no foundation in nature. He was simply
not enough of a philosopher to make the point clear. The notion
might be suggested by a passage in his early poem, *Of True
Greatness*:

'Tis strange, while all to greatness homage pay,
So few should know the goddess they obey;
That men should think a thousand things the same,
And give contending images one name.
. . . .
To no profession, party, place confined,
True greatness lives but in the noble mind.

(XII, 249–57)

But he is more likely thinking of the *quality* of greatness than of the *idea*, and probably he believed, in accordance with the Neoplatonic and antinominalistic traditions of Christian humanism, that abstract terms were the audible and visible symbols (however imperfect) of "real" values, independent of any thinking mind. "What we look on as *Power, Honour, Wisdom, Piety*, etc.," he wrote in the *Champion* for November 22, 1739, "are often not the Things themselves, but the Appearance only." But the assumption underlying such a statement is that "the Things themselves" do have a "real" existence. Again his view of the relationship of words and ideas seems close to that of Robert South: "Honour is indeed a noble thing, and therefore the word which signifies it must needs be very plausible. But as a rich and glistening garment may be cast over a rotten, fashionably diseased body, so an illustrious, commending word may be put upon a vile and an ugly thing; for words are but the garments, the loose garments of things. . . . But the body changes not, though the garments do."[32]

Still, Locke was not preaching a cynical nominalism of the kind Fielding attributed to Mandeville, who "proves religion and virtue to be only mere names."[33] He did not attempt to reduce the great moral and spiritual questions to a simple affair of words. The ideas words stood for were still important to him, however little foundation they might have in objective nature, and if Fielding could not follow him in rejecting "real" universals, there was yet no reason why he could not accept the proposition that it was words which gave these ideas form and permanence in human thought. He may have rejected the notion of nominal

---

[32]*Sermons Preached upon Several Occasions*, 3: 3.
[33]See above, p. 21.

essence, but he could still recognize the practical validity of the idea that words "preserve essences and give them their lasting duration" in the cultural tradition, and this was reason enough why they should be valued and preserved intact. Sophia, we are told, "honored Tom Jones, and scorned Master Blifil, *almost as soon as she knew the meanings of those two words*" (III, 157; my italics).

The emphasis, so Fielding probably thought, was where it belonged: on the connection between words and ideas in the human mind, for here was where corruption (or "abuse," to use Locke's own term) originated and was perpetuated, and only here could it be effectively resisted. "I am apt to suspect," he wrote in his essay on good nature, "when I see sensible Men totally differ in Opinion concerning any general Word, that the complex Idea in their several Minds which this Word represents is compounded of very different Simples. . . . I will venture to illustrate this by a familiar Instance: Suppose an Apothecary (as perhaps they often do) after mixing up a most pleasant Cordial, and a most nauseous Potion for different Patients, should write the same hard Word (*Haustipotiferous Draught* for Example) on each of the Bottles, would not these two Patients ever after conceive very different Ideas of *Haustipotiferous*?"[34] What Fielding "took" from Locke, as we have already suggested, was not a systematic philosophy of words so much as a working rationale of his own intuitive concerns about language, and these were all directed to the practical questions of its imperfections and abuse.

Locke's analysis was eminently useful in this respect because it provided an explanation not only of how words and their ideas were united but also of how, in the normal give and take of communication, they often became separated and confused. For though he assigned words a high purpose in the system of human knowledge, Locke's concept of language as a man-made structure (as opposed to the traditional view of a divinely ordained institution) also made him acutely aware of its limitations. He seemed to believe of language (as he did of civil government) that it was the artificial result of a contract or agreement among the members of a given society. The connection between "words and

---

[34]*Champion*, Mar. 27, 1740.

things," therefore, is purely illusory. Nor is there any *necessary* connection "between particular, articulate sounds and certain ideas . . . but by a voluntary imposition, whereby such a word is made arbitrarily the mark of such an idea" (III, ii, 1). Words do not mean something by divine *fiat* or natural law, but are mere "signs" of ideas in the mind of the speaker. The principal "imperfection" (i.e., inherent defect) of language, then, is simply that words have "naturally no signification." Even those standing for simple ideas refer to a standard in nature which is imperfectly known, while those standing for abstract ideas have "no settled standard anywhere in nature existing, to rectify and adjust them by" (III, ix, 5).

Yet for purposes of communication this connection between words and ideas must be respected and, if possible, preserved. For "there comes, by constant use, to be such a connexion between certain sounds and the ideas they stand for, that the names heard, almost as readily excite certain ideas as if the objects themselves . . . did actually affect the senses" (III, ii, 6). It is this arbitrary connection, institutionalized by usage, which makes communication possible in language, and "unless a man's words excite the same ideas in the hearer which he makes them stand for in speaking, he does not speak intelligibly" (III, ii, 8). The liberty which the originators of language enjoyed "of affixing any new name to any idea," we have still today. But there is this difference:

that, in places where men in society have already established a language amongst them, the significations of words are very warily and sparingly to be altered. Because men being furnished already with names for their ideas, and common use having appropriated known names to certain ideas, an affected misapplication of them cannot but be very ridiculous. He that hath new notions will perhaps venture sometimes on the coining of new terms to express them: but men think it a boldness, and it is uncertain whether common use will ever make them pass for current. But in communication with others, it is necessary that we conform the ideas we make the vulgar words of any language stand for to their known proper significations, . . . or else to make known that new signification we apply them to. (III, vi, 51)

At its best, then, "common use" is the expression of the original compact or "tacit consent" of society which makes communication possible. It is the lawgiver of language and the principle of its continuity. But at the same time it is the lawless force of revolution and chaos, for the constancy of language depends on its individual users, each of whom retains the power to ignore the "agreed" connections between words and ideas and to rearrange them as he pleases. The more abstract the word, the more complex is the combination of ideas it expresses and the more liable it is to be used in private and unusual senses. The result is that the traditional connections are broken down and the words cut adrift from their established meanings. They become, at worst, literally meaningless because the social contract which made their meanings generally available has been violated and the word is reduced to its "natural" state of mere sound. Hence Fielding's frequent assertions that such terms as "virtue" and "religion" were "words of no meaning" or "no more than a sound" were more than just satiric exaggerations. There was a sense, founded on the Lockean theory of language, in which this was the simple truth.

The first obligation of the responsible speaker or writer, therefore, is to established usage, and when Locke comes to consider the "abuses of words" (those "*wilful* faults and neglects," above and beyond the natural imperfections of language, "which men are guilty of in the way of communication, whereby they render those signs less clear . . . than naturally they need to be" [III, x, 1]), he gives special prominence to the vice of applying "the words of any language to ideas different from those to which the common use of that country applies them . . . without defining [one's] terms" (III, x, 29); and his specific examples of this abuse recall not only Fielding's attacks on the verbal corruptions of hypocrisy but also Pope's ironic recommendation, in *The Art of Sinking in Poetry*, of "the method [of] converting Vices into their *bordering* Virtues." ("A man who is a Spendthrift and will not pay a just Debt, may have his Injustice transform'd into Liberality; Cowardice may be metamorphos'd into Prudence; Intemperance into good Nature and good Fellowship, Corruption into Patriotism, and Lewdness into Tenderness and Facility.")[35] "I may have the ideas of virtues or vices," says Locke, "and names

---

[35]Steeves ed., p. 79.

also, but apply them amiss: v.g. when I apply the name *frugality* to that idea which others call and signify by this sound, *covetousness"* (III, x, 33).

But once traditional usage has been violated by enough individual users of a word to make its "agreed" sense uncertain, the appeal to "common use" is no longer valid, particularly for purposes of "Philosophical Discourses," "there being scarce any name of any very complex idea (to say nothing of others) which, in common use, has not a great latitude, . . . and even in men that have a mind to understand one another, [does] not always stand for the same idea in speaker and hearer" (III, ix, 8). This abuse, originating with individuals, is perpetuated by the haphazard way in which words are learned, "especially the most material of them, *moral words.*" For "the sounds are usually learned first; and then, to know what complex ideas they stand for, [men] are either beholden to the explication of others, or (what happens for the most part) are left to their own observation and industry; which being little laid out in search of the true and precise meaning of names, these moral words are in most men's mouths little more than bare sounds; or when they have any, it is for the most part but a very loose and undetermined, and, consequently, obscure and confused signification" (III, ix, 9).

One "great abuse of words," therefore, is *"inconstancy* in the use of them." This is a "plain cheat, . . . the wilful doing whereof can be imputed to nothing but great folly, or greater dishonesty" (III, x, 5). Another is "an *affected obscurity,"* (III, x, 6) which may take the form of old words used in new and unusual senses, new words introduced without good reason and clear definition, or ordinary words brought together in ambiguous combinations —the "learned gibberish" (III, x, 9) which Fielding satirizes in the disputes of Thwackum and Square (ironically recalling Locke in Square's assertion that "It was a mere abuse of words to call those things evil in which there was no moral unfitness") (III, 211), in his Scriblerian burlesques of literary criticism (whose practitioners "have very confused Ideas, and but few Words to express them"),[36] and in his tireless attacks on professional jargon ("to which it will be very difficult to assign any certain Idea").[37] Still another abuse—which Locke allows may not be accepted as such by many of his readers—is the use of figurative language. For "all the artificial and figurative applications of words eloquence hath invented, are for nothing else but to insinuate wrong ideas, move the passions, and thereby mislead the judgment; and so indeed are perfect cheats" (III, x, 34).

This was a principle which Fielding, like any imaginative writer (and like Locke himself, whose most famous passage, perhaps, is the one involving the figure of the *tabula rasa*) could not follow implicitly. But his habit of "translating" his more florid metaphors into "plain English" indicates that he is conscious of the obfuscation figurative language can lead to. This distrust of the metaphor, moreover, is at least partly Lockean in its rationale. As we have seen in the instance of "turncoat," Fielding's objection is not to the device of analogy as such but only to the loss of meaning which occurs when the metaphorical usage of a word becomes habitual and its "original idea" is forgotten. In the chapter of *Tom Jones* entitled "A Comparison between the World and the Stage," he explains this objection. He has nothing against the classic comparison of the world and the stage in itself; in fact, he goes on to develop the idea in his own way in the same chapter. But he does feel that "This thought hath been carried so far, and is become so general, that some words proper to the theatre, and which were at first metaphorically applied to the world, are now indiscriminately and literally spoken of both; thus stage and scene are by common use grown as familiar to us, when we speak of life in general, as when we confine ourselves to dramatic performances; and when transactions behind the curtain are mentioned, St. James's is more likely to occur to our thoughts than Drury Lane" (III, 331). As always, of course, one must not overlook the satiric intent of such a passage (here the cut at the covert political manipulations which make these terms appropriate to St. James's), but the satire rests on Fielding's exposure of the abuse of metaphorical language: the words in question have been cut loose from their original ideas, and what he asks of his readers is not that they should stop using the words of the theater in connection with St. James's,

[37]*Champion*, Jan. 17, 1739/40.

but rather that they should remain fully alive to the normative implications of this transference of terms.

For the most basic and iniquitous abuse of language, according to Locke, is simply "the using of words without clear and distinct ideas; or, which is worse, signs without anything signified" (III, x, 2). "The whole mischief which infects . . . our [political] economy," Fielding writes in *The Journal of a Voyage to Lisbon*, "arises from the vague and uncertain use of a word called Liberty, of which, as scarce any two men with whom I have ever conversed, seem to have one and the same idea, I am inclined to doubt whether there be any simple universal notion represented by this word" (XVI, 239). And of the word "Humour," in the *Covent-Garden Journal* No. 19: "perhaps there is no Word in our Language of which Men have in general so vague and undeterminate an Idea. To speak very plainly, I am apt to question whether the greater Part of Mankind have any Idea at all in their Heads, when this Word drops (perhaps accidentally) from their Tongue." But Fielding does not agree with Locke that this abuse is serious only on the level of philosophical discourse and that it is of small consequence in the "ordinary occurrences of life" (III, x, 4). He is being facetious when, in *Tom Jones*, he applies the test of "clear and distinct ideas" to the words uttered by Mrs. Waters in the comic scene at the inn, but once again there is a serious edge to his mockery. The occasion is the one in which the jealous Fitzpatrick, searching for his wife, bursts into Mrs. Waters' room and discovers her with Jones. As the two men struggle in the dark, she sits up in bed and begins "to scream in the most violent manner, crying out murder! robbery! and more frequently rape! which last, some, perhaps, may wonder she should mention, who do not consider that these words of exclamation are used by ladies in a fright, as fa, la, la, ra, da, etc., are in music, only as the vehicles of sound, and without any fixed ideas." But the serious implications of such an empty use of words are suggested a moment later when Mrs. Waters, fearful now for her reputation rather than for her safety, continues to scream the same words and, when help arrives, pretends to believe that both Jones and Fitzpatrick had entered the room "with an intent upon her honor" (IV, 199–200). Perhaps Fielding, as a magistrate, had had experience with the loose way some women could use the language of accusation—not to mention that much abused word "honor."

He is also, however, more conscious than Locke of the emotional content of words and of the question of sincerity involved in their use. Locke is inclined to attribute most abuse of words to sheer negligence, and when he turns, in the final chapter of Book III, to a consideration of the "Remedies" for these abuses he is therefore confident that, on the level of the individual speaker or writer, all that is needed is greater care in using words with clear and distinct ideas, more attention to consistency of meaning, and more frequent use of definitions, synonyms, and examples. Fielding, as we shall see in Chapter IV, is less optimistic than Locke regarding these remedies, and one of the reasons for his pessimism is his sensitivity to the nonrational elements of language. We have already seen how Fielding's awareness of these elements causes him, in *An Essay on Conversation*, to defend words and phrases which "have in a philosophical sense no meaning" (i.e., which have been separated from their original ideas) on the grounds that they convey impressions of esteem necessary to the conduct of society. We have also seen, however, that he more often attacks these same words and phrases for their insincerity and that even in *An Essay on Conversation* his defense is grudging and ambivalent. Mrs. Waters' use of words is another case in point. The cry "Rape!" is not the sign of an "idea," but, in the first instance, a way of summoning aid and, in the second, a means of safeguarding her reputation. Such "ideas" as the word conveys are to her purely secondary and accidental; her primary objective is not the communication of thought but the conveyance of emotional attitudes important to her own self-interest. In short, in the second instance at least, she is a hypocrite, and her use of the word is a lie.

But again the "common use" of such words in such contexts is corrupting because it separates the words from their proper ideas and infects them with the suspicion of insincerity. If enough boys cry "Wolf!" when there is no wolf, it is not only the liars who will fall under suspicion but the word itself, and this is also true of ladies who cry "Rape!" Even on the simplest levels of speech this can have serious consequences when the wolf or the rape are real, and on the higher levels of discourse the principle is the same. "Honor," "virtue," "religion," and the other words Fielding identifies as "corrupt" have been reduced in efficacy not only by the process of specialization but also by the erosions of insincere usage, and however much this sincere speaker may try to apply Locke's rationalistic remedies he cannot be certain that his words will be accepted at their face values, he cannot be sure that they have been purified of the associations of insincerity. Certain terms, as a result, are all but removed from the vocabulary of truth: "The Words *curious, eminent, learned,*" for example, are according to Fielding like the false labels which unscrupulous merchants use to pass off cheap wine as champagne: "all of them certain Marks of Perry."[38] The word "grace" (which Locke himself, in a passage quoted by Fielding, identifies as an "abused" word)[39] was similarly contaminated by insincerity. Charles DeLoach Ashmore has observed that "The word *grace*, as used by the Methodist pickpocket [at the beginning of *Amelia*] was particularly offensive to the novelist. Not only in the mouths of sectarians, but also on the lips of orthodox clergymen, the word seemed to have an ugly sound in Fielding's ears. . . . Apparently he felt that *grace* was at best used by men to throw upon God responsibilities that they themselves ought to shoulder. At worst, it was a cant word used by hypocrites as a substitute for Christian virtue in action."[40] The hypocritical Parson Barnabas uses the word in *Joseph Andrews*, as does Joseph's sister Pamela (repeatedly) at the end of that novel (I, 72, 343). In *Tom Jones*, Captain Blifil attempts to persuade Allworthy to abandon the infant Jones by arguing that grace is more important than good actions; and it is surely no accident that the easy-virtued chambermaid, at the inn where the puppet show is given, is named Grace (III, 82; IV, 324)—a living symbol, like Mrs. Honour in the same novel (and like Jonathan Wild's three sisters, Grace, Charity, and Honour) of the corruption of words.

Fielding, in fact, is nearly always conscious of the "ideas" conveyed by proper names. "Whatever sour Ideas may be annexed to the Name of *Vinegar*," writes the irascible *persona* of the

---

[38]*Covent-Garden Journal*, Mar. 3, 1752.
[39]See above, pp. 22–23.
[40]"Henry Fielding's 'Art of Life': A Study in the Ethics of the Novel" (Ph.D. diss., Emory University, 1957), p. 257.

Champion, Captain Hercules Vinegar, "no Family hath been more remarked for Sweetness of Temper than ours; and as for myself, those who know me thoroughly, agree in calling me the best natured Man in the World."[41] And in another *Champion* paper an explanation of how names acquire "ideas" foreign to their original significations serves Fielding as a sort of paradigm of one of the processes of linguistic corruption. The reason, he says, why some names are regarded as lucky or unlucky, foolish or grave, good or bad, is not "as some think, from any greater Agreement, that certain Sounds bear [to certain ideas], nor from any of the other chimerical Reasons ludicrous Persons assign; but it is, indeed, because the Name hath been made odious by some Person who hath borne it, *and hath transformed it to Posterity with his Iniquity annexed*"[42] (my italics). This is the same process, clearly, which makes it necessary for Fielding to apologize, in the *Jacobite's Journal* for January 23, 1748, for using the words "Patriot" and "Critic": "The Persons who have, without any just Pretensions, assumed these Characters, must answer for the disadvantageous Light in which they have placed these Words."

It is also very close to the kind of contamination by "the grossness of domestick use" (in Dr. Johnson's phrase)[43] from which poetic diction was supposed to protect the language of poetry,[44] the process whereby a word, according to Addison, may "contract a Kind of Meanness by passing through the Mouths of the Vulgar," and thus become "debased by common Use."[45] "The best expressions," explained a seventeenth-century rhetorician, "grow low and degenerate, when profan'd by the populace, and applied to mean things. The use they make of them, infecting them with a mean and abject Idea, causes that we cannot use

[41]Mar. 27, 1740.

[42]June 7, 1740.

[43]*The Life of Dryden.* Cited by James Sutherland, *A Preface to Eighteenth-Century Poetry* (Oxford: Clarendon Press, 1948), p. 131.

[44]A concept almost exactly contemporaneous in its development with the Restoration and eighteenth-century critique of language. See Thomas Quale, *Poetic Diction* (London: Methuen, 1924), p. 6; F. W. Bateson, *English Poetry and the English Language* (Oxford: Clarendon Press, 1934), pp. 69–70; and Geoffrey Tillotson, "Eighteenth-Century Poetic Diction," *Essays and Studies by Members of the English Association*, 25 (1939; Oxford: Clarendon Press, 1940): p. 76.

[45]*Spectator*, Jan. 26, 1712, Everyman ed. (London: Dent, 1958), 2: 349–50.

them without sullying and defiling those things, which are signified by them."[46] The difference, of course, is that Fielding, who ridiculed the pretensions of poetic diction in *The Tragedy of Tragedies* and in innumerable burlesque passages in the novels and who had to defend himself throughout his career against the charge of being a "low" writer, was not troubled by "domestick" use so much as by *hypocritical* use. But the effect is strikingly similar: the word so contaminated is no longer fit, in the one case, for poetry, in the other, for truth.

But if Fielding was more pessimistic than Locke about the condition of the language, if he used the charged word "corruption" where Locke invariably employed the more neutral "abuse," it was not entirely because he was more sensitive to the emotional content of words. Locke's optimism, for all his emphasis on individual responsibility for effective communication, rested finally on a faith in the basic solidarity of society. The contract theory of language presupposes a society homogeneous enough to have an "agreed" standard of meaning and responsible enough to observe it. For Locke, it is clear, such a society still existed. He had witnessed social upheaval in his time—much more than Fielding was to experience in his—but his belief in the Revolutionary Settlement of 1689 was supreme. Here, so he thought, was the social contract of civil government affirmed in actual fact, palpable evidence of the fundamental unity of English society under the unalterable laws of reason. The laws of language, he realized, were neither so reasonable nor so unalterable. In their original framing, in fact, they were quite arbitrary, and men still possessed their original power to use words in an arbitrary fashion. But for practical purposes they no longer had the *right* to do so, not only because arbitrary tampering with the "agreed" meanings of words would lead to confusion in communication but also because language was itself "the great bond that holds society together" (III, xi, 1), and widespread violation of the linguistic contract could only result in eventual breakdown of the social contract. But Locke, though he recognized the threat of this eventuality, clearly did not see it as present and immediate. He believed that the reasonableness

---

[46][Bernard Lamy], *The Art of Speaking*, 2d ed. (London, 1708), pp. 50–51. Translated from a French treatise of *ca.* 1668.

of men would cause them to respect "agreed" meanings and that his "remedies" would suffice for those cases in which "agreed" meanings had already been lost or were otherwise inadequate.

To Fielding, however, a generation later, the situation looked different. He believed as devoutly as Locke in the Settlement of 1689, but he did not find it so easy to believe in the solidarity and reasonableness of English society on which this setlement must rest. Everywhere he looked he saw not homogeneity but factionalism, "interest," and party, not a sense of social responsibility but crass opportunism, not reasonableness but fatuous "enthusiasm." And nearly always he saw the effect of these forces on language and, conversely, the effect of "corrupted" language on society. From Locke, Fielding took a method and terminology of linguistic criticism, but his interest in the problems of communication was not, like Locke's, epistemological so much as social and moral, and his sense of the corruption of words was deeply rooted in his own experience of the language and society of his day. The next chapter will consider that experience as it is given expression in Fielding's attacks on those elements of society he held most responsible for the corruption of words— the persons who, he was convinced, should be made to "answer for the disadvantageous Light in which they have placed these Words."

Chapter III
LANGUAGE AND SOCIETY

"When a man speaks to another," wrote Locke, "it is that he may be understood: and the end of speech is, that those sounds, as marks, may make known his ideas to the hearer" (III, ii, 2). Fielding never quotes this passage, nor does he ever have occasion to frame his own definition of the purpose of language. But there is no doubt that he shared Locke's view, which was, in this instance, merely the orthodox attitude of the age and the basic assumption underlying the whole of the seventeenth- and eighteenth-century critique of language: the principal purpose of speech was the disinterested communication of ideas. The notion had been stated by Hobbes in very similar terms,[1] was implicit at least in earlier treatises on language, and, after Locke, was echoed by nearly every eighteenth-century grammarian or lexicographer who felt the need of some prefatory remarks on the nature and function of speech. It was also repeated, as we have seen, by such occasional commentators on the subject as Jonathan Swift.[2] In all of the eighteenth century, in fact, there was only one dissenting voice which made itself heard above the general chorus of agreement, and this was, not surprisingly, the voice of that professional cynic, Bernard Mandeville. "The first Design of Speech," said the author of *The Fable of the Bees* (1729), "was to persuade others either to give Credit to what the speaking Person would have them believe; or else to act or suffer such Things, as he would compel them to act or suffer, if they were entirely in his Power."[3] Alone in the age, Mandeville

---

[1] "The generall use of Speech, is to transferre our Mentall Discourse, into Verbal; or the Trayne of our Thoughts, into a Trayne of Words," and therefore the use of words to "declare that to be [the speaker's] will, which is not" is an "abuse of Speech." *Leviathan*, ed. A. D. Lindsay (New York: Dutton, 1950), pp. 23–24.
[2] See above, p. 12.
[3] *The Fable of the Bees: or, Private Vices, Publick Benefits*, ed. F. B. Kaye (Oxford: Clarendon Press, 1924), 2: 289.

provided a statement of the purpose of language which would accommodate the saying of *the thing which was not* as a legitimate function of speech. It is little wonder that he was looked upon, by Fielding and others, as a dangerous and subversive influence.

For to all the rest what Mandeville called "the first Design of Speech" was a perversion of its true purpose. Locke, as we have seen, ascribes the abuse of words chiefly to negligence, but he recognizes that certain "by-interests" (III, x, 13) are sometimes responsible as well and in the chapter on "Remedies" he names three possible motivations for this abuse which stand opposed to the true purpose of speech. These are "vain-glory, ambition, or a party" (III, xi, 7). But where Fielding went beyond Locke was in seeing such deviations from the true purpose of language not only as an abuse of particular words and phrases but also as a corruption of the whole process of verbal communication—a discrediting of language itself as a medium of truthful expression. He would not have agreed with Mandeville that the use of language as an instrument of power and self-interest was right because it was natural, but he would have admitted that the age in which they lived furnished abundant evidence that this kind of use was rapidly displacing the disinterested exchange of ideas as "the end of speech." Where Locke saw reasonable men eager to cultivate an effective medium of discourse, Fielding, like Mandeville, saw mostly self-seeking opportunists willing to exploit the powers of language for their own gain. The Orator in the "Pleasures of the Town" sequence of *The Author's Farce* (1730) boasts that he is superior, as a purveyor of nonsense, to any other member of society, and his song is a fairly complete survey of the exploiters of language whom Fielding held principally responsible for its corruption:

> The lawyer wrangling at the bar,
> While the reverend bench is dozing,
> The scribbler in a pamphlet war,
> Or Grub Street bard composing:
> The trudging quack in scarlet cloak,
> Or coffee-house politic prater;
> Can none come up to what I have spoke
> When I was a bold orator.

> The well-bred courtier telling lies,
>   Or levée hunter believing;
> The vain coquette that rolls her eyes,
>   More empty fops deceiving;
> The parson of dissenting gang,
>   Or flattering dedicator,
> Could none of them like me harangue,
>   When I was a bold orator.

(VIII, 247)

All of these diverse members of society have in common the use of language as a means to unworthy ends and hence the power to corrupt it. For all of them language is an important stock in trade, but none of them respects its integrity of purpose. They are concerned not with the communication of ideas but with persuasion, not with understanding but with personal advantage or reward, not with truth but with form or effect. They may be loosely divided, for purposes of the analysis which follows, into four main categories: writers, particularly the Grub Street variety (the scribbler, the bard, the dedicator); politicians (the courtier, the place-seeker, the "coffee-house politic prater"); polite society (the coquette, the fops); and the professions (the lawyer, the quack, and the parson). Fielding attacked these groups repeatedly throughout his career. He did not limit himself by any means to their linguistic transgressions, and frequently, as we have had occasion to remark before, his exposure of these transgressions is as much a means of getting at some more general corruption of the age as it is an end in itself. But it is surely significant that he so often chose this particular method of attack.

WRITERS, CRITICS, AND HACKS

In the underworld scene of *The Author's Farce*, recalling Lucian and anticipating Pope, Fielding has the various literary genres competing for a prize before the Court of Nonsense. William Coley describes it as follows: "The irrational modes of art are here at their irrational best. . . . Language is either circumvented entirely [by Monsieur Pantomime], . . . or heroically inflated (by Don Tragedio), or confused and Babel-like (by Sir Farcical

Comic, who understands no language at all), or spoken shout-
ingly (by Dr. Orator), or, finally, set to music (by Signior
Opera)."⁴ Opera wins the contest, probably because it was a
perfect symbol both of the age's degeneracy of taste and of its
debasement of language: it treated words in literal fact "only as
the vehicles of sound." Fielding was not, of course, in his
dramatic burlesques, acting entirely as a disinterested guardian
of public taste and morals when he attacked the opera and other
subliterary theatrical spectacles of the day such as rope dancing,
tumbling, and pantomimes. Drury Lane and Covent Garden,
both dominated by the author-impresario John Rich (the
"Machine" of Fielding's *Tumble-Down Dick*) were the rivals of
Fielding's own theater, the Haymarket, and his burlesques of
Rich's popular "entertainments" were skirmishes in the incessant theater war of the time. But Swift and Pope, with no such
immediate provocation, were equally alarmed at the threat to
"regular" comedy and tragedy represented by the growing
popularity of debased theatrical forms, and there is no doubt
that their concern was sharpened, like Fielding's, by the anti-
verbal implications of these forms. The theater, so much more
integral a part of the cultural milieu in the eighteenth century
than it is today, was recognized as a formative influence not only
on manners and morals but also on language. Gilbert Burnet,
in the Preface to his translation of More's *Utopia* (1684), placed
the stage on an equal footing in this regard with the pulpit, for
though "the two places . . . ought not to be named together, much
less to resemble one another; yet it cannot be denied, but the
Rules and Measure of Speech is [*sic*] generally taken from
them."

But for Burnet, writing before the heyday of Rich and his
"entertainments," the major threat was not the banishment of
language from the stage but its corruption by "false Rhetorick"
—notably the pseudo-sublime bombast of the heroic drama. He
believed, however, that "that florid strain" was by his day
"almost quite worn out and is now as ridiculous as it was once
admired." The language of the stage, he confidently concluded,
"is now certainly properer, and more natural than it was formerly,

chiefly since the correction that was given by the *Rehearsal*."[5]
Fielding, who was the principal upholder of the *Rehearsal* tradition in his own time, clearly did not agree. Not only had the
revival of the classical ideal of tragedy, in which Burnet apparently placed his trust, failed to fulfill its promise (Addison's *Cato*
had been its only major success and even it was ridiculed by
Fielding, in *The Tragedy of Tragedies*, for its hollow rhetoric),
but the heroic drama of the Restoration continued to hold the
stage and to wield its influence over contemporary dramatists.
Dryden, Lee, Banks, and Otway, still popular in Fielding's time,
are burlesqued (and identified in the Scriblerian Notes) in *The
Tragedy of Tragedies*, but so are Young, Theobald, John Dennis,
Rowe, Nahum Tate, Charles Johnson, Gay, and other eighteenth-
century authors. Whatever Burnet may have thought, the threat
to the language of the "false Rhetorick" which had so "much
corrupted . . . the Stage" was for Fielding still immediate and
even more potent than that of debased entertainments because
the language of tragedy was taken more seriously and was more
openly admired.

Addison, though he did not in Fielding's view escape it himself,
recognized where the fault of the heroic dramatists lay: in the
disparity between "the Stile . . . [and] the Sentiments of their
Tragedies. Their Language is very often noble and sonorous,
but the Sense either very trifling or very common. . . . For my
own part, I prefer a noble Sentiment that is depressed with
homely Language, infinitely before a vulgar one that is blown up
with all the Sound and Energy of Expression." English writers
of tragedy would do well, he thought, to write down their notions
first "in plain *English*" before turning them into verse, and
readers should try to separate thought from expression in tragic
speeches. "By this means, without being imposed upon by
Words, we may judge impartially of the Thought."[6] In short, as
Locke would have said, the trouble with the language of heroic
tragedy was that it separated words from their proper ideas, and
this was precisely its trouble for Fielding as well, who resented
being "imposed upon by Words" in any form. Abstractions like
"love" and "honor" acquired "specialized" meanings in the

---

[5]Cited by Williamson, *The Senecan Amble*, p. 227.
[6]*Spectator* No. 39, Apr. 14, 1711, Everyman ed., 1: 117–18.

heroic drama not much different from the reductionist senses
Fielding assigned these words in his ironic vocabulary. The
heroic playwrights "have made the . . . great characters of a Hero
to be Love [and] Honour," wrote an anonymous Restoration
critic, but "they have made Love to be the hot passion of an
hour, . . . [and] their Honour consists in . . . maintaining the fiery
ground of Fame; to vanquish Reason and generosity in the contempt of life; *gathering the spreading glory of a Hero into a single
punctilio*" (my italics).[7]

But such specialization of "general words" was always, for
Fielding, the prelude to pure meaninglessness, the total separa-
tion of words and ideas. It is this feature of tragical rhetoric
which he most vigorously burlesques in *The Tragedy of Trage-
dies*. "Here I shall beg only one Postulatum," writes H. Scriblerus
Secundus in the Preface, "*viz*. That the greatest Perfection of the
Language of a Tragedy is, that it is not to be understood. . . .
What can be so proper for Tragedy as a Set of big sounding
Words, so contrived together, as to convey no Meaning; which
I shall one Day or other prove to be the Sublime of *Longinus*."[8]
Even the names of the characters (Lord Grizzle, Queen Dollal-
lolla, Princess Huncamunca), as William Coley observes, "are
mouth-filling, sense-fracturing, stature-diminishing honorifics
that do no honor."[9] This was probably Fielding's complaint
against the whole of the heroic drama he was burlesquing—that
its unrelieved hyperbole and sublimity of language defeated its
own purpose by draining heroic words of their heroic power and
reducing them to empty commonplaces. *The Tragedy of Tragedies* simply carries this process to its logical conclusion. Traditionally heroic terms like "soul" and "genius," repeated *ad
nauseam* in every kind of inappropriate context, become feeble
and ridiculous echoes of once mighty concepts. "Be still my
Soul," emotes the Queen upon hearing Tom Thumb request
the hand of Princess Huncamunca; "A Tragical Phrase much in
use," comments Scriblerus. Speeches delivered always in the
larger-than-life superlative style succeed finally in producing
only comic incredulity. When the Queen tells the King that she

---

[7]*Remarques on the Humours and Conversations of the Town* (London, 1673), p. 53.
[8]Hillhouse ed., pp. 83–84.
[9]*Fielding's Comic*, p. 191.

is weeping for joy, he replies,

> If it be so, let all Men cry for Joy,
> 'Till my whole Court be drowned with their Tears;
> Nay, till they overflow my utmost Land,
> And leave me Nothing but the Sea to rule;

and Scriblerus, citing examples from Lee and others, notes, "These Floods are very frequent in the Tragick Authors." Heroic ranting is exposed as mere alliterated sound: "I'll rave; I'll rant; I'll rise; I'll rush; I'll roar"; and Scriblerus refers the reader to "a late Ode called the *Naval Lyrick*," a bombastic Pindaric poem by Edward Young. The heroic metaphor, as represented by the lines

> He is indeed, a Helmet to us all,
> While he supports, we need not fear to fall,

is defended by Scriblerus in a note which makes Fielding's objection to pointless conceits abundantly clear. Against an alleged charge by Dennis that the epithet is confused, Scriblerus ranges a whole battery of equally absurd similes and epithets from Dryden and others and expresses his contempt for "so ignorant a Carper, who doth not know that an Epithet in Tragedy is very often no other than an Expletive." The pretensions of poetic diction are revealed (through the patent Scriblerian device of bathos) by the fact that a single "unpoetic" word can bring a whole passage of inflated loftiness crashing down to earth in empty ruin: "All Nature wears one universal Grin."[10]

Critical opinion has always ranked *The Tragedy of Tragedies* high among Fielding's works as an extraordinarily successful exercise in pure comedy, a sort of magnificent sport. But because its rollicking burlesque seems so far removed from the social and ethical themes which inform his greatest works it has not generally been given much attention by students of his thought and method. It is, according to a fairly typical estimate, "a general burlesque. No specific heresy was being hunted. No particular poet was being savaged. . . . [Fielding] was out for a laugh,

---

[10]Hillhouse ed., pp. 90, 93–94, 98, 103, 134.

not for chastisement."[11] The play is remarkably free, it is true, of any feelings of rancor or personal animosity, and it would be wrong to try to play down its spirit of good humored comedy in order to claim for it the dignity of thematic seriousness. But the Augustans rarely laughed without some earnest reason, and the name of Scriblerus on a title page was an imprimature of serious purpose. Viewed in the context of Fielding's lifelong preoccupation with the corruption of language, the theme of the play, the "specific heresy" Fielding is hunting, is the abuse of language by the false rhetoric of the heroic stage, a rhetoric which not only defeated its own purpose as the vehicle of heroic sentiments but, in so doing, weakened the language as a whole by robbing honorifics of honor.

The Tragedy of Tragedies, however, is a double-edged burlesque. The text of the play mocks the linguistic absurdities of heroic tragedy, but the Preface and notes do more than merely identify the real sources of these absurdities. They also—again in the best Scriblerian tradition—satirize the pedantic verbal quibbling of a literary criticism which presumed to justify itself as a contribution to "the Intelligibleness of Language."[12] The annotations of such modern critics and commentators as John Dennis, Dr. Bentley, Professor Burmann, Lewis Theobald, Leonard Welsted, and Nathan Salmon are caricatured in the form of little essays in obfuscation which darken rather than illuminate an already murky text. The satire arises in part from the application of pedantic subtlety to so worthless a subject and is therefore as much at the expense of the modern writing which spawns such commentary as of the critics who perform it so ponderously and self-importantly. In a long expository note on a heroic simile in *The Vernoniad* (which has a similar burlesque apparatus of scholarly annotations), Fielding ironically calls for more commentary on modern writers. This might, he explains,

---

[11]V. C. Clinton-Baddeley, *The Burlesque Tradition in the English Theatre after 1600* (London: Methuen, 1952), p. 54. But cf. Martin Price, who treats *The Tragedy of Tragedies* as an example of the "mock form," which "begins by attacking a false language. . . . The Augustans were deeply concerned with the breakdown of language. They saw it as a symptom of a decline of culture, and the greatest satires of the age have this as their theme." *To The Palace of Wisdom* (New York: Doubleday, 1964), pp. 204, 250, 255–57.

[12]Robert Baker, *Reflections on the English Language* (London, 1770), p. 115. Cited by Leonard, p. 105.

prove them superior to the ancients because "certainly it will not be said, that the moderns are less obscure; for though Persius be the most obscure of all the Latin authors, and Lycophron of all the Greeks, yet they are, notwithstanding the great distance of time, to be understood even by foreigners; whereas many of the moderns are not intelligible even to their own countrymen, without the help of some commentator, who with infinite pains . . . arrives at the meaning" (XV, 54).

But Fielding was also aware of the positively harmful job of obfuscation which pedantic criticism could do when turned loose on a really serious work of literature. Having explicated, in a burlesque fashion, a turgid passage from one of Cibber's birthday odes, he concludes "by observing that if Dr. Bentley had never given us his comment on Milton, it is more than possible few of us would have understood that poet in the same surprisingly fine manner with that great critic" (XV, 55). But if to obscure the language of Milton was a crime against one of the "pure sources of genuine diction," a poisoning of "the wells of English undefiled,"[13] then how much more heinous were the crimes committed in the name of verbal criticism against the language of Shakespeare. A "Correspondent" to the *Covent-Garden Journal* No. 31 (actually Fielding himself), noting that "there is nothing in this Age more fashionable, than to criticise on Shakespeare," submits some emendations of Hamlet's "To be or not to be" soliloquy in which false principles of "correctness" and "propriety" are allowed to destroy completely the sense and beauty of the original. A similar attack on the travesties of Shakespearian emendation occurs in *A Journey from This World to the Next* when the narrator reports a conversation between the shades of Shakespeare and some of his commentators and idolaters. The poet is called upon to pass judgment on a disputed line in *Othello*—"Put out the light, and then put out the light." Each of the critics offers his interpretation or emendation, the readings becoming more and more ingenious as they warm to their work, until finally Shakespeare interrupts to say that he does not remember what he had intended in the line. But

---

[13]In the Preface to the *Dictionary*, Dr. Johnson appeals to the precedent of "the writers before the restoration, whose works I regard as *the wells of English undefiled*, as the pure sources of genuine diction." The "wells of English undefiled" is a paraphrase of Spenser's tribute to Chaucer in *The Faerie Queen*, Bk. IV, Canto ii, Stanza 32.

"this I know, could I have dreamt so much nonsense would have been talked and writ about it, I would have blotted it out of my works. . . . I marvel nothing so much as that men will gird themselves at discovering obscure beauties in an author. Certes the greatest and most pregnant beauties are ever the plainest and most evidently striking; and when two meanings of a passage can in the least balance our judgments which to prefer, I hold it a matter of unquestionable certainty, that neither of them is worth a farthing" (II, 247–48).

For Fielding (who would not, one suspects, have cared for twentieth-century methods of criticism any more than he did for those of his own age) the ideal of good writing was perspicuity. In that he was at one with the tradition of linguistic reform from Bacon through Locke, and just as the seventeenth-century reformers of pulpit oratory fought the influence on language of a "metaphysical" style of preaching which elevated the "imperfections" of language into rhetorical virtues,[14] so Fielding battled against the same tendencies in the verbal quibbling and ambiguity-hunting of eighteenth-century criticism.

But an over zealous pedantry was not the only evil which threatened language and letters through literary criticism. Even more pernicious was the descent of criticism into the hands of the totally ignorant and irresponsible, the transformation of a highly exacting art, demanding wide learning and a trained sensibility, into a fashionable parlor game at which any number could play, with no qualifications required but those of a carping disposition and an acquired jargon, and with no rules except those imposed by whim and prejudice. "A few general Rules extracted out of the *French* Authors, with a certain Cant of Words, has sometimes set up an illiterate heavy Writer for a most judicious and formidable Critick," wrote Addison in the *Spectator*, and this thought led him into the statement that critics would do well to study Locke's *Essay Concerning Human Understanding* so as to learn "the Art of distinguishing between Words and Things" and thereby avoid polluting the language with further "Confusion and Obscurity."[15]

---

[14]See R. F. Jones, "The Attack on Pulpit Eloquence in the Restoration," *The Seventeenth Century*, p. 142.

[15]No. 291, Feb. 2, 1712, Everyman ed., 2: 368–69.

Fielding, who in the "Modern Glossary" says that "Critic" is "Like *Homo*, a Name common to all human Race," waged war from the beginning of his career to the end against this leveling of the name and office of criticism. In the *Champion* for November 27, 1739, observing (characteristically) that "this Word Criticism" is derived "from a *Greek* Word, implying no less than Judgment," he sets up "some Qualifications, without which no person shall henceforth presume to censure any Performance whatever"—qualifications so ironically minimal that the modern sense of the word (like the modern art of criticism itself) is revealed to be an empty mockery of its ancient original. But if the name and office of criticism were debased, so also was its special language, and it is hardly surprising to find Fielding returning again and again to the "certain Cant of Words" behind which modern critics tried to conceal their ignorance and spite. "I would recommend to all Persons," he continues, "to be extremely cautious in the Use of the Words *Low*, *Dull*, *Stupid*, *Sad Stuff*, *Grub-Street*, etc. which, with some more, I wish heartily were banished out of our Language, and that it was reckoned as certain a Mark of Folly to use them, as it would be of Indecency to use some others. Tho' I must own at the same Time, this might be as fatal to Criticism, as the Banishment of Indecent Words hath been to Gallantry; and that some Persons of admired Judgment would be as hard put to talk critically without the one, as some noted Beaus are to talk wantonly without the other."

What Fielding demanded of critics was simply a genuine exercise of the judgment that their name implied and a forthright expression of that judgment in specific, meaningful terms. It is true, of course, that his attacks on the critics were again not altogether free of the elements of personal resentment, and if he particularly objected to the use of words like "low" as critical terms it was at least partly because these were the kinds of terms that hostile critics applied to his own works throughout his career. The *Grub Street Journal* branded him as a "low" writer in the thirties for trafficking with such "low" theatrical forms as the farce and the ballad opera (even when he was using these forms as vehicles for burlesque and satire), and he was still being charged with "lowness" in his novels twenty years later by Dr.

John Hill and the *London Daily Advertiser*.[16] But Fielding's objection to such criticism (or at any rate the grounds on which he chose to do battle with it) was not that it was hostile but that it was *vague*, that it was a mere parroting of words which conveyed the hostility but not the reasons for it, in short, that it used words without clear and distinct ideas. Captain Vinegar's son Tom is assigned the job of dramatic critic in the first number of the *Champion* on the strength of the fact that "He frequently useth the Words *Damned Stuff*; *That is Low*, etc. in Conversation, with which Words alone, together with his *Cat-call*, he often brags he can damn the best Play in the Universe."[17] But this is to debase criticism to mere indiscriminate condemnation and to reduce its terminology to the level of the cat-call.

Any writer who broke away from the established genres, as Fielding did in both his dramatic and his narrative writings, ran the risk in the eighteenth century of being identified with the retailers of subliterary entertainments and hence of being classed as a "low" writer according to the strict neoclassical hierarchy of literary values. The burlesque and the prose romance were by neoclassical definition "low" forms of writing. But in actual practice the word was used not merely as a classification of form but also as a prejudicial means of ranking the presumed subject matter of such works ("low life" as opposed to "high life"), the audience (the lower classes to which they were supposed to cater), and, by extension, the author (who must, it was reasoned, be himself of "low" mind and morals in order to purvey such "stuff"). Fielding satirized this abuse of the word by putting it in the mouths of speakers who were as ill-placed to pronounce social judgments on works of art as they were ill-equipped to pronounce esthetic ones. "The lowest of all wretches are the aptest to cry out low in the pit," he remarks in *Tom Jones*, and if a scene was natural and true to life, the "young critics of the age, the clerks, apprentices, etc., called it low, and fell a groaning." Again, in the puppet-show scene, Jones protests the retirement of Punch and Joan in favor of an expurgated puppet version of Cibber's *Provoked Husband*, but his opinion is roundly con-

---

[16]Cross, 1: 114 ff. and 2: 392 ff.

[17]Nov. 15, 1739. For similar attacks on the debased language of criticism, see *Tom Jones* (Henley ed., IV, 242–47), and the *Covent-Garden Journal* Nos. 3 and 13.

demned by the puppet master, a clerk, and an exciseman, all of
whom decry the "low" quality of Punch and Joan; and the
exciseman defends the expurgated *Provoked Husband* by citing
his own experiences of the original version which he had seen as
a footman in London: the "gentlemen in our gallery could not
bear any thing so low, and they damned it" (III, 334–35; IV, 323).

It was partly to escape this kind of prejudicial categorization
and partly to mock it that Fielding proposed, in the Preface to
Joseph Andrews, his own half-jesting classification of the "comic
epic poem in prose," or, in *Tom Jones*, of "prosai-comi-epic
writing." He would, as he says in the latter instance, be free
under such a classification to lay down his own rules and would
not be intimidated by whatever "the modern judges of our
theatres mean by that word *low*; by which they have happily
succeeded in banishing all humor from the stage, and have made
the theatre as dull as a drawing-room" (III, 206). For the real
trouble with the word "low" as a critical term (and Fielding's
objection to it *as a word*) was that while masquerading as an
esthetic category it was actually an expression of social snobbery,
a confusion of the stultifying genteelness of the drawing room
with the proprieties of art and so separated from its original idea.
A footnote in the *Champion* for June 12, 1740, identifies "low"
(in a manner which anticipates the definitions of the "Modern
Glossary" a dozen years later) as "A Word much used in the
Theatre, but of such uncertain Signification, that I could never
understand the Meaning of it." Fielding did not succeed, in his
own time, in banishing the word "low" from the vocabulary of
criticism, but it was largely due to his relentless ridicule of the
term (and even more to his own unparalleled success in "low"
forms) that it lost its authority as an expression of critical disdain,
and by 1780 George Colman (the elder) could pay him a compliment which would have pleased him both as an author and as a
reformer of the language:

> When Fielding, Humour's fav'rite child appear'd,
> *Low* was the word—a word each author fear'd!
> 'Till chac'd at length, by Pleasantry's bright ray,
> Nature and mirth resum'd their legal sway.[18]

[18] *Prose on Several Occasions* (London, 1787), 3: 227. Cited by Blanchard, p. 208.

But though Fielding was willing to defend even Colley Cibber against the meaningless charge of being "low," he did not spare the laureate on other grounds. He became, in fact, by virtue of his free-wheeling, devil-may-care literary style, Fielding's archetypal desecrator of the English tongue. In *The Author's Farce* Cibber is Sir Farcical Comic, who, when he is told that his rival Don Tragedio (probably Lewis Theobald) "does not only glean up all the bad words of other authors, but makes new bad words of his own," replies triumphantly, "Nay, egad, I have made new words, and spoiled old ones too, if you talk of that. . . . I have as great a confusion of languages in my play, as was at the building of Babel" (VIII, 238–39). The allusion is to the Preface of the same *Provoked Husband* (1728) which Fielding champions in *Tom Jones* against the footmen's cries of lowness. Describing Mrs. Oldfield's costume in the original production of the play, Cibber wrote: "The Ornaments she herself provided . . . seem'd in all Respects, the Paraphonalia of a Woman of Quality," and the mistake (whether typographical or orthographic) was quickly taken up by the *Grub Street Journal* and other self-appointed guardians of taste and linguistic purity as a symbol of Cibber's ignorance of and lack of respect for the English language. No one imagined, of course (least of all Fielding, whose ridicule of Cibber was always good humored), that the blunder was important in itself. But there was a sense, which Fielding made clear in his Preface to the second edition of *Tom Thumb* (1730), in which such errors represented a serious threat to the purity of the tongue. Referring to Locke's complaint of "confused Ideas in Words," Fielding suggests that an excellent way of avoiding this fault is to cultivate the current "Prefatical" style in which words are stripped of all ideas whatsoever, and he offers as an example of this technique Cibber's method of rendering a word meaningless by the simple device of altering one or two letters, as in turning "Paraphernalia" into "Paraphonalia." "For a Man may turn Greek into Nonsense, who cannot turn Sense into either *Greek* or *Latin*."[19]

In part Fielding's contempt (and that of Cibber's other detractors) for the laureate's ignorance of the classical languages

---

[19]Hillhouse ed., p. 49.

was a reflection of the resentment felt by the established *literati* against the encroachments on their domain by a writer who lacked the accepted credentials of the man of letters. But it also implied a genuine concern over the fate of the language at the hands of uneducated writers who, lacking knowledge of the "original" Latin or Greek roots of words, could inflict real harm on the tongue by using these words in ways which would separate them from their "true" meanings. One of the causes Dr. Johnson mentions in the Preface to his *Dictionary* for the "corruption" of words is that "illiterate writers will at one time or another, by publick infatuation, rise into renown, who, not knowing the original import of words, will use them with colloquial licentiousness, confound distinction and forget propriety."[20] Nor was faulty spelling a matter to be taken lightly. The rationale which George Harris offers in *Observations upon the English Language* (1752) for his preoccupation with orthography is that the "Manner of Spelling sufficiently declares the Original of the Words in Question,"[21] and Anselm Bayly, in *An Introduction to Languages* (1758), maintains that "uncertainty in Orthography" will introduce "confusion in Roots: and these, the change, ignorance, and loss of a Language . . ., [for] what would be the consequence but the ignorance of their precise meaning and derivation from the Latin [or other original tongue]"? The important thing is to preserve in spelling the original root form of the word, "For if you injure the root, you effectually destroy the tree and its branches."[22]

But Cibber played fast and loose with the English language in other ways besides his orthography. In the Preface to *Tom Thumb* Fielding offers as an example of a "Second Method of stripping Words of their Ideas" (that of "putting half a dozen incoherent ones together") a paradoxical line from the Prologue to *The Provoked Husband* asserting that "*the People of our Age shall be Ancestors*" in which "one discordant Word, like a surly Man in Company, spoils the whole Sentence, and makes it

---

[20]"The word *illiterate*," according to Lord Chesterfield, "in its common acceptation, means a man who is ignorant of those two languages [Greek and Latin]." Quoted by James Sutherland, *Preface to 18th Century Poetry*, p. 59 n., after a citation in *OED*.
[21]P. 12.
[22]P. 58.

entirely Prefatical."[23] In *The Opposition, a Vision* (1741) he ridicules Cibber's use, in the *Apology for the Life of Mr. Colley Cibber* (1740), of the "remarkable expression, ... Here I met the revolution," which he finds so puzzling that, "having considered and turned it every way in my thoughts, I was at last obliged to lay down the book in despair of ever finding out what the Author meant by that extraordinary sentence" (XIV, 323–24).[24] And in the *Champion* he seizes upon the

barbarous instance ... of the poor Word *Adept* [also in the *Apology*]; a Word which I apprehend no School-Boy hath ever wantonly employed, unless to signify the utmost Perfection; for Ignorance they cannot plead who have gone beyond the Accidence, since they must then find that *adipiscor vult adeptus*: Nay an *Englishman* may learn from *Hudibras*,

> *In* Rosicrutian *lore, as learned*
> *As he that* verè Adeptus *earned.*

This Word our great *Master* hath tortured and wrested to signify a *Tyro* or *Novice*, being directly contrary to the Sense in which it hath been hitherto used.[25]

Actually Cibber's eccentric use of language was probably as much due to a kind of exuberant carelessness as to ignorance, but his willingness to confess to such a fault (not, one suspects, without a certain amount of perverse self-satisfaction) could scarcely have been expected to appease writers like Pope and Fielding who believed that an author had a special responsibility to the language in which he wrote. "I grant," Cibber wrote in the *Apology*,

that no Man worthy of the name of an Author is a more faulty Writer than myself. That I am not a Master of my own Language, I too often feel, when I am at a loss for Expression. I know too that I have too bold a Disregard for that Correctness which others set so just a Value

[23]Hillhouse ed., p. 49. Cibber had written that the play would be remembered "when the People of this Age shall be Ancestors." Pope ridicules the same passage in *The Art of Sinking in Poetry*, Ch. XVI.
[24]Cibber meant that he was a member of the party which welcomed William III at Nottingham in 1688. *Apology*, p. 34.
[25]Apr. 22, 1740. Commenting on the English debut of a certain opera singer, Cibber had written, "Mrs. Tofts, who took her first Grounds of Musick here in her own Country, ... was then but an ADEPT in it." *Apology*, p. 34.

upon. . . . Whenever I speak of any thing that highly delights me, I find
it very difficult to keep my Words within the Bounds of Common
Sense: Even when I write too, the same Feeling will sometimes get
the Better of me: of which I cannot give you a stronger instance, than
in that wild Expression I made use of in the first Edition of my
Preface to the *Provoked Husband*; where, speaking of Mrs. *Oldfield's*
excellent Performance in the part of Lady Townley, my words ran
thus, *viz*. It is not enough to say, *that here she outdid her usual Outdoing*. A most vile Jingle, I grant it. You may well ask me, How could
I possibly commit such a Wantonness to Paper? And I owe myself the
Shame of confessing, I have no Excuse for it, but that, like a Lover in
the Fulness of his Content, by endeavouring to be floridly grateful, I
talk'd Nonsense.[26]

It is probably with this passage in mind (and particularly
Cibber's comparison of himself with a transported lover) that
Fielding in *Joseph Andrews* develops a burlesque heroic simile
comparing the powers of love to "metamorphose and distort the
human senses" with the powers of "the great Cibber, who confounds all number, gender, and breaks through every rule of
grammar at his will, [and so] hath . . . distorted the English
language" (I, 46). Cibber's approach to language was irrational,
like love; it was, by his own admission, an *enthusiastic* approach
and therefore subject to the same criticism which the reformers
of pulpit oratory lodged against the preaching of the puritan and
metaphysical divines: that it was a perversion of the rational
purpose of speech. The charge that he flouted grammar, a theme
which Fielding pursued relentlessly in a series of papers in the
Champion, was in a larger sense an attack on Cibber's lack of
respect for this rational principle of language. We have already
seen that Fielding seems not to have regarded Cibber's grammatical transgressions as very important in themselves. But a
disregard for the logical (as the age believed) laws of language
was symptomatic of the irresponsibility of uneducated writers
and of the threat they posed to the condition of the tongue.

Fielding opened the attack in the *Champion* for April 22, 1740,
by offering to prove that Cibber's *Apology*, despite accusations
to the contrary, *was* written in English, because "Whatever Book

[26]Pp. 31–32.

is writ in no other Language, is writ in *English*. This Book is writ in no other Language, *Ergo*, It is writ in *English*: Of which Language the Author hath shewn himself a most absolute Master; for surely he must be absolute Master of that whose Laws he can trample under Feet, and which he can use as he pleases." In a succeeding issue (April 29) he returns to the theme by affecting to disagree with Cicero's opinion "That he who commits his Thoughts to Paper without being able methodically to range them, or properly to illustrate them, gives us an Instance of the most intemperate Abuse of his own Time and of Letters themselves." Suggesting Cibber as a notable exception to this rule, Fielding pretends to wonder "whether Learning be of such Consequence to a Writer as it is imagined," and he quotes liberally from the *Apology* "to shew the little Advantage of . . . Grammar, to an Author" and to prove that Cibber "is generally to be understood without, and *secondly*, That he is sometimes not to be understood with it," taking particular note of the Cibberian rule that "*Wherever the* VERB OUTDO *comes in*, . . . *the* PLEASANT ACCUSATIVE CASE OUTDOING *is sure to follow*." The next paper (May 6), arguing the proposition that "One might almost say, *He hath even a Language to himself*," concentrates on Cibber's prolixity of style and incoherency of syntax and includes a parody of his prose in which "I have endeavoured to use my Author's own Words in the same Sense which he hath attributed to them." This concludes with a Cibberian simile which makes, however, a serious Lockean criticism of Cibber's style. It is, says Fielding, like a rapid stream in which "the Waves of Words pass by so quick, that it is very difficult to separate or fix distinct Ideas. . . . You cannot distinguish one Wave from another and you have from the whole, only an Idea of a River." The *Champion* of May 10 announces that a "Court of Judicature" will be convened in a subsequent issue and that among the cases to be tried is that of "*Col. Apol*. . . . for the Murder of the *English* Language." The May 17 number has the first "PROCEEDINGS *of a Court of Censorial Enquiry held before Capt.* HERCULES VINEGAR, *Great Champion and Censor of* Great Britain," in which, as we have seen, Cibber is acquitted on the strength of the plea that other writers have done greater damage to the language than he has and that errors of grammar and orthography such as he excels in are not so harmful as the total pedantic meaninglessness which marks certain other literary productions of the day. Citing his own confession in the *Apology* that he frequently "talk'd Nonsense," Cibber argues that "It is impossible I should have any Enmity to the *English* Language, with which I am so little acquainted."

The indictment itself, in fact, softens the charge against Cibber (though scarcely the satiric insult) by describing the "wounds" which he has inflicted on the English language as "broad . . . but of no Depth at all," and this would seem to represent Fielding's real opinion of the harm which a writer like Cibber could do. Ignorance, carelessness, enthusiasm—the faults which Cibber personified so well—were a nuisance and, insofar as they were propagated by the writings of popular authors like Cibber and stood a chance of becoming established in the language, a positive danger. But for the most part the harm was not deep. If Sir Farcical Comic made up new words "and spoiled old ones too," he did not really strike at the heart of language because his perversions were basically innocent. If he did not use language for the disinterested exchange of ideas, neither did he pervert it systematically to the service of the lie. The ends he applied it to were unworthy, perhaps, but they were not evil. Fielding had personal and political reasons for attacking Cibber. The laureate had called him a "broken wit" in the *Apology* and had composed hired panegyrics (or so Fielding charged) on the Walpole ministry which Fielding hated.[27] But if there is no malice in Fielding's attacks it is probably because there was clearly no malice or wicked intent in Cibber himself. He made an ideal symbol of the Grub Street threat to language in the person of the ignorant and irresponsible scribbler, but Grub Street's more serious menace, as Fielding realized, lay elsewhere.

To represent the blacker depths of corruption to which Grub Street could sink, Fielding turned from Cibber to John ("Orator") Henley. Henley was a free-lance preacher of the day who had established an "Oratory" in London and charged admission for sermons and lectures which were often, so Fielding alleged, merely thinly disguised eulogies of Walpole and (later) Jaco-

---

[27] *Apology*, p. 164. *Champion*, Sept. 6, 1740. Not included in the 1741 reprint.

bitism. He advertised his "Oratory" programs in the press in a vulgarly sensational and impudent manner which, in view of the quasi-religious nature of their subject matter, was constantly flirting with the blasphemous.[28] He was also an author who wrote treatises on rhetoric in which nearly the whole emphasis was on gesture and modulation of the voice and who, according to Pope, "had an hundred pounds a year given him for the secret service of a weekly [pro-ministerial] paper of unintelligible nonsense, called the Hyp-Doctor."[29] "Set up an oratory and preach non-sense," Witmore cynically advises the penniless author Luckless in *The Author's Farce.* "If you would receive applause, deserve to receive sentence at the Old Bailey" (VIII, 204). And in "The Pleasures of the Town," Henley is the Dr. Orator who boasts to the Goddess of Nonsense that he is superior to any other cor-rupter of the language.

If Cibber is the archetype of the upstart scribbler who spoils words out of ignorance and unrestrained exuberance, Henley is the archetype of the unscrupulous hack who perverts them to evil causes for cash received. Something both of his way with language and of his dedication to the profit motive can be glimpsed in a letter he wrote in March, 1724, offering his literary services to Sir Robert Walpole. "My intentions are both honour-able and sincere," he concluded graciously, "and I doubt not but they will meet with a suitable return."[30] In the *Champion*

[28]For example: "At the Oratory in Newport Market, tomorrow, at half an hour after ten, the Sermon will be on the Witch of Endor. At half an hour after five the Theological Lecture will be on the conversion and original of the Scottish nation, and of the Picts and Caledonians: St. Andrew's relicks and panegyrick, and the character and mission of the Apostles. On Wednesday, at six or near the matter, take your chance, will be a medley oration on the history, merits, and praise of Confusion and Confounders in the road and out of the way. On Friday, will be that on Dr. Faustus and Fortunatus, and Conjuration; after each the Climax of the Times, Nos. 23 and 24.—

   "N.B. Whenever the prices of the seats are occasionally raised in the week-days notice of it will be given in the prints. An account of the performances of the Oratory from the first, to August last, is published, . . . and if any bishop, clergyman, or any other subject of his Majesty, or any other foreign prince or state can, at my years, and in my circum-stances and opportunities, without the least assistance of any partner in the world, parallel the study, choice, variety, and discharge of the said performances of the Oratory by his own or any others, I engage forthwith to quit the said Oratory.—J. HENLEY." Quoted by Charles Knight, *London* (London, 1844), 5: 44–45.

[29]In a note to the 1743 *Dunciad*, Book III, lines 199–212, Twickenham ed., 5: 330. For an example of Henley's oratorical treatises, see his *Art of Speaking in Publick* (London, 1727).

[30]*Notes and Queries*, 2d ser., 2: 443.

Henley's doings are regularly reported under "Puffs," a department devoted to pillorying false advertisements, and his paper is
generally referred to as "the *Quack Doctor*." Along with items
from the lottery brokers, apothecary shops, and linen drapers
appear such "puffs" as "From the Orator, alias Puff-Master
General, two, one to thank his Benches for their Company, and
the other to bespeak a ready furnish'd Apartment in Moor-
Fields" (suggesting that Henley was not above hawking real
estate from the pulpit if there was money in it) and, in a later
issue, "the Orator's Panegyrick on his own Modesty."[31] Under
the first "Proceedings at the *Court of Criticism*, held before *John
Trot-Plaid*, Esq; Censor of *Great Britain*" in the *Jacobite's
Journal* for January 16, 1748, appears "A Petition from Orator
Handlie [*sic*] . . . praying to be Crier of the Court, offering to
write, preach, or swear any thing, and to profess any Party or
Religion, at a cheap rate; rejected," and in the *True Patriot* he
becomes "McHenley the Ordinary," the symbol of the hireling
Jacobite press and, as always, of the menace to language and
society involved in the buying and selling of the word.

Fielding's most productive years were exactly coincident with
the decline of literary patronage and the rise of a new middle-
class reading public, those years of uneasy transition between the
time when authors could still harbor the comfortable illusion of
independence under an enlightened and disinterested patron[32]
and the acceptance of authorship as a profession dependent upon
the favor of the reading public and governed by the economics
of bookselling. This shift of literary responsibility from aristocratic patrons to popular readership was another evidence of the
relaxing grip of the traditional ruling classes on the repositories
of culture, language and literature. With the emergence to prosperity and self-awareness of a new commercially minded middle-
class, with the spread of literacy fostered by the charity schools,
new demands were being made of writers; and when the estab-

---

[31]Jan. 29, 1739/40; Feb. 14, 1739/40. Henley apparently did operate a real estate office
on the side at the Oratory. Advertisements in *The Hyp Doctor* for houses frequently
direct interested parties to "Enquire . . . of Mr. HENLEY, at the ORATORY, by Lincoln-
inns-fields." See, for example, No. 518, Sept. 30, 1740.

[32]Fielding himself acknowledges the help of the Duke of Bedford in the Dedication to
Tom Jones and probably enjoyed also the aid of George Lyttelton and others. See
A. S. Collins, *Authorship in the Days of Johnson* (London: R. Holden, 1927), pp. 185–86.

lished authors of the age, schooled in the tradition of aristocratic values and classical learning, were unwilling or unable to supply these demands, a new kind of writer appeared on the scene who was eager to grasp at the opportunity. More often than not, he was ill-educated, at least by the standards of a Pope or a Fielding, and, since the pressures of the journalism, political pamphleteering, and other hack activities in which he was principally engaged required haste, he was frequently careless with his language. The clownish Cibber personified these faults to perfection, but more serious was the damage done to the reputation of authorship, and to the efficacy of language, by the commercial orientation of the new kind of writer. Middle-class himself in his origins and sympathies, sharing that class's respect for trade and its material rewards, he had little of the traditional writer's sense of responsibility to "truth, . . . honour, and . . . posterity."[33] He wrote for money. His services were usually for sale to the highest bidder, and, since he was interested in an immediate return for his labors, he wrote wholly for the present, careless of any responsibility to the continuity of thought and language which is the basic principle of literary tradition. The *Covent-Garden Journal* for May 19, 1752, contains a work, supposedly sent in by a "Correspondent," entitled *Peri Tharsûs*—an imitation of Pope's *Peri Bathous, or the Art of Sinking in Poetry*. It is described as: "A TREATISE ON THE CONFIDENT and PERT. A Modern Improvement in Writing; OR, The Art of Swaggering in Print. A Work useful to all Kinds and Classes of Authors at this Day, but more particularly to Polemic Divines, Paradoxical Historians, Self-taught Commentators, Hypothetical and Heretical Physicians, Daily-Essay Writers, Quack-Bill Writers, and Advertisers." The "author" of this treatise shows that the pert style is a modern art, not mastered by the Ancients, who were too much occupied with fame and posterity to cultivate it, whereas the Moderns have mastered it because "they conclude, that a Book [is] calculated not to last Ages, but to produce an immediate Effect."

[33]The phrase is Pope's. Writing to dissuade Swift in 1726 from lending his pen to Pulteney against Walpole, he argued that "They have scoundrels enough to write for their passions and their designs; let us write for truth, for honour, and for posterity." *The Correspondence of Alexander Pope*, ed. George Sherburn (Oxford: Clarendon Press, 1956), 2: 413.

Money, of course, was corruptive of other and more basic values besides those of language and letters, but such was the age's conviction of the interdependence of social, ethical, and linguistic values that corruption in one sphere was certain to be discovered in the others as well. In the *Covent-Garden Journal* for May 2, 1752, Fielding has a "Correspondent" calling himself "Misargurus" writing from Bedlam (where he has been committed for disposing of his money in the Thames) and arguing that as "the certain Cause of all that national Corruption, Luxury, and Immorality, which have polluted our Morals . . . [is] Money," the use of this commodity should be immediately abolished. "Thus a certain Method called Election, which is of very singular Use in a Nation of Freedom, will be again revived; otherwise it may possibly sink only to a Name." Also, this measure "would restore certain excellent Things, such as Piety, Virtue, Honour, Goodness, Learning, etc. all of which are totally abolished by Money, or so counterfeited by it, that no one can tell the true from the false; the Word Rich indeed is at present considered to signify them all."

Grub Street, as both this passage and the excerpts from *Peri Tharsûs* indicate, had no monopoly on the mercenary corruption of language. Politicians, polite society, and the professions, as we shall see, were regarded by Fielding as equally culpable. But the Grub Street hack was particularly well situated to do harm because, having assumed the title of authorship and taken over the traditional forms of literary expression, he was boring from within. By diverting literature from the service of "truth, . . . honour, and . . . posterity," he was undermining its traditional power as a force for good, discrediting it, rendering authorship suspect in the eyes of the world.

The devotion of Grub Street to profit and "immediate Effect" is satirized in the scenes at the writing factory in *The Author's Farce*. Bookweight, the money-grubbing bookseller (probably modeled on the notorious Edmund Curll), keeps a whole stable of salaried hacks to whom he assigns literary tasks strictly according to the law of commercial supply and demand. "Do you consider, Mr. Quibble," he chides one of them, "that it is above a fortnight since your letter from a Friend in the Country was published? Is it not high time for an Answer to come out? At this rate, before your Answer is printed your Letter will be forgot. I love to keep a controversy up warm. I have had authors who have writ a pamphlet in the morning, answered it in the afternoon, and compromised the matter at night." Enter Scarecrow, another hack: "Sir, I have brought you a libel against the ministry." Bookweight: "Sir, I shall not take anything against them (*aside*) for I have two in the press already." Scarecrow: "Then, sir, I have another in defense of them." Nor will Bookweight risk publication of Scarecrow's "translation" (copied out of Dryden) of the *Aeneid*, "for that bubble is almost down." Mr. Index, however, a specialist in mottos who charges more for Latin mottos ("sixpence per each") than for Greek ones "for as no body now understands Greek, so I may use any sentence in that language, to whatsoever purpose I please," meets with better success. Bookweight tallies up the account: " 'For *Omnia vincit amor et nos cedamus amori*, sixpence. For *Difficile est satyram non scribere*, sixpence.' Hum, hum, hum. Ah. 'A Sum total for thirty-six Latin mottos, eighteen shillings; ditto English, seven, one shilling and ninepence; ditto Greek, four, one shilling.' "[34]

One consequence of this application of merchandizing techniques to literature is the degeneration of its special terminology to the level of advertising jargon. In a passage from the *Covent-Garden Journal* for March 3, 1752, which we have already examined in another context, Fielding compares title page blurbs and booksellers' puffs with the labels of fake champagne: "The Words *curious, eminent, learned, the 6th or seventh Edition. Done into English from the original French Vessels*, etc. written upon the Label, are all of them certain Marks of Perry." Dash, one of the hacks in *The Author's Farce*, has "nothing to do but to put a set of terrible words together on the title page" of Bookweight's publications. "It becomes an author," he muses, "to be diffuse in his title page. A title page is to a book what a fine neck is to a woman, therefore ought to be the most regarded as it is the part

---

[34]The text here is that of the original 1730 version, ed. Charles B. Woods, pp. 29–30, which I prefer in this instance to the version printed in Henley from a later revised edition of the play. The relevant scenes in the latter version are truncated and considerably weakened. For other examples of Fielding's views on the Grub Street commercialization of language and letters, see *Amelia*, Book VIII, Ch. 5, and the *Covent-Garden Journal*, June 27, 1752.

which is viewed before the purchase."[35] In the "Introduction" scene of *The Welsh Opera* (1731) a player asks the author (Scriblerus Secundus) why he calls the play "Welsh," since not a word of that language appears in it. Will not this disappoint audience expectations? "No Sir," Scriblerus answers, "the Town is too well acquainted with Modern Authors to expect any thing from a Title. A Tragedy often proves a Comedy, a Comedy a Tragedy; and an Opera nothing at all."[36] The Court of Criticism in the *Jacobite's Journal* hears a plea in defense of "*Porcupinus Pelagius*, . . . convicted of having writ a Panegyry-Satyri-Serio-Comi-nonsensi-unintelligi . . . Poem, called the *'Piscopade*." The defense argues that the conviction is unjust because "the Word Poem was a Misnomer; for . . . whatever was not written in any Numbers could not be called a Poem." Furthermore, "the Word *Satire* or *Satirical* is improperly used, . . . for an unmannerly Abuse of a whole Body of Men, (as here of the whole Bench of Bishops) is Scandal and not Satire." The court allows the justice of these objections but, being bound by the rules of Equity, pronounces "Sentence of Contempt upon the Author and his Works."[37]

But the real trouble, so Fielding seems to have felt, was that the "Sentence of Contempt" was passed not only on the authors and works which were actually guilty of such crimes against language and letters but also, in the public mind, against *all* authors and *all* literary works. Even Bookweight in *The Author's Farce* is alarmed because "People begin to be afraid of authors since they have writ and acted like stockjobbers,"[38] and when Fielding defines the word "Author" in the "Modern Glossary" as "in general an Object of Contempt" he is not in this case ridiculing the usage of polite society so much as the corruption of the title by hack writers who had "transformed it to Posterity with [their] Iniquity annexed." Thanks to "those base and scandalous Writings, which the Press hath lately poured in such a Torrent upon us," he complains in the *Covent-Garden Journal*

---

[35]P. 28.
[36]P. i. *The Welsh Opera* was the original title of the play later revised and reprinted as *The Grub Street Opera*. The original has never been reprinted.
[37]Feb. 13, 1748. The *'Piscopade* (London, 1748) was a satiric poem in quantitative verse (probably by William Kenrick) which included an attack on Fielding.
[38]P. 31.

No. 5, "the Name of an Author, is, in the Ears of all good Men, become almost an infamous Appellation." In 1741, in the poem *Of True Greatness*, he was already attacking "this Gothic leaden Age,"

> When wit is banish'd from the press and stage,
> . . . .
> When nonsense is a term for the sublime,
> And not to be an idiot is a crime;
> When low buffoons in ridicule succeed,
> And men are largely for such writings fee'd,

and concluding,

> Leave, scribblers, leave the tuneful road to fame,
> Nor by assuming damn a poet's name.
>
> (XII, 254–55)

Not only were the "names" of author and poet corrupted by such practices and the names of literary forms (satire, comedy, tragedy, etc.) made meaningless by the inflated claims of title pages, but all literature, the art of writing itself, was brought under suspicion. True authors, Fielding declares in the *True Patriot* for February 4, 1746, are "those . . . who, by their Writings, have either improved the Understanding, corrected the Will, or entertained the Imagination," but as these aims in recent years have been increasingly "attempted by some Men of mean and inadequate Capacities, while others have perverted great Talents to darken and corrupt the Minds of Men, by dressing up Falshood in the Colours of Truth, and Vice in those of Virtue, such Writers have justly raised the Contempt and Indignation of the Wise and Good, and have been stigmatized with the Appellation of *Scribblers*; a Name which from the Persons on whom it was properly fixed, hath contracted much Scorn and Abhorrence," but which "likewise hath been applied with great Indifference and Impropriety," until now "the Word is immediately given to all the Gang." Or again, in the *Jacobite's Journal* for January 9, 1748: "A great Number of loose, idle, and disorderly Persons, calling themselves Authors, . . . have . . . conspired together to mix up great Quantities of Ribaldry and Nonsense; and have afterwards endeavour'd to do their utmost to spread the said Mixtures abroad among the People, often under false Names and Colours; and by means of a certain wicked, base, deceitful, and diabolical Art, vulgarly call'd Puffing, . . . to the utmost Abuse, Disgrace, and Discouragement of Literature, and to the great Scandal of this Nation."

Satire, the great moral art of Horace and Juvenal, of Swift and Pope, had become so discredited by the scandalmongering and truthless libel which had assumed its name that it no longer carried conviction. The rhetoric of satire, like Pope's personified Rhetoric in *The Dunciad*,[39] had degenerated into billingsgate. "Our Satyr," wrote Steele, "is nothing but Ribaldry, and *Billingsgate*. Scurrility passes for Wit."[40] A session of the Court of Criticism in the *Jacobite's Journal* for February 13, 1748, listens to a dispute between "the Corporation of *Grubstreet*, Plaintiff, and the Corporation of *Billingsgate*, Defendant," over "the Right to claim all low, scandalous Invectives, without the least Wit, Humour, Argument, or Fact"; and Article 3 of the "Treaty of Covent-Garden" (ending the "Paper War" between Sir Alexander Drawcansir, of the *Covent-Garden Journal*, and "the low Republic" of Grub Street) declares "That Billinsgate [*sic*] shall be acknowledged for ever, to be a Fief of the low and unmighty Republic; and that Sir Alexander, and all the High Allies do renounce any Right, Title, or Claim, to that Fief for ever."[41]

It was not so easy, however, even in allegorical terms, to dissociate the "High Allies" of the true Republic of Letters from the Grub Street debasement of the language of panegyric. Unjust satire could be distinguished from the genuine article by its very crudity, its reliance on billingsgate as opposed to "true wit." But the language of praise, which depends for its efficacy entirely on the reader's belief in the sincerity of the writer and the worthiness of the subject, could be more easily counterfeited and hence was more thoroughly corruptible. "The first Quality which every Man ought to be possessed of, who promises himself to make any Figure in this Hemisphere," writes a cynical "Correspondent" to the *Champion* for January 29, 1739/40, very much in the

[39]Bk. IV, lines 23–26.
[40]*Spectator* No. 451, Aug. 7, 1712, Everyman ed., 3: 393.
[41]Jan. 14, 1752.

ironic vein of *Jonathan Wild*, "is the Art of Lying. This Word, as it regards our Interest, however it came to be scandalous I will not determine, comprehends Flattery and Scandal, a false Defence of ourselves, and a false Accusation of other People." The latter, he warns, can be overdone and so exposed as untruth, "but this regards only the Le [*sic.*, Lie?] scandalous; if you come to the Le panegyrical you need set no Bounds." Particularly offensive to Fielding as an author was the application of this principle to the traditional dedicatory epistle. Despite the efforts of Swift and Pope to restore the concept of dedications as sincere, disinterested, and honorable tributes of esteem or expressions of gratitude, the prevailing practice in the first half of the eighteenth century was to dedicate indiscriminately for cash on the line or, in the case of political patrons, for "interest"—"panegyric for a pension sung" as Fielding put it in *Of True Greatness* (XII, 255).[42] "These Fellows," complains Mercury in *An Interlude* (1743), "prevent the very use of praise" (XVI, 92–93).

Grub Street's prostitution of the language of praise was not limited, however, to the dedicatory epistle or the formal pane-gyric. On a lower but no less pernicious level was its development of the art of advertising, a medium in which the buying and selling of the word was reduced to its purest form. Advertising was in its infancy in the eighteenth century and one wonders what Fielding would have thought of its growth in the twentieth century into a science of public manipulation. But even in his own time it made a useful symbol of the deliberate cultivation of the language of deceit for monetary motives. When Tom Jones is treated respectfully by the landlady of an inn, the author accounts for her solicitude by observing that "this was one of those houses where gentlemen, to use the language of advertise-ments, meet with civil treatment for their money" (IV, 67). But the hollowness of the phrase (and the ironic literalness of the qualifying "for their money") is revealed when the landlady,

---

[42]For an account of the eighteenth-century practice of selling dedications, see Collins, *Authorship in the Days of Johnson*, pp. 180–84. For further examples of Fielding's attacks on the practice, see his mock dedication of *Shamela*, his dedicatory epistle to *The Intriguing Chambermaid*, and *Pasquin* (Act III, Sc. 1). For Pope's attacks, see *The Art of Sinking in Poetry* (Ch. XIV) and the *Guardian* No. 4, for Mar. 16, 1713. For Swift's views, see the Bookseller's Dedication and the Preface of *A Tale of a Tub*, "Directions for Making a Birth-Day Song," and "On Poetry, a Rhapsody."

upon hearing that Jones is a disinherited foundling, abruptly drops her civil attitude. Even in such an early exercise as *Part of Juvenal's Sixth Satire Modernised in Burlesque Verse* (published in the 1743 *Miscellanies* but written much earlier) Fielding has a note referring to the phrase "play-bills By Desire" which ridicules the false claims of advertisements and exposes their threat to the language. The phrase in question, he says, is "A constant puff at the head of our play-bills; designed to allure persons to the house, who go thither more for the sake of the company than of the play; but which has proved so often fallacious (plays having been acted *at the particular desire of several ladies of quality, when there hath not been a single lady of quality in the house*) that at present it hath very little signification" (XII, 313).

"Puff," which Fielding in another note in *The Vernoniad* testifies was a word, like "the thing itself, . . . at present in great vogue" (XV, 48), had particular reference in the eighteenth century to "the applause that writers and booksellers give their own books, etc. to promote their sale,"[43] the kind of self-praise disguised as public commendation which Fielding satirizes in the Letters to the Editor (one of which is signed "John Puff") at the beginning of *Shamela*, parodying the commendatory letters which Richardson immodestly prefixed to the later editions of *Pamela*. The desire for literary reputation, Fielding writes in the *Champion* for March 1, 1739/40, is a "Malignancy [which] hath given Rise to several Inventions among Authors, to get themselves and their Works a Name. And has introduc'd that famous Art call'd Puffing, which, as it is brought to great Perfection in this Age, affords us a constant Article in one Column of our Paper." The "article" mentioned is one which does not appear in the reprint edition of the *Champion* but in the original numbers is called "Puffs," a regular department dedicated to a mocking review of literary publicity as well as, by logical extension, of the hyperbolic advertisements inserted in the back pages of newspapers by tradesmen, purveyors of quack cures for venereal disease, gout, and other maladies of man and beast, teachers of classical and foreign languages (who promised painless lessons and quick results), dancing masters, lottery touts,

---

[43]*London Magazine*, 1 (1732): 81. Cited in *OED*.

waxworks exhibitors, and others for whom the more or less artfully contrived lie was the essence of salesmanship.[44]

Here was another potent symbol of the debasement of authorship, for since the advertisements appeared in newspapers which in their front pages laid claim to the dignity of literature, it was only logical, in the absence of a distinct advertising profession, that Grub Street should bear the onus of their dissemination. Addison, in the *Tatler* No. 224, scornfully refers to the writers of advertisements as "diminutive authors" and, developing the proposition that "a collection of advertisements is a kind of miscellany; the writers of which, contrary to all authors, except men of quality, give money to the booksellers who publish their copies," wonders what their compositions might yield to the searching analysis of literary criticism. "The great art in writing advertisements," he decides, "is the finding out a proper method to catch the reader's eye," and he especially ridicules such subverbal techniques as the use of little pointing hands, asterisks, N.B., etc. "But the great skill in an advertiser," he concludes, "is chiefly seen in the style which he makes use of," for it is his whole task to boast of " 'the universal esteem, or general reputation,' of things that were never heard of."[45]

Fielding, in the Puffs department of the *Champion*, seizes upon the same kinds of shams and absurdities, quoting or paraphrasing actual advertisements currently appearing in the newspapers. The entries in the *Champion* for March 27, 1740, are typical:

[44]It is impossible to be sure, of course, whether Fielding was personally responsible for the Puffs department or whether it was compiled by James Ralph or some other editorial assistant on the paper. Criteria of style are of little help here since the bulk of the matter in question is quoted or paraphrased. But appearing in a paper of which Fielding was the chief editor, the column doubtlessly reflects his point of view, and the fact that there are similar departmentalized features in each of his later journals, in which Ralph had no part, strengthens Fielding's claims of authorship. Also, the Puffs column seems to have been discontinued after Fielding left the *Champion* in June, 1741, or at any rate it does not appear in any of the later numbers of the paper which I have been able to examine.

[45]Sept. 12, 1710, Everyman ed., pp. 232–34. Addison parodies advertisements in the *Spectator* No. 547, Nov. 27, 1712, in which he prints testimonials from readers of the paper written "in the Stile and Phrase of the like Ingenious Compositions which we frequently meet with at the ends of our News-Papers," particularly the type inserted by physicians and apothecaries "where it is usual for the Patients to Publish the Cures which have been made upon them, and the several Distempers under which they laboured." Everyman ed., 4: 224.

Mr. Lowe's French Grammar exceeds all others, positively, comparatively, and superlatively, in the Opinion of (one that should know)—*himself*.

Dr. Milward's *invitatory* Letter to all Orders of Men to buy his Book, Price 1s.

Mrs. Stevens has receiv'd 5000 l. for discovering a new Method of making Soap, a round about Way.

Nor does he spare the ads which grace the back pages of the *Champion* itself. In the issue for October 11, 1740, for example, he reports a puff for "A Parcel of *curious* Brown, Copper Tea Kettles to be sold that *need no Commendations*," an ad which appeared fairly regularly in the *Champion* both before and after Fielding singled it out for ridicule.[46] The italics, which Fielding, according to the usage of the time, uses in a rather haphazard way to indicate direct quotation, call attention not only to barbarous, ungrammatical, or pretentious words and phrases ("Dr. Milward's *invitatory* Letter") but also to the debasement of good words to mean purposes: "Mr. Vick's *lively* Representation of Versailles, and *beautiful* Night Piece, seen and *admir'd by great Numbers* of the Nobility, and other *curious Inspectors* into Art and Rarity."[47]

A column similar to Puffs called "Appeared" is a regular feature of the *True Patriot*, but with the difference that here, having perhaps sustained a loss of advertising revenue in the *Champion* by virtue of his mockery of advertising wherever it might appear, Fielding promises not to ridicule the ads in his own paper. But even in an announcement of the paper's advertising rates and policy he cannot resist a gibe at the insubstantiality of the claims of his prospective customers: "N.B. Mrs. Cooper the Publisher of this Paper is provided with several walking Licenses for Ghosts, by our Authority; which she issues forth to the said Ghosts at various Prices, from Three Shillings to Half a Guinea, according to the Length and Breadth of the respective Ghosts; and all Shadows which for the future shall venture to *appear* abroad in the Shape of Puffs or Advertisements, without such Licence, shall be instantly lay'd in

[46] See, for example, Sept. 20, and Oct. 16, 1740.
[47] *Champion*, Apr. 3, 1740.

this Paper."[48] Some typical entries are those in the *True Patriot* for November 12, 1745: "*Appeared*. Several Ghosts in the Shape of Puffs, as usual. Particularly, . . . Lottery-Mongers, who keep but one Office *out of Gratitude to the Public*, of which several News-Writers *think it incumbent on themselves* to inform their Readers. . . . Brandy Merchants *determined* to keep up their Brandy to its usual Goodness, which has for 10 Years *withstood all Contrivances in opposition to it.*"

Fielding's case against the newspapers was not, however, confined to their back pages. If the "Art of Lying" flourished here in its purest form, it was strongly in evidence in the other pages as well. While Puffs concentrated on exposing sham advertising, other departments of the *Champion* (Advices, Rumours, Prophecies, Preferr'd) satirized the notorious unreliability of eighteenth-century newspapers, their preoccupation with trivia and ephemera, their rumormongering, their dependence on biased sources, their distortions, and their pure invention; and similar departments in his later papers, often accompanied by italicized ironic commentary by the editor, served the same function. The newspaper was, to Fielding's mind, the characteristic Grub Street medium for the debasement of the arts of language. Here there was no tradition of "truth, honour, and posterity" to deflect the industrious hack from his pursuit of gain and his cultivation of immediate effect. Yet for the very reason that journalism, like advertising, was still an infant science and had therefore, again like advertising, no tradition of its own, no separate system of values and standards, it presented itself to the world as a new form of *literary* endeavor and seemed to invite judgment in literary terms. "The World, it is certain," writes Fielding in the *Covent-Garden Journal* No. 1, "never more abounded with Authors, than at present; nor is there any Species more numerous than of those Writers who deal forth their Lucubrations in small Parcels to the Public, consisting partly of historical, and partly, to use their own Word, of *literary* Matter." But what they actually "deal in," he goes on, the "Wares which they . . . vend to the Public," are nothing else but politics, personal slander, scurrility, and "Dullness."

[48] *True Patriot*, Dec. 10, 1745.

The most serious charge Fielding leveled against the newspapers of his day—that their political bias led them to place
"party and interest" above truth—will be considered in the
next section of this chapter. But that his objections to them were
not motivated entirely by his own political commitments is indicated by the fact that he repeatedly attacked them on other
grounds as well. Even when politics were not at issue, he felt,
they retailed the most baseless rumors, the most fanciful conjectures, and the most pointless gossip under the guise of an
objective presentation of the "news" and thereby contributed
in no small way to the growing discredit of the printed word.
Justifying his establishment of the *True Patriot*, Fielding argues
ironically in the first issue that as "*no body at present reads any
thing but News-Papers*," an author who wants to be read has no
choice but to write in that medium. And then too, despite the
large number of papers already in circulation, "I fancied I had
discovered two or three little Imperfections in them all . . .":

The first little Imperfection in these Writings, is, that there is scarce
a Syllable of TRUTH in any of them; . . . 2dly, There is no SENSE in
them; . . . 3dly, There is, in reality, NOTHING *in them at all*. And this
also must be allowed by their Readers, if Paragraphs which contain
neither Wit, nor Humour, nor Sense, nor the least Importance, may
be properly said to contain nothing. Such are the Arrival of my
Lord _____ *with a great Equipage*, the Marriage of Miss _____ *of
great Beauty and Merit*, and the Death of Mr. _____ *who was never
heard of in his Life*, Etc., Etc.

Introducing a minor character (Mrs. Miller) in *Tom Jones*,
Fielding explains that he has delineated her in some detail because she will later assume an important role in the story, "as
our history doth not, like a newspaper, give great characters to
people who never were heard of before, nor will ever be heard of
again" (V, 53). This aspect of the newspaper, particularly in
death and marriage notices, irritated him throughout his life.
The *Champion* for February 28, 1739/40, reports puffs on
behalf of "Several Persons dead, who were never heard of while
they liv'd. And some preferr'd, who will never be heard of any
more till they die." The relevance of this practice to the corruption of the language can be seen in Fielding's sardonic use of
italics, interpolations, and commentary (in questionable taste,

to say the least of it, from the modern point of view) in the obituary notices of his own papers, copied, in accordance with the standard practice of the day, from other newspapers. The following example is from the *True Patriot* for November 19, 1745:

Dead. . . . Mr. Tillbury, *an eminent Scarlet Dyer.* Mr. Bick, *an eminent Wax Chandler.* The Rev. Mr. Strange, much esteemed by all that knew him. Mr. Samuel Russell, *an eminent Linen-Draper. . . .* Thomas Tonkin of Polgar in Cornwal, Esq., universally lamented by his Acquaintance. Upwards of 40 Cows belonging to one at Tottenham Court, *universally lamented by all their Acquaintance.*

N.B. If great Men and Cattle die so fast, we shall scarce have room to bury them in our Paper.

The question of taste must have been raised by some of his contemporary readers as well, for in any case Fielding in a later issue of the paper (January 7, 1746) attached the following apologetic but not altogether contrite note at the end of the death and marriages column: "*Note.* To prevent giving Offence to the many eminent dead Persons, as well as to several young Ladies of great Beauty, Merit, and Fortune, we shall for the future register all Marriages and Deaths as they come to Hand, and leave all Distinctions to the Public; after having premised that every Word printed in *Italics* is our own, and of these, and these only we will be answerable for the Truth." Hereafter the *Married* and *Dead* columns of the *True Patriot* are distinctly more sober, but the point had been made and Fielding apparently felt that it was worth making again two years later when he inaugurated a new paper. The *Jacobite's Journal* for February 13, 1748 reports:

MARRIED. Mess. _____ _____ all eminent, to the Misses _____ _____ very agreeable young Ladies of great Beauty, Merit, and Fortune.

DEAD. The Hon. Peregrine Widdrington. — Lieut. Col. Barrington. — Capt. Hannaway. — James Maningham, Esq; of Shropshire. — *And several Persons of great Eminence — in the News-Papers.*

N.B. For the future no Marriages nor Deaths of eminent Persons, whose Names were never before heard of, will be inserted in this Paper, unless Certificates be left with the Printer that such Persons were *really born.*

Still later, in the *Covent-Garden Journal*, he notes the wedding of
"a Lady of great Beauty and Fortune, *and truly possessed of the
Sweetness of Mind which is so necessary to the Happiness of the
married State*," and adds a query of his own which exposes the
meaninglessness of such trite compliments: "Q. *What are the
Accomplishments necessary to render the State truly happy?*" A
later number ridicules once again the use in death and marriage
notices of the word "*eminent*," particularly as applied to such as
"Builders, Soap-boilers, Shoemakers, Butchers, etc."[49]

Here was the linguistic process of "degradation" caught in
action, the transformation of originally serious and meaningful
words into faint and facetious expressions of middle-class notions
of the genteel. The slatternly Laetitia, in *Jonathan Wild*, is
"thought to be possessed of every qualification necessary to
make the marriage state happy"; and it is little wonder that the
word "eminent" took its place, along with "honor," "virtue,"
"learned," etc., among the staples of Fielding's ironic vocabulary
of corrupt words. When we are told, for example, that Laetitia
was once "the handmaid (or housemaid as the vulgar call it) of
an eminent pawnbroker" (II, 65, 118), we may understand why
Fielding felt it was necessary to "translate" one euphemism in
the sentence and not the other. "Eminent" had already been
translated by popular usage and reduced to absurdity by the
newspapers.

The inaccuracy of contemporary news reporting, which the
newspapers presumed to dignify under the title of "history," is
ridiculed by Fielding in the same way that he ridiculed inflated
advertisements and social notes—by reprinting or paraphrasing
sentences culled from rival papers. A regular feature of the
True Patriot, for example, is the "Apocrypha, Being a curious
Collection of certain true and important WE HEARS from the
News-Papers," in which are presented excerpts of more than
usual thinness or absurdity (often nothing more than wild
rumors) usually followed by a brief editorial comment from
Fielding. A variant heading for this column is "Gallimatias,"
which the *OED* defines (under *Galimatias*) as "confused
language, meaningless talk, nonsense." He particularly delights

[49]Jan. 7 and 11, 1752. Cited by Jensen, 2: 164 n.

in printing under this heading, during the Jacobite invasion, contradictory accounts of the doings, whereabouts, and intentions of the Pretender and his followers and in exposing their inconsistencies. After a passage from *The General Advertiser* describing the capture of a certain lord, Fielding adds, "*We hope his lordship will not regain his Liberty as easily as he return'd to Life, after having been killed by the Historians of last Week.*"[50] The emptiness of such reports, founded on rumor and speculation, is satirized in *The Coffee-House Politician* (1730) when a character reads from "*The Lying-Post*" (one of the papers of the day was called the *Flying-Post*): "Berlin, January the 20th. We hear daily murmurs here concerning certain measures taken by a certain northern potentate; but cannot certainly learn either who that potentate is, or what are the measures which he hath taken—meantime we are well assured, that time will bring them all to light" (IX, 142). All in all, Fielding probably felt that he was not really exaggerating so very much when in *An Essay on Nothing* (published in the *Miscellanies* of 1743) he takes exception to the "vulgar error among persons unacquainted with the mystery of writing, who imagine it impossible that a man should sit down to write without any meaning at all! whereas, in reality, nothing is more common" (XIV, 314).

POLITICS AND POLITICIANS

Captain Vinegar, in the *Champion* for February 14, 1739/40, advances the theory that politics "first came into the World at the Building of *Babel*; . . . the Builders of this Tower have by the best Critics been thought no other than a Set of Ministers, which I suppose to have been collected from their confounding one another by their Language, a Circumstance in which all their Successors have imitated them, it being the chief Excellence, and earnest Endeavour of a Minister to avoid being understood by any of his Fraternity." It would be a mistake, of course, to represent Fielding's numerous political utterances as expressions solely or even primarily of his preoccupation with language and its perversions. Just as he was frequently motivated by personal considerations in his thrusts against debased theatrical

---

[50] *True Patriot*, Dec. 3, 1745.

entertainments, literary criticism, and journalism, so were his pronouncements on political matters often inspired by his own involvement in party politics and sometimes, probably, by hopes of personal reward for his services. The passage just quoted, for example, is not entirely the generalized piece of satire it seems. No reader of the *Champion* in 1740 would have misunderstood that the particular "Set of Ministers" Fielding had in mind was the government of Sir Robert Walpole, then nearing the end of its long hegemony and about to be toppled from power by the election of 1741—an eventuality which the *Champion* was wholeheartedly devoted to bringing about.

There is no doubt that Fielding was writing in the *Champion*, as indeed he had in the dramatic satires of the previous decade which had led to the Licensing Act of 1737 and his enforced retirement from playwriting, in support of the anti-Walpolian Whig Opposition, the Country Party "Patriots." His turnabout attack on the Patriots themselves in *The Opposition, a Vision* (1741) was motivated in part by his disillusionment with men whose elevation to power had revealed them to be self-serving hypocrites, but he made no secret of the fact that he was also personally stung by their neglect of himself and James Ralph, his collaborator on the *Champion*.[51] His political tracts of 1745, *A Serious Address to the People of Great Britain* and *A Dialogue between the Pope, the Devil, and the Pretender*, were calculated to awaken an apathetic nation to the perils of the Jacobite uprising in Scotland, and his return to political journalism in the *True Patriot* that same year showed him during this national emergency to be in the service (and possibly in the pay) of the Pelham Ministry. He was still defending the Ministry against the lingering effects of Jacobitism two years later in *A Dialogue between a Gentleman of London and an Honest Alderman* and in the *Jacobite's Journal*.

But again it is significant that the form this political concern takes, whatever Fielding's immediate ends or larger purposes, is so often one which represents the political rhetoric of persuasion and equivocation as a corruptive perversion of language. Lying, that most fundamental of all the perversions of speech, had been

---

[51]See Martin C. Battestin, "Fielding's Changing Politics and *Joseph Andrews*," *Philological Quarterly*, 39 (1960): 39–55.

cultivated by the Grub Street hacks and advertisers in a desultory and amateurish way, but it was left to the politician to elevate it into a profession and a way of life. "He applies his Words to all Uses, except to the indication of his Mind,"[52] Gulliver explains to the Houyhnhnm master who had earlier reminded him that the "Use of Speech" was perverted if anyone *said the thing which was not*; and the Mayor's wife in Fielding's *Pasquin* wants to know, "What has a man's heart to do with his lips?" (XI, 189).

The worthlessness of the political promise and its role in the corruption of language are a recurring theme in Fielding's works. Politicians have "peculiar Phrases," he notes in the *Champion* essay on the abuse of words, "which some Persons imagine to have a Meaning among themselves, but give no more Idea to others, than any of those unintelligible Sounds which the Beasts utter; such are, upon my Honour, believe me, depend on me, I'll certainly serve you another Time, this is promised, I wish you had spoken sooner; and some hundred others of this kind, very frequent in the Mouths of . . . great Men."[53] In the *Covent-Garden Journal* "Modern Glossary" he defines "Promise" as "Nothing,"[54] and when the narrator of *Jonathan Wild* speaks of "those great arts which the vulgar call treachery, dissembling, promising, lying, falsehood, etc., but which are by great men summed up in the collective name of policy, or politics, or rather pollitrics" (II, 73), the word "promising," it will be observed, is the only one of the "vulgar" synonyms which is not properly a pejorative term. But the point of its inclusion in the list, of course, is that its corruption (both as a word and as a political practice) has made it as pejorative as the rest. The characteristic Fielding irony of the "translated" euphemism is here double, since it is not only the tenor term (politics) which is treated as corrupt but the vehicle (promising) as well, and Fielding never tires of showing how the political promise has acquired this evil reputation.

Parson Adams, we are told, has repeatedly been the victim of betrayed political promises, but he still naively believes in the oily assurances and excuses of his latest parliamentary "patron"

[52] *Gulliver's Travels, Prose Works,* 11: 239.
[53] Jan. 17, 1739/40.
[54] Jan. 14, 1752.

Sir Thomas Booby: "He promised me a living, poor man! and I believe I should have had it, but an accident happened, which was that my lady promised it before, unknown to him. . . . Since that time, Sir Thomas, poor man! had always so much business that he never could find leisure to see me" (I, 155). Dr. Harrison, however, in *Amelia*, is not so gullible. When he asks a powerful nobleman to aid Booth, the lord affects great concern. "You may be assured," he tells Dr. Harrison, "I shall do him all the service in my power." But this, Fielding tells us, was "a language which the doctor well understood; and soon after took a civil, but not a very ceremonious leave" (VII, 253).

Mrs. Western, in *Tom Jones*, is associated throughout the novel with the language of politics. "Parliamentary language has been used *without doors*," wrote Richard Cambridge in an essay on "Fashionable and Court Phrases" in *The World* five years after the publication of *Tom Jones*. "Our country squires made *treaties* about their game, and ladies *negotiated* a meeting of their lap-dogs."[55] Aunt Western is a perfect example. She manages Sophia's affairs like a cynical diplomat, reading her lectures on "matrimonial politics" (V, 230), persuading the squire that his daughter should not "be treated with such arbitrary power," and demanding his "full ratification of all the concessions stipulated" since he is himself clearly "not qualified for these negotiations. All your whole scheme of politics is wrong" (V, 214–15). He accuses her of speaking a "Hanoverian linguo" which he cannot understand, but he recognizes her claim to superior political skill and soon "a league was struck (to borrow a phrase from the lady) between the contending parties" (V, 167). But Mrs. Western's affectation of "parliamentary language" is more than just a comic "humour." It is symptomatic of the extent to which the political corruption of words has infected the language at large and rendered it suspect. When Squire Western tells her that Allworthy, despite the obvious advantage to both families, may disapprove of the proposed match between Sophia and Blifil because "money hath

---

[55]Quoted by William Matthews, "Polite Speech in the Eighteenth Century," *English*, 1 (1937): 502. I am indebted to Robert M. Wallace, "Henry Fielding's Narrative Method" (Ph.D. diss., University of North Carolina, 1945), p. 408, for pointing out the relevance of this passage to the speech of Mrs. Western.

no effect o' un," Mrs. Western replies, "Brother, . . . your politics astonish me. Are you really to be imposed on by professions? Do you think Mr. Allworthy hath more contempt for money than other men because he professes more? Such credulity would better become one of us weak women, than that wise sex which Heaven hath formed for politicians. Indeed, brother, you would make a fine plenipo to negotiate with the French. They would soon persuade you that they take towns out of mere defensive principles" (III, 279). The "Use of Speech" has been corrupted indeed when even an Allworthy cannot speak without suspicion of insincerity and equivocation.

But the meaningless promise and the diplomatic lie were not the only contributions which politicians were making to the perversion of language. Equally corruptive was factionalism, which placed party loyalty higher than truth and treated language solely as a means of persuasion. The common cause of the decline of "our Conversation, our Stage, and our Press," Fielding declared in the *Covent-Garden Journal* No. 16, was the "Spirit of Party." Language, the medium of truth, was being debased to sloganeering, whitewashing, and propaganda. The passage from *A Voyage to Lisbon* quoted in the previous chapter in which he argues that "the whole mischief" of the British political system "arises from the vague and uncertain use of a word called Liberty" is only one among many expressions, both serious and ironic, of Fielding's sensitivity to the perversions of this potent political word. In *A Charge to the Grand Jury* (1749) he apologizes to his distinguished audience for using "this word liberty," which "I am afraid, gentlemen, . . . though so much talked of, is but little understood," and then defines it as "the enjoyment of our lives, our persons, and our properties in security" (XIII, 209). For he was aware that in political rhetoric the term was frequently nothing more than an emotional catchword. Is not "our Liberty . . . in danger"? asks the misguided anti-Hanoverian alderman in the *Dialogue between a Gentleman of London and an Honest Alderman*, and the gentleman answers, "First let me know what you mean by the Word *Liberty*; for though it is in every Man's Mouth, I have often doubted whether we have annexed to it any settled and certain Idea. Many indeed seem to understand by it the Liberty of doing what they please."

"By the Liberty of an *Englishman*," replies the alderman, "I mean the Enjoyment of all those Privileges which the Law allows him," and when the gentleman forces him to admit that the present ruling house does not abridge liberty in this sense, the alderman falls back on the form of words which insists that it is nevertheless "in danger." "This of *our Liberty being in Danger*," says the gentleman impatiently, "is a Cant Phrase invented for the same seditious Purpose with that ever-memorable Cant Phrase of the Church being in Danger" (a shamefully exploited political slogan during the reign of Queen Anne), and is an example of the dangerous political emotions which "Words alone without Truth, nay, without Meaning, are capable of raising."[56]

It was thus, for Fielding, a natural candidate for the vocabulary of irony. When Jonathan Wild is imprisoned in Newgate he soon organizes a party to overthrow the reigning bully, Roger Johnson. His purpose, of course, is to install himself in Johnson's place and so enjoy the spoils which the "head of all the *prigs*" traditionally exacts from the other prisoners, but his rallying cry is that Johnson was "undermining THE LIBERTIES OF NEWGATE." So successful is his campaign that "all Newgate resounded with WILD *forever*, . . . and the poor debtors re-echoed *the liberties of Newgate*, which, in the cant language, signifies *plunder*, as loudly as the thieves themselves" (II, 152–54). The "cant language," identified with the criminal cant which has to be glossed for the benefit of uninitiated readers, is of course, the language of politicians, with particular reference to the alleged rule by corruption of Walpole and his faction and their incessant squabbling over the spoils of office. But by logical extension (and it should be remembered that *Jonathan Wild* was published *after* Walpole's

---

[56]Pp. 22–23. Never reprinted. In the *Covent-Garden Journal* No. 49, Fielding mentions as one of the causes of the present power of "the Mob" in English politics "the mistaken Idea which some particular Persons have always entertained of the Word Liberty" and promises to treat the matter "in a future Paper." No full paper on the subject appears, but he does return to it briefly (and in the same vein) in Nos. 55 and 58. See also the *Champion* for June 28, 1740, where the explorer Job Vinegar, describing the strange language of the Ptfghsiumgski nation, cites the word "LBRTY" and comments that "During my whole Stay among them, tho' I often heard this Word repeated, I could never comprehend what they meant by it." Not included in the 1741 reprint edition, but now available in the Augustan Reprint Society series, No. 67, *The Voyages of Mr. Job Vinegar from the Champion* (*1740*), ed. S. J. Sackett (Los Angeles: Augustan Reprint Society, 1958), p. 5.

defeat) it is the language of *all* politicians. When the critic Sneer-well in *Pasquin* suggests that "interest" would be a more accurate word than "conscience" for the Mayor's speech in "The Election," the author Trapwit replies, "Ay, interest, or conscience, they are words of the same meaning; but I think conscience rather the politer of the two, and most used at court" (XI, 194).

Fielding's disillusionment with the Patriot Opposition to Walpole is expressed in similar terms. In the allegorical *Opposition, a Vision*, the large box labeled "Public Spirit" which the Opposition keeps always on prominent display turns out to be really full of "ambition, malice, envy, avarice, disaffection, disappointment, pride, revenge, and many other heavy commodities" (XIV, 328). The word "Patriot" itself, which the "Modern Glossary" defines as "A Candidate for a Place at Court" ("Politics" being "The Art of getting such a Place") was contaminated for the same reason. In the *Dictionary* Dr. Johnson defined "Patriot" as "One whose ruling passion is the love of his country." But in the fourth edition he added: "It is sometimes used for a factious disturber of the government," and Boswell remarks in the *Life* that "to factious men, who consider a patriot only as an opposer of the measures of government," the title of Johnson's own pro-ministerial pamphlet *The Patriot* "will appear strangely misapplied"—though Boswell is somewhat shocked himself at Johnson's later description of "patriotism" as "the last refuge of a scoundrel" and hastens to explain that the speaker meant not "a real and generous love of our country, but that pretended patriotism which so many, in all ages, have made a cloak for self-interest."[57] The *OED* reports that the word "fell into discredit" in the first half of the eighteenth century, and indeed in 1728 Pope is quite casual in his suggestion that in "converting Vices into their bordering Virtues" it is no trick at all to transform "Corruption" into "Patriotism."[58] As early as 1681, however, Dryden was already speaking scornfully of "a Patriot's name, whose Modern sense / Is one that would by Law supplant his Prince,"[59] and in 1686 Robert South had singled out "Patriots" in one of his sermons on the "Fatal Imposture and

[57] *The Life of Johnson*, Hill-Powell ed., 2: 286, 348.
[58] *The Art of Sinking in Poetry*, Steeves ed., pp. 78–79.
[59] *Absalom and Achitophel*, lines 965–66.

Force of Words" as among those "rabble-charming words, which carry . . . wildfire wrapped up in them."[60] But in any case, by the 1740's the name had virtually, as Macaulay observed, become "a by-word of derision": "Horace Walpole scarcely exaggerated when he said that . . . the most popular declaration which a candidate could make on the hustings was that he had never been and never would be a patriot."[61]

For Fielding, then, when he became reconciled with the Patriot party in 1745 and undertook to defend the Pelham Ministry in the *True Patriot*, the immediate problem (as his title indicates) was to dissociate himself, his paper, and the Ministry itself from the corrupt associations which the term had acquired by virtue of having served for so long as the shibboleth of every disgruntled politician out of power and as a false front for the same kind of vices he had found concealed behind the term "Public Spirit." The elder Walpole himself, in a speech delivered in Commons on February 13, 1741, had accused the Opposition of having prostituted "a venerable word" to their own selfish ends,[62] and apparently Fielding agreed:

It must be confess'd, indeed, that this Word *Patriot* hath of late Years been very scandalously abused by some Persons. . . . Ambition, Avarice, Revenge, Envy, Malice, every bad Passion in the Mind of Man, have cloaked themselves under this amiable Character, and have misrepresented Persons and Things in unjust Colours to the Public. . . . But, however the Word *Patriot* hath been abused, or whatever Odium it may have thence contracted among the honest Part of Mankind, the Word itself, so far from deserving Contempt and Abhorrence, doth certainly set before us the most amiable Character in human Nature. For what less is meant by Patriotism, than the Love of one's Country carried into Action. . . . The Difficulty is the same in this as in other Virtues, to distinguish Truth from Falshood and Pretence.[63]

But the particular purveyors of "Falshood and Pretence" to whom Fielding was concerned, in the *True Patriot* and later in

[60] *Sermons*, 2: 523.
[61] *Horace Walpole* (1865). Cited in *OED*.
[62] F. Homes Dudden, *Henry Fielding, His Life, Works, and Times* (Oxford: Clarendon Press, 1952), 1: 299.
[63] *True Patriot*, Nov. 12, 1745.

the *Jacobite's Journal*, to deny the name of patriots were, of course, those who supported the Pretender in the Jacobite rebellion or who in any way questioned the Hanoverian Succession. "Their Words, 'tis true, are the Words of Patriots and honest Men," he quotes from a contemporary pamphlet on the Tory Opposition, "but their Actions are the Actions of concealed Jacobites."[64] The covert nature of Jacobitism, its refusal to declare itself openly, its hypocritical way of mouthing the very principles (according to Fielding) that is sought to overthrow, made it especially insidious as a perverter of language. In the *Jacobite's Journal* for March 12, 1748, he offers a parody of Ovid's *Art of Love*, entitled "De Arte Jacobitia," in which he lays out the secrets of this special skill. "First of all," the treatise begins, "learn the Art of Lying, and Misrepresenting. . . . The next thing you are to remember, is to feign a Love to your Country and Religion. The less you have of both, the better you can feign both. O Liberty, O Virtue, O my Country! Remember to have such expressions in your Mouth. Words do Wonders with silly People." The result of such abuse is an inability on the part of the public to distinguish truth from falsehood (since both come clothed in the same "colours") and a consequent distrust of *all* political language. "The Court, my Friend," argues the honest alderman of the *Dialogue*, "hath long cheated us with Names: the term *Jacobite* is a mere Bugbear, and hath served well to deceive and amuse the Multitude; but empty Sounds will not impose on me."[65] But the grim irony of this, as Fielding sees it, is that in 1747 the term "Jacobite" was *not* a mere bugbear; it was the name of a real menace. Politicians, like Mrs. Waters shouting "Rape" in *Tom Jones*, had cried "Wolf!" so often that the watchman who cried true was credited no more than any other.

The political perversion of language was at its worst, however, when it enlisted the aid of Grub Street and availed itself of the quasi-literary machinery of the hack pamphlet and the hireling newspaper. Of all the kinds of writers who have debased the

[64] *Jacobite's Journal*, Jan. 16, 1748. The pamphlet from which Fielding quotes is *An Historical Essay upon the Ballance of Civil Power in England* (1748), by Samuel Squire, Bishop of St. David's.
[65] P. 7.

name of author into a synonym for "Scribbler," Fielding declares
in the *True Patriot* for February 4, 1746, "those who meddle
with Politics" are the most culpable. For though Grub Street
was a power in its own right in the corruption of language, it
became, when it lent its skills to the dissemination of the political
lie, a positive force of evil. "If a lying Tongue be so dreadful a
Weapon as the wisest of Men seem to think it is," Fielding asks
in the *Jacobite's Journal*, "in what Light shall we see a lying Pen,
which can circulate a Falsehood over the whole Kingdom in a
Day, and may be said to be telling Lies in several thousand
different Places at one and the same Time?" The evil of such
writing, moreover, was not political alone. It also undermined
the very foundations of language as a medium of objective truth,

because, as the Generality of Readers consider [newspapers] only as
the Relaters of mere Matters of Fact, they are apt to give almost an
implicit Faith to what they read. The Mind is, as it were, put upon its
Guard against the Impressions of Argument or Ridicule. But an
Author (if we must debase the Name by so applying it) who professes
only to tell you the Occurrences which happen from such a Day to
such a Day, is sure to be read without any Diffidence or Caution. And
we no more doubt him when he assures us, that "It appears to be
literally true, by authentic Accounts from H[anover] . . ., that the
Foreign Adm[inistratio]n of Br[itis]h Affairs, is, at present, in the
Hands of a *High German Doctor*." than when he tells us, in the same
Paper, That seven Asses started for the Purse at Newcastle.[66]

But the original evil genius of political propaganda, to Fielding's mind, was not Jacobitism but Sir Robert Walpole, and in
his plays and early journalistic writings Fielding expended enor-
mous energy to expose that master politician's prostitution of the
language. No spellbinding orator, Walpole could not be accused
of any extraordinary abuse of words in his own person. If Sir
Robert was "Liar Robin" to Fielding it was rather because of
his maintenance of a paid ministerial press dedicated to defending his policies and promoting his character. The leading ministerial newspaper received direct financial payment from the
government, and Walpole himself later admitted spending 5,000

[66]Sept. 24, 1748. The quoted passages are from the *London Evening Post*, Aug. 11, 1748.

pounds a year (out of Treasury funds)[67] on what might today be
called public relations but what Fielding, with an eye for the
satiric analogy with trade advertising and publishers' blurbs,
called "Ministerial Puffs." In the *Champion* Puffs department
of February 16, 1739/40 appears the following notice:

Whereas many Persons, Novices in the Art of *Puffing*, have rashly
undertaken though greatly to their own Detriment, to puff their own
Wares, Writings, Projects, Merits, and Accomplishments: This is to
certify, for the Good of the Publick, that I *Gustavus Puffendorf*, first
student under the great Professor of *Rose-Street*, then Fellow Practi-
tioner with the admir'd antient *Pistol*, and lastly Co-Rival in Renown,
with that consummate Master of Art, erst of *New-port Market*: This
is to certify, I say, that Puffs, *secundum Artem*, of all Degrees and
Magnitudes, for all Arts, Mysteries, and Professions, are to be had of
me, if *properly bespoken*, at my House, the Sign of the Powder Puff, in
Blow-Bladder-Street, and no where else in the Three Kingdoms.

It was in the person of the hireling publicist Puffendorf that
Fielding carried on his campaign against the ministerial gazet-
teers in the back pages of the *Champion* while he and Ralph were
attacking Walpole and his policies direct in the leading articles,
and Puffendorf's credentials made it clear that hereafter all
attempts at panegyric and whitewashing defenses of the ministry
would be considered as mere advertising puffs. The "great
Professor of Rose Street" was Edmund Curll, who was not only
a notorious puffer of his own publications but had taken the
unusual step in the eighteenth century of having one of his hacks
write the biography of a living man—the idolatrous *Brief and
True History of Sir Robert Walpole and His Family* (1738) by
William Musgrave—which was printed and sold at Curll's shop
in Rose Street. The "admir'd antient *Pistol*" was Theophilus
Cibber, the son of Fielding's arch-desecrator of the language but
also, according to Fielding, no mean corrupter of the word in
his own right. His nickname Pistol was not so much a tribute to
his memorable success as an actor in the role of Shakespeare's
ranting soldier as it was a reflection of his off-stage character as
a blustering man about town and occasional polemicist. In *An*

[67]See David Harrison Stevens, *Party Politics and English Journalism* (Chicago: University
of Chicago Press, 1916), pp. 119–20.

Apology for the Life of Mr. T——— C———, Comedian (1740), a
work which has sometimes been attributed to Fielding, the
younger Cibber is represented as writing an autobiography,
modeled on his father's *Apology*, in which he boasts among other
early accomplishments of how he "shew'd such an *uncommon
Genius* for writing and composing a *Playhouse Bill*, . . . and wrote
them in such a *promissory Way*, (a Way which has been since
call'd *Puffing*) that they engross'd the Attention of the Town. . . .
From such small Beginnings, my Genius soar'd to an unequal
Height; and I have had, for this Species of writing, no one
hardy enough to become my Competitor in Fame." But it is a
later passage, describing how this special gift led him to become
a "Writer for the M———st———y" hired to write "occasional
Gazeteers,"[68] which explains why Fielding singled him out for
attack in the *Champion*.

The *Daily Gazetteer* was at this time the leading ministerial
paper, and though Cibber seems to have been strictly a second-
string contributor his twin talents of invective and panegyric
made him, for Fielding's purposes, an ideal type of the political
hack. The Ministerial Puffs for March 29, 1740, for example,
notices "In Tuesday's Gazetteer, a curious Epitome of the whole
Art of Political Billingsgate; with Examples of all the Tropes,
Figures, etc. used therein by Antient Pistol," and one is delighted
to find the writer of this paper (presumably Cibber) defending
himself against the charge that his attacks on the Opposition are
"an Endeavour to *frighten with hard Words, and to overpower with
the superior Force of Noise and Bluster*" by arguing that the
Opposition writers who make such charges are nothing but "a
Tribe of Pretended Patriots, . . . mighty Advocates of Liberty
[who] chiefly consist of the very Scum and Refuse of all Nations,
Professions, and Religions; Fellows that have beggar'd themselves by their Debaucheries in their Youth, and are obliged to
turn to Hackney Writing to support themselves in their Age;
*Libertines, Atheists, Scotch Presbyterians, Jacobites, Romish
Priests*, and *Irish Papists*!"[69] Pistol, it would seem, was Pistol

---

[68]Pp. 13, 118. I do not myself believe Fielding to be the author of this piece, its style
seeming to me very unlike his usual manner. Fortunately, however, my point does not
depend on Fielding's authorship.
[69]*Daily Gazetteer*, Mar. 25, 1740.

indeed, and though Fielding offers us no examples of his panegyrical vein we may perhaps take him on trust that it was equally
destructive of good words.

The third of Puffendorf's colleagues, "that consummate
Master of Art, erst of *New-port Market*," was none other than
Orator Henley, whose Oratory in Newport Market had been
closed by a presentment of the Grand Jury of Middlesex in
January, 1729, only to be reopened in Clare Market, where the
Orator, having raised the admission charge from two pence to
one shilling, continued to preach his blasphemous sermons and
deliver his seditious orations until he was arrested in 1746 on the
charge of "endeavouring to alienate the minds of his Majesty's
subjects from their allegiance by his Sunday harangues."[70] The
appropriateness of his appearances in the Puffs column as a
promoter of his own sermons and an advertiser of real estate has
already been considered, but it was as the salaried author of the
pro-ministerial *Hyp Doctor* that he gained entry to the sub-
department of Ministerial Puffs. A particularly labored essay in
The Hyp Doctor for March 4, 1739/40, for example, in which
Henley argued that the septennial Parliament was more con-
ducive to liberty than the triennial system urged by the Opposition, is noticed by Fielding in the *Champion* for March 8, as "a
new World of Words; or a Specimen of a Political Dictionary in
the Hyp-Doctor."[71]

Puffendorf himself, if he was intended to represent any real
person, was probably modeled on Ralph (or Raphael) Courteville, the principal writer for the *Daily Gazetteer*, who signed himself (to Fielding's great irritation, no doubt) "R. Freeman."[72] As

[70]*Gentleman's Magazine*, Dec., 1746. Cited by Miriam A. Locke, *True Patriot*, p. 58.
Henley was soon released on bail and was apparently never brought to trial, but the
charge would seem to lend some weight to Fielding's later allegations (in the *True
Patriot*) that Henley was a Jacobite tool. See also Henry B. Wheatly, *London Past and
Present* (London, 1891), 2: 595.

[71]"A new World of Words" probably alludes to Edward Phillips' popular dictionary of
"hard terms," *The New World of Words* (London, 1678).

[72]Cross and Dudden identify Freeman as one Thomas Pitt (Cross, 1: 266; Dudden, 1:
163–64), confusing him, apparently, with the James Pitt who also wrote for the *Daily
Gazetteer*, under the name of Francis Osborne. But the anonymous author of *An
Historical View of the Principles, Characters, Persons, Etc. of the Political Writers of Great
Britain* (1740) declares that "The *Gazetteer* is wrote chiefly by one Mr. C——le. . . .
His political name is . . .*R. Freeman*" (pp. 52–53); and Fielding himself makes the same

chief ministerial propagandist and as the author of the *Memoirs
of the Life and Administration of William Cecil, Baron Burleigh*
(1738) in which he had included a "Parallel between the State of
Government Then and Now" lavishly complimentary to Walpole's administration, Courteville had a clear title to the office
of "Puff-Master General . . . of *Great Britain*" to which Puffendorf proclaims himself elected in the *Champion* for February 21,
1740. He was, besides, the organist of St. James's Church in
Westminster (a "blower" according to the vernacular of the
time) and hence peculiarly well fitted to operate the "Air Pump"
which Puffendorf boasts he is master of in the same Puffs column.

But in any case, it is Courteville (or Freeman) who is the main
target of Fielding's Puffs notices. "R. Freeman, Esq., his
Panegyrick for the Ministry" is almost a regular entry in the
column. Of all the ministerial writers, Courteville seems to have
been the most adept at the art of whitewashing Walpole's
methods and promoting his claims to "honor" and "greatness"
—those spurious Walpolian attributes which Fielding satirizes
in *Jonathan Wild* as ironic corruptions of language. The way in
which this satiric fable exploits the parallels between Walpole's
career and that of the criminal Wild is too familiar to need
recapitulation here.[73] W. R. Irwin, in *The Making of Jonathan
Wild*, has admirably explored its broader implications as a satire
on the notion of Machiavellian ethics which regarded "the great
man" as one whose superhuman ambitions exempted him from

---

[72]*continued*
identification by punning on Courteville's name. A burlesque advertisement in the
Champion for Oct. 16, 1740, announces "PROPOSALS for printing, by Subscription, an
Apology for the Life, Actions, and Writings of RALPH FREEMAN, alias, COURT-EVIL,
Esq.; containing an authentic History of the several wonderful Stages, thro' which he
hath passed in the World; together with the successful Progress of *Corruption, Baseness*,
and *Treachery*, during his Time. *Written by* HIMSELF." See also Robert L. Haig, *The
Gazetteer: 1735–1797* (Carbondale: Southern Illinois University Press, 1960), pp. 7,
13; and William B. Coley, "The 'Remarkable Queries' in the *Champion*," *Philological
Quarterly*, 41 (1962): 433 n. The report in the *Champion*, Oct. 14, 1740, of "Puffendorf
press'd into HIS HONOUR'S [i.e., Walpole's] Service by the *Political Hyp Doctor*," refers
to *Hyp Doctor*, Oct. 14, in which Henley played into Fielding's hands by appealing
fortuitously to the theories of the German philosopher Samuel Puffendorf as sanction
for Walpole's peace policy. A long letter signed "Gustavus Puffendorf" is the leading
article in the *Champion*, Dec. 19, 1741, but this was after Fielding had left the journal
and the piece bears none of the marks of his style.
[73]See J. E. Wells, "Fielding's Political Purpose in *Jonathan Wild*," *PMLA*, 28 (1913):
1–55.

ordinary codes of morality. But the extent to which *Jonathan Wild* is also a satire on the political corruption of language, particularly as practiced by Walpole's hired panegyrists, has not received the attention it deserves.

If Walpole was "His Honour" and "the Great Man" it was not because he advanced any special claim to these epithets himself but because these were the terms employed by his publicists. The prime minister whom Julian the Apostate meets in *The Journey from this World to the Next*, it is true, tells him that "honour" and "honesty" are "words without meaning" (II, 257). But the precise process whereby such words are "transformed to Posterity" with their "Iniquity annexed" is described by Jonathan Wild in his famous discourse on "honor." No man, he tells his gang, can "possibly entertain a higher and nobler sense of that word, nor a greater esteem of its inestimable value," than himself:

> But alas! gentlemen, what a pity is it that a word of such sovereign use and virtue should have so uncertain and various an application that scarce two people mean the same thing by it. . . . In what then doth the word honor consist? Why, in itself alone. A man of honor is he that is called a man of honor; and while he is so called he so remains, and no longer. Think not anything a man commits can forfeit his honor. Look abroad into the world; the PRIG, while he flourishes, is a man of honor; when in jail, at the bar, or the tree, he is so no longer. And why is this distinction? Not from his actions; for these are often as well known in his flourishing estate as they are afterwards; but because men, I mean those of his own party or gang, call him a man of honor in the former, and cease to call him so in the latter condition. (II, 42–43)

Walpole's own shrewd application of this principle, Fielding implies, lay in ensuring that he would be "called a man of honor" by paying hacks to do just that. Starting with the September issues of the *Champion* (and occasionally, perhaps, earlier) Walpole is usually referred to, in the leading articles and news reports as well as in the Puffs column, as "HIS HONOUR," with obvious ironic emphasis on the inappropriateness of that title. A letter appearing in the October 7, 1740 number underscores the irony by observing that "Your Distinction of HIS HONOUR is certainly very just and applicable, for who is more deserving of that Title than One that never *prevaricated*, *trifled*, or *falsified* his *Word* in a *Public Assembly*, and is *eminent* in all the Courts of *Europe*, as in his own Country, for his *Personal* and *Political Resolution*, *untainted Virtue*, and *Public Spirit*." I have not been able to find the original of this statement (if any such ever existed) but it is clearly intended to represent, in keeping with Fielding's method in the *Champion* of quoting verbatim from the ministerial press, the kind of paid panegyric on which Walpole's reputation was supposed to have been built. The satiric technique is to assume the corruption of the italicized words, at least in the context of their applicability to Walpole, and so to rest confident that they will be read as meaning the exact opposite of what they "say."

It was in this kind of panegyrical corruption of words, according to Fielding, that Courteville excelled, and the extent to which the "Puffs" notices in the *Champion* of his whitewashing of Walpole anticipate the ironic method of *Jonathan Wild* (whose eulogizing narrator is perhaps Courteville magnified to the nth power) is remarkable. "Even *Corruption* itself affirm'd to be a Virtue in his HONOUR by one of his virtuous Scribes" reports Puffs in the *Champion* for October 25, 1740, compressing the progress from perverse usage to irony (the word "virtuous" being equivalent to "corrupt") into one sentence; and though the notice scarcely does justice to Courteville's defense of Walpole in the paper in question it is close enough to the mark to suggest that Fielding was seriously troubled by the political juggling of words, particularly since Courteville himself chose to make the matter an issue of language. Citing an example from Roman history of a man who prospered so much that he was accused by his neighbors of witchcraft and who defended himself by exhibiting his carts, plows, and harrows and saying, "Behold, O Romans, . . . the Spells and Incantations that I use," Courteville (in the *Daily Gazetteer* for October 24, 1740) drew a modern parallel:

To me it seems pretty clear that this is the Case of a certain Great Personage amongst us, only that in this Free-thinking Age, Conjuring being no Imputation, it has been thought proper to pitch on a better sounding, tho' full as unintelligible a Term, that is, Corruption. . . .

I say, then, gentle Readers, that Corruption in the Mouths of a Minister's Enemies, signifies much the same Thing that Witchcraft did in the Mouth of the *Roman* mob. It stands . . . for a Cause they know nothing of, but to which they would willingly give an Ill Name, because they do not like its Effects; . . . the very Enemies of the present Ministry allow, that he [i.e., Walpole] is affable, courteous, and easy of Access. These Carts, Ploughs, and Harrows, are so ever-lastingly in the Way, that there is no charging him with Conjuring. In such a Case what is to be done? Why, . . . charge him with Corruption; that is an Accumulative Vice, and you may give his very Virtues in Evidence.

But an earlier Puffs notice, in the *Champion* for August 9, 1740, is more interesting still. It may well be, in fact, along with the *Daily Gazetteer* essay to which it refers, the very germ of *Jonathan Wild*. "An Acquaintance of *Squire Freeman's*," Fielding notes, "owes all his *Greatness* to his many *useful, good Qualities*, and, in the midst of that *Greatness*, is as *humble* as if he had none." The allusion is to the *Daily Gazetteer* for August 8. "We have often heard it said," Courteville had written,

That the Great do what they have a mind to, That such an Action would be a base thing to a meaner Man, and such an Expression would not have been borne, but from a Person of his Quality; all these Phrases seem to insinuate that a different Kind of Measure is to be made use of, when we compute the Morals of ordinary sort of People from that which is apply'd to Men in a superior Sphere. Yet, I presume to say, that this is far from being grounded either upon Reason or Experience; there ought to be no such Distinction amongst Men, there really is none such. . . . The Intent of Speech is to be understood, and, of consequence, perverting the Sense of a Phrase is a Sort of false Coining in Language, which whoever detects does a Service to the Publick. With this View, I write this Paper: In which I shall attempt to prove, that it is against Reason and against Experience to believe, that those whom we call in common Speech People of Fashion, are looser in their Manners than other People; as by a long Habit in using a Phrase, at first maliciously perverted, the Mass of Mankind usually apprehend. . . . But Men of true good Sense, and of impartial Spirits, . . . esteem such as are Good, tho' they happen at the same Time to be Great; and are especially desirous of *honouring that* Man who *owes* all his Greatness to *his many useful Good Qualities*, and who, in the Midst of all that *Greatness*, is as *humble* as if he had none.

The issue, it will be observed, is once again seen—by Courteville as well as by Fielding—as a question of language, and Courteville even appeals to Locke's doctrine of "the Intent of Speech" in support of his own position, a form of defense which must have struck Fielding as an instance of how the Devil may quote Scripture. But two more diametrically opposed interpretations of the same set of verbal data could scarcely be imagined. For Courteville, serving the interests of the Court Party in general and of "the Great Man" Walpole in particular, is denying that the words in question have been corrupted by "the Persons who have," in Fielding's phrase, "without any just Pretensions, assumed these Characters" and is arguing instead that they have been maliciously perverted by the *enemies* of the persons in question. Fielding, though he duly registered the matter in the *Champion* Puffs column, did not rise to the challenge immediately. We have already seen, however, how first in *Joseph Andrews* and later in the *Covent-Garden Journal* he treats the phrase "People of Fashion" as an instance of "the barbarous Corruption of Language"[74] for which, Courteville to the contrary notwithstanding, "those whom we call in common Speech People of Fashion" are themselves plainly held responsible. In *Jonathan Wild* "greatness" in the sense of social status is regarded in the same ironic light, particularly in the chapters describing Jonathan's courtship of Laetitia, which is conducted "all in the GREAT style" (II, 59).

But it is "greatness" in the sense of political power which is Fielding's main subject in *Jonathan Wild*, and here again he reverses Courteville's judgment by treating the term as one corrupted not by the enemies of so-called "great men" but by their friends, their flatterers, and apologists. When he makes his narrator speak of "greatness, or, as the vulgar erroneously call it, villainy," and has him report that Wild distrusted his henchman Fireblood, "knowing him to be an accomplished rascal as the vulgar term it, a complete GREAT MAN in our language" (II, 124, 136), Fielding intends his readers, of course, to understand "the vulgar" as meaning honest, plain-spoken men and "our language" to be taken as referring to the language of Wild's

[74]See above, p. 39.

(or Walpole's) party and, by extension, to that of all indiscriminate eulogizers of the politically powerful. *Jonathan Wild* is
indeed, then, as W. R. Irwin has shown, a satire on the worship
of brute power, but Irwin is mistaken, I think, in taking quite
seriously Fielding's distinction between "greatness" and "goodness" and believing that he meant the former term to be understood literally as a pejorative word.[75] It is true that Fielding himself, speaking in his own person in the Preface to the *Miscellanies*,
seems to subscribe to this distinction:

Perhaps some apology may be required of me, for having used the
word greatness to which the world hath affixed such honourable ideas,
in so disgraceful and contemptuous a light. Now if the fact be, that
the greatness which is commonly worshipped is really of that kind
which I have here represented, the fault seems rather to lie in those
who have ascribed to it those honours to which it hath not in reality
the least claim. The truth, I apprehend, is, we often confound the
ideas of goodness and greatness together, or rather include the former
in our idea of the latter. . . . In reality, no qualities can be more
distinct: for as it cannot be doubted but that benevolence, honour,
honesty, and charity, make a good man; and that parts, courage, are
the efficient qualities of a great man, so must it be confessed, that the
ingredients which compose the former of these characters bear no
analogy to, nor dependence on, those which constitute the latter. A
man may therefore be great without being good, or good without
being great. (XII, 244–45)

But in fact he is using the words "great" and "greatness" here
in the same way—as ironic corruptions of language—as he does
in the text of *Jonathan Wild*, for otherwise the moral and verbal
incongruity of Jonathan's claim to the epithet "Great Man"
would be lost. Actually, then, Fielding himself (as he makes clear
in the poem *Of True Greatness*,[76] first published in 1741 and reissued in the *Miscellanies* along with *Jonathan Wild*) "affixed . . .
honourable ideas" to the word "greatness" and included the idea
of goodness in its meaning. But he felt that in its popular application to Walpole and others of his stripe it was becoming debased
into a synonym for "power," or rather that its specialized sense

[75] *The Making of Jonathan Wild* (New York: Columbia University Press, 1941), pp. 43–79.
[76] See above, p. 42.

(as in Alexander the Great) of *temporal* bigness was threatening to drive out its more general and abstract meaning of moral grandeur, largeness of spirit or mind, and it is this corruptive process which his irony exploits and thereby seeks to expose. Just as in the "Modern Glossary" paper (in which "great," "applied to a Thing, signifies Bigness; when to a Man, often Littleness, or Meanness") he pretends to champion popular "Custom" against the traditional usage of moral and religious writers, so in the first chapter of *Jonathan Wild* he has his narrator dissociate himself from that "set of simple fellows, called, in derision, sages or philosophers, [who] have endeavored, as much as possible, to confound the ideas of greatness and goodness; whereas no two things can possibly be more distinct from each other, for greatness consists in bringing all manner of mischief on mankind, and goodness in removing it from them" (II, 2–3). But the "philosophers," here as elsewhere in Fielding, really stand for the "proper and original" meanings of words, and in fact he makes his belief in such a proper and original meaning of "greatness" all but explicit when he goes on, in the Preface to the *Miscellanies*, to say,

Now as to that greatness which is totally devoid of goodness, it seems to me in nature to resemble the false sublime in poetry; whose bombast is, by the ignorant and ill-judging vulgar, often mistaken for solid wit and eloquence, whilst it is in effect the very reverse. Thus pride, ostentation, insolence, cruelty, and every kind of villainy, are often construed into true greatness of mind, in which we always include an idea of goodness. This bombast greatness . . . is the character I intend to expose. (XII, 246)[77]

The distinction in *Jonathan Wild* between "greatness" and "goodness" is not a cynical acquiescence in the political corruption of language but a way of resisting it by revealing how ironically empty a moral term can be when it is separated from one of its essential ideas.

---

[77]Cf. *An Essay on Conversation* (also published in the *Miscellanies*) in which Fielding writes, "There are [some] who consider [pride] as the foible of great minds; and others again, who will have it to be the very foundation of greatness; and, perhaps, it may be of that greatness which we have endeavoured to expose in many parts of these works; but to real greatness, which is the union of a good heart with a good head, it is almost diametrically opposite, as it generally proceeds from the depravity of both, and almost certainly from the badness of the latter." Henley ed., 14: 259–60.

POLITE SOCIETY

When in the "Modern Glossary" paper Fielding pays ironic deference to "Custom (the absolute Lord and Master, according to Horace, of all the Modes of Speech)" he is thinking to some extent of popular usage in general, and the verbal corruptions of literature, criticism, and politics are well represented in the Glossary. But the kind of usage he has chiefly in mind, as the introductory essay makes clear, is that of "the polite Part of Mankind." It is interesting, therefore, to find Bernard Mandeville (the proponent of the subversive view that "the first design of Speech was to persuade others either to give Credit to what the speaking Person would have them believe; or else to act or suffer such Things as he would compel them to act or suffer if they were entirely in his Power") paying tribute to the same kind of Custom and in the same kind of terms, though his tone, to be sure, is entirely different. It is "the *beau monde*," says Mandeville, "who in all Countries, are the undoubted Refiners of Language," not "the Preachers, Playwrights, Orators, and fine Writers." The latter "make the best of what is ready coin'd to their Hands; but the true and only Mint of Words and Phrases is the Court; and the polite Part of every Nation are in Possession of the *Jus & norma loquendi*. . . . Orators therefore, Historians, and all wholesale Dealers in Words, are confin'd to those [terms] that have been already well receiv'd," and their language "must first have the Stamp of the Court, and the Approbation of the *beau monde*, before it can pass for current, [since] whatever is not used among them, or comes abroad without their Sanction, is either vulgar, pedantick, or obsolete."[78]

The idea that the class of society which was generally acknowledged to be its arbiter of taste exercised also a special power over its language was neither surprising nor new. In *Remarques sur la langue française* (1647), an early statement of the principle of usage (*l'usage*) as "le Maistre & le Souverain des langues vivantes" which influenced English language theorists of the Restoration and eighteenth century, the French grammarian Favre de Vaugelas maintained that "l'élite des voix . . . est veritablement celuy que l'on nomme le Maistre des langues"

---

[78]*The Fable of the Bees*, Kaye ed., 2: 289–92.

and made it clear that by "l'élite des voix" he meant the upper classes.[79] The French philosopher Bernard Lamy, in a treatise of 1668 translated into English as *The Art of Speaking*, was of the same opinion. "When we advance Custom to the Throne," he wrote, "and make it Sovereign Arbiter of all Languages, we do not intend to put the Scepter into the hands of the Populace. There is a good, and there is a bad Custom. . . . But it is no hard matter to discern betwixt the . . . depraved Language of the common People, and the noble and refin'd Expressions of the Gentry, whose condition and merits have advanced them above the other."[80] John Hughes, writing in 1698, recommends that for an understanding of "general Acceptation, which is the only Standard of Speech," writers would do well to familiarize themselves "with the Conversation of People of Fashion."[81]

To the English writers of the Restoration, with their conscious emulation of the refinements of French letters and society, the claims of polite society to the *jus et norma loquendi* did not seem either an encroachment on their own domain or a threat to the condition of the tongue. Theirs was, after all, the age of the "mob of gentlemen who wrote with ease," and never before nor since in the history of English society have the *literati* and the *beau monde* been on such excellent and intimate terms of mutual respect. "Restoration literature," as James Sutherland says, "was dominated by the aristocracy, who set the tone and exercised a control over the mode of expression. Restoration prose is, in the main, a slightly formalized variation of the conversation of gentlemen."[82]

So long, then, as the conversation of gentlemen could be relied upon to furnish a worthy standard of speech, the writers had no reason to complain. It was in their interest, in fact, to do what they could to maintain the high standards which the art of conversation had achieved, and Fielding's *Essay on Conversation*,

---

[79]Preface.
[80]P. 41. This is the second English edition (1708). I have not been able to locate a first edition, but Pepys praises "a little book concerning speech in general, a translation late out of French," which sounds like the same work, in the *Diary* for Dec. 6, 1668.
[81]"Of Style," *Critical Essays of the Eighteenth Century*, ed. Willard Highley Durham (New Haven: Yale University Press, 1915), p. 80. The essay was not published until 1735.
[82]"Restoration Prose," *Restoration and Augustan Prose*, p. 5.

with its underlying assumption of the social values of polite discourse, belongs to a tradition of Renaissance and seventeenth-century "conversation books" which includes also Swift's *Hints towards an Essay on Conversation* and, on the negative side, his *Polite Conversations*.[83] As one moves from the Restoration into the eighteenth century, however, it is impossible to escape the conclusion that "the negative side"—the reaction against polite society's abuse of its privileged position as the arbiter of speech —was beginning to outweigh the positive celebration of the ideal. The curious ambivalence we have noted in Fielding's contribution to this literature of celebration is, partly at least, a matter of the conflict between his loyalty to the traditional ideal of conversation and his conviction that in the practice of his own time this ideal was forgotten or travestied beyond recognition.

What was happening, the critics of the age agreed, was not that polite society had abdicated the rule of speech but that it was ruling badly, irresponsibly. Swift had still confidence enough in polite society to address his *Proposal for Correcting, Improving, and Ascertaining the English Tongue* (1712) to "all the learned and polite Persons of the Nation."[84] But in a *Tatler* essay of 1710 complaining of "the continual corruption of our English tongue . . . by . . . false refinements," he included a letter abounding in slang, abbreviations, and contractions and full of new words such as "*banter, bamboozle, . . .* and *kidney*," which was, he insisted, "in every point an admirable pattern of the present polite way of writing,"[85] and his *Polite Conversations* left no doubt as to which class of society he held most directly culpable for these corruptions of speech. Addison, in the *Spectator* for August 4, 1711, complained that current slovenly habits of conversation "miserably curtailed some of our Words," reducing them to "all but their first Syllables, as in *mob. rep. pos. incog.* and the like; and as all ridiculous Words make their first Entry into a Language by familiar Phrases, I dare not answer for these that

---

[83]See Sutherland, "Some Aspects of Eighteenth-Century Prose," *Essays on the Eighteenth Century Presented to David Nichol Smith* (Oxford: Clarendon Press, 1945), p. 96; and Herbert Davis, "The Conversation of the Augustans," *The Seventeenth Century*, pp. 181–97.
[84]*Prose Works*, 4: 6.
[85]*Ibid.*, 2: 173–77.

they will not in time be looked upon as a part of our Tongue."[86]
The corruptions cited by Swift and Addison, like many of those
reported by Fielding, seem trivial until we remind ourselves once
again that to the Augustans language was "the great bond that
holds society together" and that any usage which obscured the
etymological "original" or "agreed" meanings of words was
potentially dangerous. "Abbreviations," warned George Harris
in 1752, "are destructive of Language,"[87] and slang words,
whether new coinages or existing terms used in capricious new
senses, were to be shunned for the same reason. They were, as
Dr. Johnson put it, "the spawn of folly or affectation, and . . .
therefore, no legitimate derivation can be shown" for them.[88]

"O, Dear, London is quite another World," writes the modish
Prudentia Flutter to her provincial friend Lucy Rural in one of
Fielding's contributions to Sarah Fielding's *Familiar Letters*
(1747). "Was I to mention half our Diversions to you, you would
not even know the Names of them. Here are Drums, and Riots,
and Hurricanes. I warrant now, I have set you guessing what a
Drum is; nay, I'll leave you a thousand years to guess what it is
made of.—To satisfy your Curiosity then, it is made of a great
many Rooms, and a great many Tables, and a great many
Candles, and a great many People." "I own, my Dear, I have not
much Idea of a Drum," answers Miss Lucy (with an echo of
Lockean terminology that gives serious point to her objection),
"and you'll pardon me, if I say, you don't seem to entertain any
very perfect Notion of it yourself. . . . I do not find, you can give
good . . . Reason for the Name of your Assembly."[89] The same
word, as used by the fashionable personages introduced at Lady
Bellaston's, gives Fielding pause again in *Tom Jones*, and the
irritating necessity, "notwithstanding our present haste" of
narration, to stop and define a term which could not bespeak its
own meaning either by etymology or traditional usage causes
him to take comfort at least in the reflection that "our posterity,
it is hoped, will not understand [it] in the sense it is here applied"
(V, 274). In the *Covent-Garden Journal* No. 17, however, it is

[86]Everyman ed., 1: 408.
[87]*Observations upon the English Language*, p. 12.
[88]*Plan of an English Dictionary, Works*, 2: 16.
[89]2: 328–29, 334.

the ephemeral nature of such words which is the object of his ridicule as he imagines what a future historian might make of contemporary accounts of mid-eighteenth-century society. The imaginary historian discounts entirely a chronicler of the time who "says that Women of the first Quality used to make nightly Riots in their own Houses," and he is sorely puzzled by another's assertion that "The Ladies of St. James's Parish . . . used to treat their Company with *Drums*; . . . some Copies, I know, read *Drams*, but the former is the true Reading, nor would the latter much cure the Absurdity."

The satire in these passages, of course, is striking out in more directions than one, but if the modish terms affected by fashionable ladies and gentlemen are a reflection of the triviality of their pursuits, they are also symptomatic of polite society's pollution of the language it was traditionally supposed to refine. A "Correspondent" who signs herself "An Old Gentlewoman" writes to the *True Patriot* for January 21, 1746, to ask about "a new Word being introduced, *viz.* (Intonation). . . . You that are a learned Man perhaps can tell me what Idea ought to be affixed to that Word: For I cannot find, in any of the several Dictionaries that I have searched, that there is such a Word in any Language; whether it has been lately imported by a fine foreign Fidler, or is an Epithet uttered only to astonish the Hearers, is too important a Point for me to decide. Though when I recollect, Dr. *Taylor* the Occulist declared, that he always found himself most admired when he was least understood; I am inclined to think this may proceed from the same Motive, for there are Quacks in Politeness as well as all other Sciences."

Another instance of this pollution was the irresponsible use by polite speakers of modifying words as meaningless intensifiers, a use which tended, so Fielding and others feared, to separate these words from their proper ideas and to reduce them to mere rhetorical counters. Fielding's "high life" characters in his plays and his novels, it will be observed, are particularly guilty of this fault, and according to a modern student of eighteenth-century usage, the polite speakers of the time were indeed "immoderately fond of emphatic adverbs and adjectives, which they used not only with frequency, but in astonishing variety. . . . This fashion begot a habit of constant emphasis which . . . took the form not only of intensive epithets" but also, in its extreme manifestation, "the *ne plus ultra* style of description favored by the Countess of Strafford—'the finest that ever I see,' 'the coldest winter I ever felt,' . . . 'My lady indeed is the best woman in the world,' etc."[90]

Fielding, then, may be regarded as reporting accurately the conversational habits of his day when he tells us, in the *Champion* paper on the abuse of words, that "certain Phrases [have] by long Custom arrived at meaning nothing, tho' often used: such as, it is very early, very late; very hot, very cold; a very good, or very bad Play or Opera; the best in the World, the worst in the World." Some of the entries in the *Covent-Garden Journal* "Modern Glossary" are clearly of the same type. "Fine," for example, is "An Adjective of a very peculiar Kind, destroying, or, at least, lessening the Force of the Substantive to which it is joined: As *fine* Gentlemen, *fine* Lady, *fine* House, *fine* Cloaths, *fine* Taste;—in all which *fine* is to be understood in a Sense somewhat synonymous with useless"; and "Shocking" is "An Epithet which fine Ladies apply to almost every Thing. It is, indeed, an Interjection (if I may so call it) of Delicacy." Similarly, when Tom Jones's guide on the road to Coventry insists that it is "impossible" he has lost his way, Fielding identifies the word in question as one "which, in common conversation, is often used to signify not only improbable, but often what is really very likely, and, sometimes what hath certainly happened; an hyperbolical violence like that which is so frequently offered to the words infinite and eternal, by the former of which it is usual to express a distance of half a yard, and by the latter, a duration of five minutes. And thus it is as usual to assert the impossibility of losing what is already actually lost" (IV, 348).

But slang and "hyperbolical violence" were not, to Fielding's mind, the worst of high society's degradations of the language. This distinction was reserved for its reduction of polite verbal forms, originally intended to express the subtle interdependencies of rank and station in a complex society and to convey the respect of one order for the other, into mere empty formulas, or, worse yet, into polite mockeries behind which operated every species

[90]William Matthews, "Polite Speech in the Eighteenth Century," *English*, 1 (1937): 500–501.

of insincerity and hypocrisy. At its best, conversation was an expression both of the social ideal of an integrated society and of the linguistic ideal of the distinterested communication of ideas, a point which Fielding, in *An Essay on Conversation*, typically makes by appealing at once to the etymological "original" meaning of the word "conversation" and to its traditional "agreed" usage: "The primitive and literal sense of this word, is, I apprehend, to turn round together; and in its more copious usage we intend by it that reciprocal interchange of ideas, by which truth is examined; things are, in a manner, turned round, and shifted, and all our knowledge communicated to each other." This marriage of the social and linguistic ideals entails the use of certain verbal forms—titles, compliments, and so forth—which, while not strictly expressive of "ideas" in the "philosophical sense" (i.e., in the Lockean sense of intellectual constructs) are yet not inconsistent with the purpose of speech because they do convey notions of esteem which are themselves "ideas" of a sort and symbols of social truth as necessary and worthy of communication as philosophical concepts. For conversation, considered as a social as well as a verbal art, is founded on "good-breeding," which, in its original sense, means "the art of pleasing, or contributing as much as possible to the ease and happiness of those with whom you converse" (XIV, 246, 249).

This, however, as Fielding's divided attitude in *An Essay on Conversation* makes clear, is the ideal only. We have seen how his manner of referring to "those two disgraces of the human species commonly called a beau and a fine lady" betrays his contempt for the current usage of such verbal forms, and in the *Champion* essay on the abuse of words he without reservation considers titles like "Captain, Dr. Esquire, Honourable, and Right Honourable" and conventional compliments like "*Sir, I am your most obedient, humble Servant*" on the same plane with the empty advertising claims of tradesmen ("very cheap, lowest Price," etc.)—as instances of words and phrases which "Custom [hath] stripp'd of their Ideas, and in a Manner annihilated." The proliferation of forms for forms' sake was the characteristic vice of a ruling class which had lost sight of the ideal of social responsibility it existed to fulfill. Most members of fashionable society, Fielding observes in *Tom Jones*, are "so entirely made up of form and affectation, that they have no character at all, at least none which appears" (V, 94), and the same was true of their speech. If there were "Quacks in Politeness as well as all other Sciences" so were there pedants in politeness. This, in fact, was the original gist of the epigram Fielding would seem to be paraphrasing in the passage from the *True Patriot* quoted above. "There are Pedants in Breeding as well as in Learning," wrote Steele in the *Spectator*,[91] and Swift elaborated on the thought in a treatise *On Good Manners and Good Breeding*: "Good Manners is the Art of making those people easy with whom we converse, . . . but as the common forms of good-manners were intended for regulating the conduct of those who have weak understandings; so they have been corrupted by the persons for whose use they were contrived. For these people have fallen into a needless and endless way of multiplying ceremonies. . . . There is a pedantry in manners, as in all arts and sciences."[92]

In its simplest form this "pedantry in manners" was mere social snobbery, and its most conspicuous manifestation was the deference accorded to titles of rank irrespective of the "original" meanings of these titles and of the worthiness of the persons who bore them. If a nobleman claims his dignity is inherent in his title, Fielding declares in *An Essay on Nothing*, "might he not be told, that a title originally implied dignity, as it implied the presence of those virtues to which dignity is inseparably annexed; but that no implication will fly in the face of downright positive proof to the contrary" (XIV, 316). The confrontation of the empty title with the "downright positive proof to the contrary" is one of Fielding's favorite satiric techniques for dealing with the succession of spindly "beaus," boorish "squires," ruffian "gentlemen," slatternly "ladies," ungallant "gallants," irreverent "Reverends," and dishonorable "Right Honourables" who strut endlessly through his works; and if the ignoble "noble lord" in *Amelia*, despite his central role in the story, is never referred to by any other name it is because this ironic confrontation is the

---

[91]No. 286, Jan. 18, 1712, Everyman ed., 2: 353.
[92]*The Prose Works*, 4: 213–15. The treatise was first published by Dr. Delany in 1754 but may have been written before Steele's *Spectator* piece. See Davis' Introduction, p. xxxvi. It may, like many of Swift's unpublished pieces, have been circulated privately in manuscript and so have come into Fielding's hands.

more effective for the relentless reiteration of his title, which, without any overt commentary by Fielding, soon tolls with brazen mockery whenever the "noble lord" is announced.

The word "gentleman," judging from Fielding's ironic usage, had become so divorced from its "original idea" of true gentility and from the concept of the gentleman as a useful member of society that it currently signified the mere outward show of dress and manners, particularly when modified by that "peculiar" adjective "fine," which, it will be remembered, "is to be under-understood in a Sense somewhat synonymous with useless." "The character I was ambitious of attaining," says Wilson in *Joseph Andrews*, relating the story of his misspent youth, "was that of a fine gentleman; the first requisites to which I appre-hended were to be supplied by a tailor, a periwig-maker, and some few more tradesmen, who deal in furnishing out the human body" (I, 229–30). But even when it stood alone the word signi-fied for Fielding, in its corrupt sense, a useless member of society, like the landlord in *Tom Jones*, for example, who "had been bred, as they call it, a gentleman; that is, bred up to do nothing," or Fitzpatrick in the same novel, who had been a lawyer's clerk in Ireland but, "choosing a genteeler walk in life, . . . came over to England, and set up that business which requires no apprentice-ship, namely, that of a gentleman" (IV, 89, 226).

The debasement of the word "gentleman" into a term which was, like Jonathan Wild's concept of "honor," appropriate to anyone who "is so called" is a constant theme in Fielding (Wild himself, of course, and his henchmen, like Macheath and his gang in *The Beggar's Opera*, are "gentlemen" to one another and to their toadying chronicler). Joseph Andrews sees no more in-appropriateness in his references to "the gentlemen of our cloth" (I, 203) than does that other footman in *Tom Jones* in his allusion to "the gentlemen in our gallery" at the theater (IV, 323). The custom which allowed that all soldiers were "gentlemen" pro-vokes Fielding's amusement in *Joseph Andrews* when a peddler assures Fanny that despite his present humble circumstances, "I was formerly a gentleman; for so all those of my profession are called. In a word, I was a drummer in an Irish regiment of foot" (I, 369). In both cases he is clearly concerned about the debase-ment of an important word, and the "gentlemen in red coats" whom Tom Jones falls in with illustrate the same point. Their officers, moreover, who might be expected to advance a more legitimate claim to the title, are shown to be ignorant, uncouth, and quarrelsome—indistinguishable, except for their insignia of rank, from their men. The only other distinction they recognize is money. When Jones settles a dispute among the soldiers over a reckoning presented to them at an inn by offering to pay it himself, "the terms honorable, noble, and worthy gentleman, resounded through the room." But even this dubious standard of gentility is not maintained to the satisfaction of all. The soldiers "call themselves gentlemen," the landlady of another inn complains to Jones, and the officers are called "your honor" by the men, but though they thus put on the airs of squires they do not spend nearly as much money as squires do. From "a good squire's family, . . . we take forty or fifty shillings of a night," whereas from a company of army officers—"la! sir, it is nothing" (IV, 27, 67).

The claim of mere wealth to the titles of gentility is not allowed by Fielding, of course, any more than any of the other spurious claims he deflates, and the landlady who measures a man's quality by the size of the bill she is able to present him is the same who might advertise, as Fielding observes with ironic literalness, that her inn was one "where gentlemen . . . meet with civil treatment for their money." But "of all the Oppressions which the Rich are guilty of," he writes in the *Covent-Garden Journal* No. 27,

there seems to be none more impudent and unjust than their Endeavour to rob the Poor of a Title, which is most clearly the Property of the latter. Not content with all the Honorables, Worshipfuls, Reverends, and a thousand other proud Epithets which they exact of the Poor, and for which they give in Return nothing but Dirt, Scrub, Mob, and such like, they have laid violent Hands on a Word, to which they have not the least Pretence or Shadow of any Title. The Word I mean is the Comparative of the Adjective Good, namely BETTER, or as it is usually expressed in the Plural Number BETTERS. An Appellative which all the Rich usurp to themselves and most shamefully use when they speak of, or to the Poor: For do we not every Day hear such Phrases as these. *Do not be saucy to your* BETTERS. *Learn to behave yourself before your* BETTERS. *Pray know your* BETTERS, etc. It is possible that *the Rich* have been so long in Possession of this, that they now lay a Kind of Prescriptive Claim to the Property; but however that be, I doubt not but to make it appear, that if the Word Better is to be understood as the Comparative of *Good*, and is meant to convey an Idea of superior Goodness, it is with the highest Impropriety applied to the Rich, in comparison with the Poor.

The word in question here, of course, is relevant to other distinctions besides those of wealth. The insistence that the poor or lower classes have a better right to the title of "Betters" than the rich or upper classes is not a serious argument so much as another instance, like that of the soldiers and the officers, of the ironic identification of high life and low life in a society where distinctions were becoming purely external and verbal. "My be-betters are wo-worse than me," sobs Mrs. Towwouse's maid in *Joseph Andrews* with considerable justice (I, 98), and her sister in *Tom Jones* who is caught *in flagrante* with the Merry Andrew from the troupe of players defends herself against her mistress' insults on the grounds that she was imitating "the fine lady in the puppet show. . . . If I am a w[hor]e . . . my betters are so as well as I" (IV, 324).[93]

"Fine lady," of course, as the preceding quotation suggests and as we have already seen in *An Essay on Conversation*, was itself a corrupt term for Fielding. "The Word Lady," concludes his imaginary future historian in the *Covent-Garden Journal* No. 17, "did not then, as it doth now, signify a Woman of great Rank and Distinction, but was applied promiscuously to the whole Female Sex." Both Lady Booby in *Joseph Andrews* and Lady Bellaston in *Tom Jones*, not to mention the long list of intriguing "ladies" in the plays, are constantly being shown as unworthy of the "My Lady's" and "Your Ladyship's" which rain about them whenever they appear, and Lady Booby is at one point confronted with the corruption of her title in a manner which is all but direct. "Nothing can be more unworthy in a young man than to betray any intimacies with the ladies," she tells Joseph suggestively in the privacy of her boudoir, but he immediately takes

[93]See also the *True Patriot*, May 13, 1746, in which a footman, speaking of "the gentlemen of our cloth," warns that "we are very near as bad as *our Betters*."

up the word and casts it (unintentionally) in an ironic light: "Ladies! Madam. . . . I am sure I never had the impudence to think of any that deserve that name" (I, 37).

The insistence that a lady or a gentleman must "deserve that name" on grounds more socially relevant than those of dress, wealth, or even gentle birth is a central theme of both *Joseph Andrews* and *Tom Jones*. The heroes have to earn their own way, so to speak, to the title of a gentleman, and the enterprise in both cases involves the exposure of the various species of false gentility which have usurped the title and corrupted it. The denouements of the two novels, it is true, discover that the title belongs to the heroes also by right of birth, and in the final analysis gentle birth would seem to be affirmed as indispensable. But it is symbolically important that the discovery takes place only *after* the heroes have demonstrated that they deserve the title on other grounds as well. Gentle birth may be a necessary qualification for the true gentleman, but it is not the only essential and alone it is nothing. True gentility is shown to consist not in the external trappings of social station but in inner qualities of mind and spirit and in a generous willingness to translate these qualities into active principles of behavior.

Sometimes, however, it was satirically effective to challenge the claims of birth more directly, or even, by implication, to reject them altogether, the better to stress the other and more important qualities of gentility. For this purpose the word "gentlewoman" (which we have already seen Fielding use, in *An Essay on Conversation*, as a synonym for "fine lady" in its original, uncorrupt sense) was well suited because, less hackneyed than "gentleman," its etymological "original ideas" were still fresh and available. In the dialogue between a philosopher and a "fine Lady" which appears in the *Covent-Garden Journal* No. 30, the latter asserts that a certain Miss Bird is no "Gentlewoman" and, when the philosopher asks why not, begins to speak of Miss Bird's father. "Her father, *Miss*!" interrupts the philosopher. "Why we are talking of the young Lady, who appears to be *genteel* in her Person, and *gentle* in her Manners: That she is a *Woman*, at present, we will take for granted. Now, *Miss*, according to my Notion of Things, if her Person and Manners are as I have described, I think Miss *Bird* may be a

Gentlewoman." "Lord! Sir," the fine lady replies, "you talk . . .
to me in a quite new Language."[94]

In fact, of course, it is not the philosopher who is speaking a
"quite new Language" (he, like the moral and religious writers in
the "Modern Glossary" paper and like the "set of simple fellows
called . . . philosophers" in *Jonathan Wild*, represents the traditional values of words) but the fine lady and the "polite Part of
Mankind." For the language they speak is one which uses words
not as Lockean "signs of ideas" but as pure forms and ceremonies. The perversions of language involved in the empty rituals
of gallantry (itself a corrupt word),[95] coquetry, courtship, and
marriage afford particularly fertile ground for Fielding's satire.
"Vows in love," says Mrs. Plotwell in *The Wedding-Day* (1743),
"have just the same meaning as compliments in conversation;
and it is as ridiculous to believe the man who swears eternal constancy, as to believe him who assures you he is your most
obedient, humble servant" (XII, 83). A report in the *Champion*
for August 5, 1740, by Mr. Job Vinegar, the Gulliver-like
traveler of the Vinegar family, is more telling yet. Commenting
on the mating customs among the "Pteghsiumgski," he describes
how "The Lover (as they call him)," having entered "into what
they call a Treaty" with the parents of the bride in which each
party must satisfy the other that he is a true devotee of the god
"MNEY," calls upon the young lady of his choice and how the
pair engage in a ceremony which seems to bear no relation to the
"religious" purpose of the marriage at all. He: "*Madam, your
Father hath thought me worthy of the great Honour of being your
Husband.*" She: "*Sir, Marriage is a Thing I have not yet thought
of.*" But the problems of translation into English soon become
too difficult for Mr. Vinegar, and he has to resort to reproducing
the rest of the conversation "in the Original, as the Strains of
Compliment are beyond the Power of our Language to reach."
The result is perhaps Fielding's most devastating account of the
fate of words separated from their "original ideas" and reduced
to the natural condition of mere sound. The suitor, reports Mr.

---

[94]Jensen expresses uncertainty about the authorship of this paper (*Covent-Garden Journal*, 2: 214 n.). But its development of a theme so characteristic of him would seem to me to argue strongly in Fielding's favor.

[95]See the "Modern Glossary" definition, p. 18 above.

Vinegar, says,

> O MAD DAM.
> TU HAD DAM.
> TOL LOL DOL.
> MY GOL MOL.
> HOC POC US.
> ALL JOC US.
> NO HOB NAIL.
> BUT BOB NAIL.
> MY ALL GAL.
> FAL LAL DAL.

And the lady replies,

> SKUR HUSH MUSH.
> RUB UP BLUSH.

Nor does the ritualistic verbalism of the Pteghsiumgski end with marriage. "After the sacrifices to MNEY are over," Mr. Vinegar goes on, it would appear that "the wives became in common [and] the least Appearance of Fondness between married People . . . is infamous; on which account they are always uneasy unless they have an Opportunity of shewing the Company the Contempt or Hatred they entertain for each other: They use two Words on this Occasion, which give a most odious Idea to the Hearer: These Words are MY DEAR; the horrible Meaning of which it is not possible to convey to an *English* Reader."[96] Mr. Vinegar's conclusion that "My Dear" is a term of opprobrium is a natural consequence of its use in polite circles as a mere form. So corrupt has such usage become that the phrase has not only lost its original ideas of endearment but has been infected with the contempt and hatred it is so often called upon to conceal. Jonathan Wild and Laetitia, whose marriage quickly degenerates into an alliance of mutual contempt, are careful to preserve such outward expressions of devotion, as are those mismatched hypocrites in *Amelia*, Colonel and Mrs. James.[97]

---

[96]*The Voyages of Mr. Job Vinegar*, pp. 16–17.
[97]The corruption of terms of endearment is also a theme in Fielding's plays. See, for example, *The Author's Farce* and *An Old Man Taught Wisdom*, Henley ed., 8: 230; 9: 336–37.

The insincerity of polite forms of speech and its effect on language as the medium of truth are subjects Fielding returns to again and again. "Your actions are as much disguised by your words, as your skin by paint," one "fine lady" tells another in *The Temple Beau*, "the virtue in your mouth no more proceeds from the purity of your heart, than the colour in your cheeks does from the purity of your blood" (VIII, 105). In *The Universal Gallant* Mondish persuades his ex-mistress Lady Raffler to be sincere with him so that he may help her in her current intrigue, but she finds it a more difficult matter than she had expected: "Then to deal sincerely with you—Lud, it is a terrible hard thing to do." "Ay, come struggle a little," urges Mondish, "a woman must undergo some trouble to be delivered of truth" (XI, 141).

Nor is Lady Raffler's "trouble" quite that of a woman who has lost the habit of plain speaking. She is also discovering that for one whose language is confined to the vocabulary of polite discourse, "sincerity has no longer distinct terms in which to express her own truths." To the extent that polite society truly enjoyed the *jus et norma loquendi* her plight was one which was shared by the whole age. "What the world generally calls politeness," concludes Mrs. Bennet in *Amelia*, "I term insincerity" (VI, 240).

The measure of polite society's fall from the ideal of conversation founded on true good breeding is the fact that in popular usage the word "good breeding" is itself, as Fielding remarks in *An Essay on Conversation*, "so horribly and barbarously corrupted, that it contains at present scarce a single ingredient of what it seems originally to have been designed to express," being now "confined to externals" (XIV, 248). The "new Language" of politeness founded on this corrupt base not only drained polite words and forms of their original ideas but also perverted them to mean and selfish ends, pressing them into the contaminating service of cynicism and deceit. "Good Breeding," declared Mandeville, whose force as a moralist rests on his ability to state matter-of-factly those propositions which seemed to his contemporaries occasions for the most savage satire—"Good Breeding is a Fashionable Habit acquir'd by Precept and Example, of flattering the Pride and Selfishness of others, and concealing our own with Judgment and Dexterity."[98] Fielding, who defined the word operatively in his ironic usage, worked on a similar but simpler equation: "good breeding," in its corrupt sense, meant simply "lying." A woman's looking glass, rhapsodizes Helena in *Love in Several Masques* (1728), "is so well-bred a thing, that it tells every woman she is a beauty. O! it is the greatest flatterer in the world to our faces; but the reverse in one thing, for it never disparages us behind our backs"; Lord Formal, in the same play, defends his cynical flattery, his false gallantry, and his hypocritical use of expressions like "Sir, your most obedient and obsequious humble servant" by appealing to the "principles of good-breeding"; and the Orator's Song in *The Author's Farce* gives us "the well-bred courtier telling lies" (VIII, 49, 80, 247). The *Champion* for August 19, 1740, makes the equation explicit. In a paper on "the Genius and Temper of the Pteghsiumgski," Mr. Job Vinegar describes "a Custom which prevails almost universally" among the people of this distant but all too recognizable nation "call'd GD BRDNG, a Phrase not to be translated into *English* by any other (how coarse soever it may seem) than LYING."[99]

But if no one is deceived by the canting forms of polite speech it is not, as Mr. Vinegar generously supposes, because there is no intent to deceive but rather because to a society which values nominal virtues more highly than real ones, the true meanings of the words in question no longer matter. "By Honour," said Mandeville, "in its proper and genuine Signification, we mean nothing else but the good Opinion of others, which is counted the more or less Substantial the more or less Noise or Bustle there is made about the demonstration of it."[100] It is precisely this cynical, reductionist sense of the word which Fielding is satirizing when he treats "honor" as a synonym for "dueling" or when he exposes its hollowness in the oaths and exclamations by which it was so mindlessly invoked. The importance of this word in the ironic vocabulary of *Tom Jones* will be considered in a later chapter, but other instances of Fielding's concern for its debasement in "polite" speech are not far to seek. Lord Richly in *The*

[98] *The Fable of the Bees*, Kaye ed., 1: 77.
[99] *The Voyages of Mr. Job Vinegar*, p. 23.
[100] *The Fable of the Bees*, Kaye ed., 1: 63–64.

Modern Husband (whose mistress, Mrs. Modern, was sold to him by her husband) advises Mr. Modern to beware the attentions to his wife of another rake, "as you love your honour" (X, 24), and the brothel scene of *Miss Lucy in Town* (1742) subjects the word to an even grimmer ironic exposure. When an old bawd demands cash before she will show her newest "virgin" to the lecherous Lord Bawble, he begins, "If I like her—upon my honour . . .," but she interrupts: "I have too much value for your lordship's honour, to have it left in pawn. Besides, I have more right honourable honour in my hands unredeemed already, than I know what to do with. However, I think you may depend on my honour; deposit a cool hundred, and you shall see her; and then take either the lady or the money" (XII, 43–44).

But if it is names, as Locke insisted, "that preserve essences and give them their lasting duration," then the real danger of such abuse of words is that the essences themselves will be lost, and when the names in question are moral terms the implications are grave indeed. "Surely it is hardly possible," declared Robert South, "for men to be virtuous or honest, while vices are called and pointed out to them as virtues, and they all the while suppose the nature of things to be truly and faithfully signified by their names, and therefore believe as they hear, and practice as they believe."[101] Polite society had no monopoly on the misapplication of moral words, but where politeness was insincerity and good breeding was lying, euphemism was the normal mode of speech, and euphemism is the very art of calling evil things good or, to recall Pope's phrase once again, of "converting Vices into their bordering Virtues." "I know not any Thing more pernicious to good Manners," wrote Steele, "than the giving of fair Names to foul Actions; for this confounds Vice and Virtue, and takes off the natural Horrour we have to Evil."[102]

Fielding expresses surprise in *Amelia* that the capacity in which Captain Trent and his wife are useful to the noble lord (i.e., procuring) "hath not as yet . . . acquired any polite name" (VII, 260); but in *The Modern Husband*, the play in which he anticipates the more sordid plot elements of the later novel, he

---

[101]*Sermons*, 2: 129.
[102]*Spectator* No. 286, Jan. 18, 1712, Everyman ed., 2: 353–54.

shows that the word "virtue" itself, considered as a mere synonym for reputation, could be debased into little better than a euphemism for vice. Mr. Modern urges his wife, now that Lord Richly is tiring of her, to let him sue the nobleman so as to wring still more money out of him, but she refuses on the grounds that this would compromise her "virtue." "Very strange," says Modern, "that a woman who made so little scruple of sacrificing the substance of her virtue, should make so much of parting with the shadow of it." "'Tis the shadow only that is valuable," answers she. "Reputation is the soul of virtue." "To me," concludes her husband, "virtue has appeared nothing more than a sound, and reputation is its echo." But the way such cynical usage cheapens the word itself, rendering it suspect on all occasions, is suggested later in the play when Lord Richly describes to Mrs. Modern his plan for striking a similar bargain of prostitution with Bellamant and his wife. "She has the reputation of the strictest virtue of any woman in town," protests Mrs. Modern. "Virtue! ha, ha, ha!" laughs Lord Richly contemptuously, "so have you, and so have several of my acquaintance; there are as few women who have not the reputation of virtue as that have the thing itself" (X, 17, 44). Similarly in *Love in Several Masques*, when Vermilia tells Malvil that she is "rigidly virtuous, and severely modest," he scoffs, "A blank verse, faith, and may make a figure in a fustian tragedy. Four fine sounding words, and mean just nothing at all" (VIII, 66).

The final degradation of the word, into a virtual synonym for its opposites, is but a single step of the ironic imagination. Thus Tawdry, in *Miss Lucy in Town*, complains that "virtuous women . . . come so cheap, that no man will go to the price of a lady of the town" (XII, 35), and thus the Argument to *Tumble-Down Dick* relates how Phaeton seeks "some indubitable mark, that should convince the world that his mother was a virtuous woman, and whore to Phoebus" (XII, 10). The speakers in these cases are not themselves representatives of the "polite Part of Mankind." But the final point of the irony, interpreted in the context of Fielding's lifetime campaign against polite society's abuse of the *jus et norma loquendi*, is that they are willy-nilly making "the best of what is ready coin'd to their Hands," and that the words they use "have the Stamp . . . and Approbation of the *beau monde*." However much Shamela may misspell or mis-pronounce the words she imitates from her "betters," she has no doubt that she has mastered their precise meanings. "I thought once of making a little Fortune by my Person," she confides to her mother. "I now intend to make a great one by my Vartue. . . . O what a charming Word that is, rest his Soul who first invented it."[103]

THE PROFESSIONS

Among the spirits recently "imported for the Goddess of Non-sense" in the underworld scene of *The Author's Farce* are not only the group of authors just "arrived from England" (Don Tragedio, Sir Farcical Comic, Mrs. Novel, and the others), a delegation of politicians ("seven ordinary courtiers"), and some representatives of the polite part of mankind ("five people of great quality"), but also, and in the greatest abundance of all, an assortment of professional men: "nineteen attorneys, eleven counselors, twenty-six justices of the peace, and one hundred Presbyterian parsons." No member of the medical profession appears on the list,[104] but this, we may be sure, was merely an oversight. For "the trudging quack in scarlet cloak" takes his place along with all the other corrupters of the language in the Orator's Song later in the play, and in the allegorical "Life and Death of Common Sense" sequence of *Pasquin* Physic joins forces with Law and with Firebrand the Priest to lead the rebellion against Queen Common Sense.

Devotion to Nonsense and enmity to Common Sense may take other forms, of course, than the linguistic, and Fielding's attacks on the professions, like his attacks on hack writers, politicians, and polite society, were not confined to their abuse of words. Nor was his exposure of this abuse an end in itself. His ridicule of medical and legal jargon, of ranting sermon oratory, and of the other verbal sins he associates with the professions is nearly always relevant to larger social and ethical evils. The doctor's unintelligible terminology is shown to be a mask for

[103]*Shamela*, Baker ed., pp. 47, 53.
[104]Pp. 44–45. Again I have preferred the 1730 version (Woods ed.) of *The Author's Farce* over the later (1750) revised version printed in Henley, which does include doctors in the list but omits the justices and parsons.

ignorance, the lawyer's impassioned plea for justice is revealed as a front for cynicism, and the preacher's unctuous exhortations to piety are exposed as a cloak for hypocrisy. But the very fact that language could be twisted to such purposes, that the words of truth could be made to do the bidding of ignorance, cynicism, and hypocrisy, was reason for concern about the extent to which these practices were undermining the efficacy of language as a trustworthy medium of communication.

Fielding did not, however, condemn the professions in toto. Colley Cibber's charge that his satiric method was "to knock all Distinctions of Mankind on the Head" and that "Religion, Laws, Government, Priests, Judges, and Ministers, were all lay'd flat, at the Feet of this *Herculian Satirist*"[105] is no more true of his ridicule of professional men than it is of his attacks on other elements of society. Fielding was always the most responsible of satirists, and when he turned his fire against the pedantic doctors, dishonest lawyers, and canting clergymen who crowd his plays and novels it was with quite as clear a conception of and respect for the ideal standards of these professions as his attacks on Grub Street scribblers, ruthless politicians, and effete politeness presuppose of the true Republic of Letters, of "real Greatness," and of "true good-breeding." In *The Coffee-House Politician* corrupt magistrates are satirized in the person of Justice Squeezum, but Justice Worthy appears in the same play as the representative of the honest ideal of his profession, and the "trading justice" Mr. Thrasher in *Amelia* is introduced by some "Observations on the Excellency of the English Constitution" which make it clear that he is to be taken as a disgraceful aberration and not as a typical example of the justice of the peace (VI, 14). *The Mock Doctor* (1732), Fielding's adaptation of Molière's *Le Medecin malgré lui*, is ironically dedicated to Dr. John Misaubin, but this notorious London quack is carefully distinguished from "the brethren of your faculty" who have denounced him "as an illiterate empiric" (X, 138). Parson Adams and Dr. Harrison are outnumbered by the many bad clergymen portrayed in *Joseph Andrews* and *Amelia* and in Fielding's other works, but it is they rather than the likes of Parsons Barnabas and Trulliber who represent the

---

[105]*Apology*, p. 164.

profession of divinity as defined and defended by Fielding in his
"Apology for the Clergy" papers in the *Champion* of March 29,
April 5, 12, and 19, 1740. "There is no practice more unfair," he
writes in the *True Patriot* for February 4, 1746,

than to ascribe the Faults of particular Members of a Profession to the
Profession itself, and thence to derive Ridicule and Contempt on the
whole. Physicians and Lawyers have very sorely experienced this
Temper in Mankind; nay, the Clergy themselves have felt its Bitterness, to the no small Advancement of Irreligion and Immorality, by
lessening that Awe and Respect which we ought to bear towards a
Body of Men, who are particularly appointed to instruct us in the
Ways of true Piety and Virtue, and who generally deserve the utmost
Regard from us. The Method in which these Slanderers have proceeded is artful enough. They at first instituted a Cant Word, by
which they pretended to denote Insufficiency and Demerit in the
several Professions; and having at length sufficiently affixed those bad
Ideas to the Words, they applied them indiscriminately to the Professions themselves: And thus Quack, Pettyfogger and Parson, have
at length come to represent the serious Characters of a Physician,
Lawyer, and Minister of the Gospel.[106]

Yet for the very reason that he held the professions in such
high esteem, Fielding was painfully conscious of the extent to
which they had become infiltrated in his time by the Quacks,
Pettyfoggers, and Parsons who thereby threatened to corrupt
and discredit them. Just as with the influx of hack writers all
authors were being indiscriminately classified as "scribblers"
until finally "author" and "scribbler" were looked upon as
synonymous terms, so "doctor," he explains, was coming to be
considered equivalent to "quack," "lawyer" to "pettyfogger,"
and "Minister of the Gospel" to "parson," and the ultimate
blame lay not with the public which failed to preserve the distinctions originally inherent in these words but with the usurpers

---

[106]See also the *Champion* for Feb. 12 and Mar. 29, 1740. The implication that "parson"
was at this time a pejorative term in the same category as "quack" and "pettyfogger" is
supported by the *OED*, which reports that the word was "usually more or less depre-
ciatory or dyslogistic" except "in rural use," which would explain the exception Fielding
makes in the case of Parson Adams. Elsewhere throughout his works he seems to reserve
the term almost exclusively for nonconformist ministers. He never refers to Adams'
counterpart in *Amelia*, for example, as Parson Harrison.

to the titles of doctor, lawyer, and Minister of the Gospel who have confused their meanings by assuming them. "Names neither do nor can alter things," wrote Robert South, "but ill things will in the issue certainly foul and disgrace the best names."[107] We have already seen that Fielding includes "Dr." among other titles "at first used to distinguish particular Degrees of Men, but [now] stript of all Ideas whatever," and in the same *Champion* essay (January 17, 1740) he concludes his examination of the linguistic abuses of physicians with the observation that "Physician itself, is a Word of very little, if any Signification."

The result of this penetration and growing domination of the professions by individual practitioners unworthy of their titles was to pervert physic, law, and divinity from their true purpose as public guardians of "our Property and . . . our Wealth, both spiritual and temporal"[108] and debase them into agencies of self-interest and personal gain. According to Queen Common Sense in *Pasquin*,

> Religion, law and physic, were designed
> By Heaven the greatest blessings on mankind;
> But priests and lawyers and physicians made
> These general goods to each a private trade;
> With each they rob, with each they fill their purses,
> And turn our benefits into our curses.
>
> (XI, 215)

As "general goods," the three learned professions represented, in the form of practical application in society, the three principal branches of human knowledge—the physical, the ethical, and the spiritual. Thus one consequence of their degeneration into "private trades" was the specialization of general truth. For since their practitioners were interested, like hack writers, only in "immediate Effect" they concerned themselves less and less with the universal principles from which their arts derived. The knowledge which the professions were supposed to represent was becoming departmentalized and fragmented. "Doctors" of medicine, far from being the "learned men" which their titles

---

[107] *Sermons*, 2: 507.
[108] *Champion*, Feb. 12, 1739/40.

proclaimed them to be, no longer felt it necessary to master natural philosophy and contented themselves instead with being mere technicians. The Lawyers were not masters of jurisprudence but only of Giles Jacobs' *New Law Dictionary* (1729), to which Fielding scornfully refers in the *Champion* for December 25, 1739/40. Ministers of the Gospel, corrupted by what Adams in a dispute with Parson Barnabas calls "the detestable doctrine of faith against good works" (I, 96), were students not of the Word of God but only of the outward forms of religion.

In fact, just as polite society, having lost sight of the principle of true good breeding, was overcome by an excessive zeal for pure forms, so the professions, cut off from the sources of general knowledge and withdrawn into themselves, were becoming more and more preoccupied with their own specialized forms and rituals, multiplying them for their own sakes. "Most Professions lose their Merit," Fielding wrote in the *Champion* for March 15, 1739/40, in a paper on the modern "talent" of overdoing or excess, "and become useless or hurtful to Mankind by this Talent in their Professors." They "have been adulterated with so many needless and impertinent Ceremonies, that they have been too often drawn into Doubt and Obscurity." The test of truth to the eighteenth-century rationalistic mind was universality, and in practical terms this meant the *consensus gentium*. But the professions, jealous of their special provinces of knowledge, seemed bent on carving truth up into isolated compartments to which the generality of mankind were denied access and in which universal opinion was declared incompetent. Observing in the *Champion* for February 14, 1739/40, that "the learned Mr. *Bailey*," in his dictionary, defines the word "Mystery" as "a *Thing concealed, a Secret not easy to be apprehended*," Fielding remarks how appropriate it is that "the several Professions . . . have laid hold on this Word to signify those Arcana, . . . which are reserv'd only for the Adepts in them; thus Divinity, Law, and Physic, contain Mysteries which are understood by Divines, Lawyers, and Physicians, though they have no Manner of Idea to any who have not been initiated into them; on which account it may not be improper to observe, that the *Greek* Word for initiating is immediately derived from that which signifies Mystery in that Language."

The most conspicuous and perhaps the most dangerous form
which this cultivation of obscurity and mystery assumed was the
development by each of the professions of a language peculiar to
itself. For if language is "the great bond that holds society
together" and if its usefulness depends on the preservation of
"agreed" meanings for words, then any usage which tends to
treat words as private symbols is a threat to both language and
society. "Varieties of Phrases in Language may seem to contribute to the elegance and ornament of Speech," wrote Bishop
Wilkins in 1668 in the *Essay towards a Real Character and a
Philosophical Language*, "yet, like other affected ornaments, they
prejudice the native simplicity of it, and contribute to the dis-
guising of it with false appearances. Besides that, like other
things of fashion, they are very changeable, every generation
producing new ones; witness the present Age, especially the late
times, wherein this grand imposture of Phrases hath almost
eaten out solid Knowledge in all professions; such men generally
being of most esteem who are skilled in these Canting forms of
speech, though in nothing else."[109] The doctor Fielding refers
to in the *True Patriot* for January 21, 1746, who "declared that
he always found himself most admired when he was least understood," is only one among many professional men in Fielding's
writings, from the Physicians' Scenes of the original *Tom Thumb*
in 1730 to the final book of *Amelia* in 1751, who are shown to
have substituted jargon and a "grand imposture of Phrases" for
"solid Knowledge."

In large measure, of course, his burlesque of professional
jargon is merely a conventional comic device which can be traced
back at least as far as the Italian commedia dell'arte, and Fielding's versions owe as much, probably, to the literary tradition
represented by Ben Jonson, Molière, and Samuel Garth (to name
no others) as to his own independent observation and concern.
But the comic tradition was paralleled by a serious criticism,
which also came in with the Renaissance and which Dr. Johnson
was still advancing in 1755 in the Preface to the *Dictionary*, of the
admission into language of "terms of art." Samuel Butler, noting
that "this Canting runs through all Professions," defended his

[109]P. 18.

own satiric parodies of the special vocabularies of trades and professions by explaining that "The Tearms of all Arts are generally Nonsense that signify nothing, or very improperly what they are Meant to do, and are more Difficult to be learn'd then [*sic*] the things they are designed to teach."[110]

Thus when Dr. Gregory, in *The Mock Doctor*, diagnoses a case of dumbness in a barbarous pseudo-Latin intermixed with phrases of French and, when pressed to speak more clearly, declares it is caused "by the acrimony of the humours engendered in the concavity of the diaphragm" (X, 158), it is not likely that Fielding sees the matter entirely as a joke or that he has forgotten Locke's warning against the "affected obscurity" and "learned gibberish" which "perplex and confound the signification of words, and thereby render language less useful than the real defects of it had made it."[111]

The three professions seem to differ somewhat, however, as Fielding represents them, in the purposes to which they apply their learned gibberish. For doctors, technical terminology becomes a way of dressing out ignorance in the language of pseudo-learning and thereby of avoiding specific diagnoses or prognoses which might later be called to account. The surgeon who attends Joseph Andrews discourses "in this learned manner" when Adams asks him his opinion of the case: "The contusion on his head has perforated the internal membrane of the occiput, and divellicated that radical small minute invisible nerve which coheres to the pericranium; and this was attended with a fever at first symptomatic, then pneumatic; and he is at length grown deliriuus, or delirious, as the vulgar express it"; whereas actually, as Adams learns in the next chapter, Joseph is suffering from nothing more than a bruised pate and the effects of "not having eaten one morsel for above twenty-four hours" (I, 76, 81). Similarly in *Tom Jones* the surgeon called to treat Jones after his fight with Ensign Northerton is questioned by the lieutenant:

"I hope, sir," said the lieutenant, "the skull is not fractured." "Hum," cries the surgeon, "fractures are not always the most dangerous symptoms. Contusions and lacerations are often attended with worse

---

[110]Quoted by Ian Jack, *Augustan Satire* (Oxford: Clarendon Press, 1957), p. 28.
[111]*An Essay Concerning Human Understanding*, Book III, Ch. x, Secs. 6, 9, 10.

phaenomena. . . ." "I hope," says the lieutenant, "there are no such symptoms here." "Symptoms," answered the surgeon, "are not always regular nor constant. . . . I was once, I remember, called to a patient who had received a violent contusion in his tibia, by which the exterior cutis was lacerated, so that there was a profuse sanguinary discharge; and the interior membranes were so divellicated that the os or bone very plainly appeared through the aperture of the vulnus or wound. Some febrile symptoms intervening at the same time (for the pulse was exuberant and indicated much phlebotomy), I apprehended an immediate mortification. . . . —But perhaps I do not make myself perfectly well understood?" "No, really," answered the lieutenant, "I cannot say I understand a syllable." (IV, 41–42)

And Dr. Harrison in *Amelia* fares no better when he asks the surgeon who is summoned to examine the wounded Robinson whether the patient is in any immediate danger of death. " 'I do not know,' answered the surgeon, 'what you call immediate. He may live several days—nay, he may recover. It is impossible to give any certain opinion in these cases.' He then launched forth into a set of terms which the doctor [i.e., Harrison], with all his scholarship, could not understand. To say the truth, many of them were not to be found in any dictionary or lexicon." From which Dr. Harrison concludes "that the surgeon was a very ignorant, conceited fellow, and knew nothing of his profession" (VII, 321).

Ignorance is often a salient characteristic of Fielding's lawyers and magistrates too, and to a certain extent their addiction to legal jargon is seen as a mere affectation, like medical jargon, of a learning which they do not in fact possess. The worst excesses of legal jargon, the barbarous mixture of law-Latin and law-French parodied by Fielding in the *Champion* for November 27, 1739, were corrected by a statute of 1733 which required the use of English in all legal documents.[112] In "The Life and Death of Common Sense," Law complains to Physic,

> Thou know'st, my Lord of Physic, I had long
> Been privileged by custom immemorial,
> In tongues unknown, or rather none at all,

[112]See B. M. Jones, *Henry Fielding, Novelist and Magistrate* (London: Allen & Unwin, 1933), pp. 41–42.

My edicts to deliver through the land;
When this proud queen, this Common-sense, abridged
My power, and made me understood by all.

(XI, 207)

But the triumph of Common Sense, as her subsequent death as
a result of the plot led by Law, Physic, and the Priest indicates, is
short lived, and Fielding's lawyers throughout his works testify
that the abolition of law-Latin and law-French did not in any
way hamper their cultivation of law-English. Far from being
"understood by all," they are quite as fluent as his physicians in
the language of obfuscation.

But they use it less as a cover for ignorance than as a means of
circumventing justice. The lawyer denounced by the "Correspondent" to the *Champion* of February 12, 1739/40, a steward
for a nobleman's estate, robs his employer and bullies his tenants
by dazzling them with legal jargon; and Lawyer Scout in *Joseph
Andrews* assures Lady Booby (who is seeking a ruling against
Joseph's right to publish the banns of his marriage to Fanny on
the grounds that he is not a legal resident of the parish) that
neither he nor any other lawyer could alter the law, which is in
Joseph's favor, but that it "was in the power of a lawyer . . . to
prevent the law's taking effect; and that he himself could do for
her ladyship as well as any other." Joseph's case, he explains,
rests on the claim that a year's service in the parish entitled a man
to settle there, but "there is a material difference between being
settled in law and settled in fact; and as I affirmed generally he
was settled, and law is preferable to fact, my settlement must be
understood in law and not in fact. And suppose, madam, we
admit he was settled in law, what use will they make of it? how
doth that relate to fact? He is not settled in fact; and if he be not
settled in fact, he is not an inhabitant; and if he is not an inhabitant, he is not of this parish; and then undoubtedly he ought
not to be published here" (I, 321–22).

Even when the lawyer has no particular motive for impeding
justice, his legal jargon clouds the issue, as when in *Tom Jones*
Squire Western asks a lawyer's opinion about the right or wrong,
in a legal sense, of Blifil's spiteful act of freeing Sophia's pet bird:
"If the case be put of a partridge, there can be no doubt but an
action would lie; for though this be *ferae naturae*, yet being

reclaimed, property vests: but being the case of a singing bird, though reclaimed, as it is a thing of base nature, it must be considered as *nullius in bonis*. In this case, therefore, I conceive the plaintiff must be nonsuited; and I should disadvise the bringing any such action." "Well," says Squire Western, "if it be *nullus bonus*, let us drink about, and talk a little of the state of the nation, or some such discourse that we all understand, for I am sure I don't understand a word of this. It may be learning and sense for aught I know: but you shall never persuade me into it" (III, 155). And on a more serious level, when Dr. Harrison in *Amelia*, seeking the title deeds which will prove Amelia's rightful inheritance, applies to a justice of the peace for a warrant to search the house of the wicked Lawyer Murphy, the magistrate loses sight of justice in his concern for subtleties of terminology: "He said title-deeds savored of the Realty, and it was not felony to steal them. If, indeed, they were taken away in a box, then it would be felony to steal the box." "Savor of the Realty! Savor of the fartalty," explodes Dr. Harrison. "I never heard such incomprehensible nonsense. This is impudent, as well as childish, trifling with the lives and properties of men" (VII, 328).

Verbal quibbling is the inevitable consequence of the substitution of jargon for solid knowledge, and if Fielding complained of the folly of this activity in literary criticism and of the threat it represented to the language, he was even more sensitive to the dangers of word-splitting at the expense of the "lives and properties of men." And sometimes, he knew, it was even their souls which were at stake. "Learned gibberish," according to Locke, was originally introduced by the scholastic philosophers, but the mischief has not "stopped in logical niceties, or curious empty speculations; it hath invaded the great concernments of human life and society; obscured and perplexed the material truths of law and divinity, brought confusion, disorder, and uncertainty into the affairs of mankind; and if not destroyed, yet in a great measure rendered useless, these two great rules, religion and justice. . . . What have been the effect of those multiplied curious distinctions, and acute niceties, but obscurity and uncertainty, leaving the words more unintelligible, and the reader more at a loss?"[113]

[113] *An Essay Concerning Human Understanding*, Bk. III, Ch. x, Sec. 12.

What Locke particularly had in mind were the "comments and disputes upon the laws of God and man," and though Fielding's bad clergymen are guilty of other sins besides those of subtilizing on the Word of God, it is significant that he always manages to indicate, if only by their names, that they are adepts in this verbal art. Thus we have in *The Author's Farce* Parson Murdertext, in *The Grub Street Opera* Parson Puzzletext, and in *Shamela* Parson Tickletext. "For when the *Gallants* of the World do observe, how the *Ministers* themselves do jingle, quibble, and play the fool with their *Texts*," argued Dr. John Eachard in *The Grounds and Occasions of the Contempt of the Clergy* (1670), "no wonder they, who are so inclined to *Atheism*, do not only deride and despise the *Priests*, but droll upon the Bible."[114]

How such quibbling can make nonsense of Scripture and confuse the signification of words is suggested in *Amelia* by the dispute between Dr. Harrison and a pedantic young clergyman over the meaning of the verse from St. Matthew, "Love your enemies, bless them that curse you, do good to them that hate you." The interpretation championed by the young clergyman is "that love is not here to be taken in the strict sense, so as to signify the complacency of the heart; you may hate your enemies as God's enemies, and seek due revenge of them for his honor; and, for your own sakes too, you may seek moderate satisfaction of them; but then you are to love them with a love consistent with these things." "That is to say, in plainer words," adds Dr. Harrison sarcastically, "you are to love them and hate them, and bless and curse, and do them good and mischief." He then gives his own opinion of the text in question, declaring that it contains "a very positive precept, delivered in the plainest words. . . . No man who understands what it is to love, and to bless, and to do good, can mistake the meaning. . . . They do not, indeed, want the comments of men, who, when they cannot bend their minds to the obedience of Scripture, are desirous to wrest Scripture to a compliance with their own inclinations" (VII, 164).

For the effect of such misapplied subtlety was to infuse doubt and obscurity where there originally was none, to dissociate words from their proper and agreed meanings in order to make

---

[114]Pp. 130–31. For a general treatment of Fielding's relationship to the Contempt of the Clergy tradition, see Battestin, *The Moral Basis of Fielding's Art*, pp. 130–49.

them fit special and often unworthy cases, and so to treat the
great ethical and spiritual abstractions as mere names; and the
danger of this nominalism in religion was that words as simple
and plain as "love," "bless," and "good" would become so confused that men might, in all honesty, "mistake their meaning."
Parson Trulliber knows "what charity is better than to give to
vagabonds,"[115] but even while he is thus operatively defining for
Adams this key word of *Joseph Andrews*, one of his parishioners
is entertaining Joseph and Fanny by praising "the goodness of
Parson Trulliber." Indeed, as Fielding explains, "he had not
only a very good character as to other qualities in the neighbour-
hood, but was reputed a man of great charity; for, though he
never gave a farthing, he had always that word in his mouth"
(I, 192, 195). Similarly Thwackum in *Tom Jones* succeeds no
better than the quibbling lawyer in satisfying Squire Western as
to the question of Blifil's guilt or merit in the case of Sophia's
bird. The divine dismisses as "a jargon of words, which means
nothing," Square's argument that the act was right according to
"the law of nature," but his own defense of it as arising from "a
Christian motive" is scarcely more precise. Squire Western—
who whatever his faults recognizes gibberish when he hears it—
again invites the company to "Drink about. . . . I don't know
what you mean, either of you, by right and wrong. To take away
my girl's bird was wrong, in my opinion; and . . . to encourage
boys in such practices, is to breed them up to the gallows"
(III, 153).

The clergy's abuse of words was more serious than that of
doctors or lawyers both because religion was a more important
sphere of knowledge and because the pulpit, as Bishop Burnet
had pointed out in 1684, exercised a more immediate influence
over "the Rules and Measure of Speech."[116] But the influence
of the other professions could be pernicious too. Pope, in *The*

---

[115]The issue here is not purely a question of words, however. Parson Trulliber reflects
the Calvinist ethic summed up in the Puritan anti-poor-relief slogan "Giving alms is no
charity," first heard during the reign of Charles I before the Civil War and still vital
enough in later dissenting circles to provide Defoe with the title and main argument of
his 1704 pamphlet *Giving Alms No Charity*. Trulliber's wife suggests this context by
complaining of "the poor's rate" in the very next sentence. See Max Weber, *The
Protestant Ethic and the Spirit of Capitalism* (New York: Scribner's, 1958), p. 268 n.
[116]See above, p. 57.

Art of Sinking in Poetry, ironically urged all writers who would affect a modern style to employ "*Technical Terms*, which estrange your Stile from the great and general Ideas of Nature: and the higher your Subject is, the lower should you search into Mechanics for your Expression."[117] For Fielding the works of George Cheyne, a Doctor of Physic of the Royal College of Edinburgh and Fellow of the Royal Society, illustrated this rule to perfection. For Dr. Cheyne wrote profusely not only on medical matters (he is the author of the classic study of melancholia, *The English Malady* [1733]) but also on philosophy, which latter subject he approached, however, from the "physical" point of view and dressed out in the technical terminology of his profession. He explained why in his best known philosophical work, the title of which is itself a fair specimen of his mechanistic pretensions: *An Essay on Regimen, Together with Five Discourses, Medical, Moral, and Philosophical: Serving to Illustrate the Principles and Theory of Philosophical Medicin, and Point out Some of its Moral Consequences* (1740). "I choose to speak in the *Mathematical* and *Medical* Language," he wrote, "because the *Analogy*, the *Similarity*, and the *Precision*, is [*sic*] here so just, so close, and so luminous, that I think it must penetrate those who can perfectly understand it, and may by a *Dictionary* be made plain to others, if they think it worth the while to deal in such abstracted Conjectures."[118]

But to Fielding the question was not whether it was worth while to deal in abstracted conjectures but whether anyone dealing in them had the right to use language so specialized and obscure that the ordinary educated reader was obliged to resort to a dictionary. In the *Champion* for May 17, 1740, Cheyne is the "very great and Eminent Physician" whom the Court of Censorial Enquiry adjudges the real culprit (instead of Colley Cibber) in the murder of the English Language. A witness testifies that "the M.D. . . . hath so mangled and mauled it, that when I came to examine the Body, as it lay in Sheets in a Bookseller's Shop, I found it an expiring heavy Lump, without the least Appearance of Sense." A passage from Cheyne's *Philosophical Discourses*, as turgid and unintelligible, nearly, as some

---

[117]Steeves ed., p. 62.
[118]P. 318.

of the pronouncements of Fielding's fictional physicians, is quoted in evidence of this assertion; and two more passages are cited in a later paper (June 12) as examples "in Physic" of the proposition that "what we write of each particular Profession will be unintelligible to all besides the Members thereof." But the real point would seem to be that Cheyne's aspirations, as a popular writer and a pretender to philosophical discourse, extended beyond the narrow sphere of his profession and thereby represented a threat to infect the language as a whole with the very disease of specialization which had already "eaten out solid knowledge in all professions" and had estranged their styles "from the great and general Ideas of Nature." "Now all this may be Sense for aught I know," says Fielding of the passages from the *Philosophical Discourses*, anticipating the very words of Squire Western upon the jargon of the lawyer, "but it can be only understood by a Physician."

In *Don Quixote in England* (1734), Lawyer Brief and Dr. Drench dispute in the jargons of their professions over which of them should take charge of Don Quixote. But as William Coley points out, "the cant jargon of the professional men attempts to define something rather great, namely, Quixote's irrepressible idealism, with the result that this idealism is completely and distortedly debased."[119] Earlier in the play, when Sancho offends Don Quixote by describing Dulcinea's equipage as he sees it, the knight exclaims, "Sancho, thou wilt never leave debasing the greatest things in thy vile phrases." But clearly the other characters in the play, notably the politicians in the election scenes and the "polite" ladies and gentlemen at the house of Sir Thomas Loveland, are also debasing great things with vile phrases, each of them speaking, as it were, a language of his own and trying to define the world in its specialized and corrupt terms. The doctor and the lawyer, then, prattling in their unintelligible jargons, are not merely conventional figures of fun. They stand for the imminent breakdown of society into disparate groups unable to communicate with each other or to comprehend the "great and general Ideas of Nature" represented by Don Quixote (whom they all dismiss as a madman), and their

---

[119] *Fielding's Comic*, p. 170.

jargon is symptomatic of the loosening of "the great bond that holds society together." "Many men, many minds," Sancho explains sententiously in reply to Don Quixote's admonition—"Many men, many minds; many minds, many mouths; many mouths, many tongues; many tongues, many words" (XI, 56).

Thus in the *Champion* paper on the abuse of words it is not technical jargon in the strict sense which Fielding singles out in his attack on the "Word-squandering . . . generally practised [by] every particular Profession" to illustrate how they "have laid violent Hands on some certain Syllables which they use *ad Libitum* without conveying any Idea whatsoever." It is rather words and phrases which they have taken over from the language at large and narrowed to their own purposes—jargonized, so to speak—and therefore corrupted: "dispatch," "reasonable," "infallible Method," etc. Thus the other special "languages" considered in the same essay—those of polite society, politicians, and tradesmen—are also jargons of a sort, forms of expression which may, Fielding says, convey meaning within the groups in which they are used but which "give no more Idea to others, than any of those unintelligible Sounds which the Beasts utter." Each segment of society, in effect, was imitating the professions in developing a language of its own, and at the expense always of the agreed meanings, the repositories of general truth and the expressions of social unity, of the words which they redefined to suit their own narrow and often perverse ends.

In an essay in the *True Patriot* for April 8, 1746, deploring the narrowness of opinion in the various orders of society, Fielding begins with a reference to "a Man who believed there was no real Existence in the World but himself." This philosophy, he says, is not much different from that of many of the "Orders and Professions" of men. "For tho' they do not absolutely deny all Existence to other Persons and Things, yet it is certain they hold them of no Consequence, and little worth their Consideration, unless they *trench* [i.e., appertain] somewhat towards their own Order or Calling." It is surely significant, then, that the principal example he offers of this tendency in modern society is that which "may be seen in the monopolizing particular Words, and confining their Meaning to their own Purposes, as if the rest of the World had in reality no Right to their Application. A signal

Instance of which is in the Adjective Good. . . . Now when the Divine, the Free-Thinker, the Citizen, the Whig, the Tory, etc. pronounce such an Individual to be a good Man, it is plain that they have all so many different Meanings." Thus a surgeon when he speaks of "a very good Subject" may be referring to a hanged criminal; and some army officers apply the words "the best Man in *England*" to one who may well be "the wickedest Fellow in the whole Regiment." Fielding's objection (as in the similar case of the word "betters" as used by the upper classes) is not to the specialized meanings of "good" in themselves but to the fact that such meanings seemed to be driving out the general and essentially *moral* sense of the word. The examples, of course, are offered partly in jest, but if a "good" man to a doctor could be a criminal and to a soldier a scoundrel, then there was reason to fear that its agreed meaning was becoming lost and that the writer or speaker who tried to use it in this original general sense might be interpreted differently by each order of society. And this, it should be observed, especially since the word "good" is only one instance of a monopolizing tendency most conspicuously manifested by the professions but evident in the other orders of society as well, boded ill for language not only as an efficient medium of communication, but also as "the great bond that holds society together."

The professions are, moreover, as Fielding represents them in their degenerate, departmentalized state, the natural breeding places of hypocrisy. For though not all of his doctors, lawyers, and clergymen are hypocrites, it will not have escaped notice that most of them are guilty of *cant* not only in the sense of jargon but also in the sense of insincerity. The logical link between these two senses of the term seems to be the feeling that the specialized language of a profession or sect, though not necessarily insincere in its inception, invites imposture by divorcing words from their proper and agreed meanings and putting them at the mercy, as it were, of each individual speaker or writer. If Parson Trulliber's sense of the word "charity" is as good as Parson Adams', then who is to give the lie to his professions of this virtue?

But an even stronger inducement to hypocrisy is that Trulliber, as a clergyman, must *profess* charity not because he sincerely believes in it but because clergymen are by definition *professors* of religion, and if this seems to be putting too fine a point on the semantic connection between professions as occupations or callings and professions as claims or avowals it is a point of which Fielding himself, with his sensitivity to the literal meanings of words, is acutely conscious. Communicating his suspicion that the prudish Lady Raffler, in *The Universal Gallant*, has arranged an assignation with a lover, Mondish mocks Gaylove's incredulity: "What, I suppose you heard her rail against wicked women —and declaim in praise of chastity—does a good sermon from the pulpit persuade thee that a parson is a saint?—or a charge from the bench that the judge is incorrupt?—If thou wilt believe in professions, thou wilt find scarce one fool that is not wise, one rogue that is not honest, one courtier that is not fit to make a friend, or one whore that is not fit to make a wife" (XI, 138). Professing is a verbal act, and professional men, as people whose business it is to profess, were corrupting language by using it in the service not of truth but of their own interests, their own "private trades." They prostitute language to their own ends, and hence the final "profession" named is that of the whore, for all professions, as Fielding sees it, in both senses of the word, are whores of language.

The doctor is perhaps less culpable in this respect than the lawyer or the clergyman because language is not for him such a basic tool of trade. Yet when Fielding gives us "the trudging quack in scarlet cloak" and the other quack doctors who populate his works we may assume that even though he may not have known the word "quack" was originally an abbreviation of the Dutch *quacksalver*, which is "one who 'quacks' or boasts about the virtues of his salves,"[120] he was fully alive to the vivid associations of the English word. For it is in the sense of the ranting promoter of Walpole rather than merely of an imposter that his references in the *Champion* to Orator Henley's *Hyp Doctor* as the *Quack Doctor* gain their point, and the observation in the *True Patriot* that "there are Quacks in Politeness as well as all other Sciences" occurs in the context of a discourse on language and its abuses.

[120]*OED*. Cf. Gulliver's definition of "physicians" as "a Sort of People bred up among us, in the *Profession or Pretence* of curing the Sick" (my italics). *Gulliver's Travels, The Prose Works*, 11: 237.

His objections to the *professional* use to which lawyers put the language, however, is more serious. "Zounds! what shall I say?" demands Sir George Boncour in *The Fathers* published post-humously in 1778 but written in 1743) when his opinion on a matter under discussion meets with a cold reception. "Shall I take the other side of the question? for, like a lawyer, I can speak on either" (XII, 186). In part, of course, this was an ethical problem and one which Fielding himself, as a lawyer, was prob-ably seriously troubled about, as was James Boswell.[121] But it was also a problem of language. Among lawyers, said the author of *Remarques on the Humours and Conversations of the Town* (1673), "the Idea of Conversation is commonly very Pedantick, and unpollisht; and in Truth, not worthy of a Gentleman; where men study not so much, things noble and generous, but the arts of palliating wrong, of defeating and deferring right."[122] Swift was of the same opinion. Describing the legal profession to his Houyhnhnm Master, Gulliver observes not only "that this Society hath a peculiar Cant and Jargon of their own, that no other Mortal can understand, and wherein all their Laws are written, which they take special Care to multiply; whereby they have wholly confounded the very Essence of Truth and False-hood, of Right and Wrong," but also that the members of this society are "bred up from their Youth in the Art of proving by Words multiplied for the Purpose, that White is Black, and Black is White, according as they are paid."[123]

But it is the clergy, as we have already seen in the cases of Parsons Barnabas and Trulliber in *Joseph Andrews*, Thwackum in *Tom Jones*, and the young clergyman in *Amelia*, whose *pro-fessional* perversions of language are most reprehensible. The Ordinary of Newgate in *Jonathan Wild*, having been plied with punch and flattery, tells the condemned Jonathan, "Never mind your soul—leave that to me; I will render a good account of it, I warrant you" (II, 195); and though it is Firebrand the Priest who finally assassinates Queen Common Sense in *Pasquin*, he nevertheless preaches a funeral sermon in which he deplores "her loss with tears" and praises her "with all my art" (XI, 225).

---

[121] *The Life of Johnson*, Hill-Powell ed., 2: 47.
[122] P. 114.
[123] *Gulliver's Travels, The Prose Works*, 11: 232, 234.

" 'Tis not what we do, but what we believe, that must save us,"[124] preaches Parson Williams in *Shamela*, summing up the doctrine of the superiority of faith to works which all of Fielding's bad clergymen affect. But what they really mean by "faith," as he makes clear time and again, is the mere profession of it.

Thus if the learned professions in Fielding stand for the fragmentation of society, the departmentalization of knowledge, and the specialization of language, they are also symbolic of his distrust of "professions" in the sense of direct avowals or declarations in language. This is not to say, however, they are alone held accountable for this state of affairs. The other orders of society, as we have amply seen, were also guilty. Bookweight and his Grub Street hacks are as ready as lawyers to write on both sides of a controversy. Dedication writers, hawking their panegyrics to the highest bidders, had "prevented the very use of praise." Orator Henley is represented as offering to "write, preach, or swear any thing, and to profess any Party or Religion, at a cheap rate." Edmund Curll, the puffer of books and of Sir Robert Walpole, is "the great Professor of Rose Street." Mrs. Western, that earnest student of politics, warns Squire Western not to believe that Allworthy "hath more contempt for money than other men because he professes more." And among People of Fashion politeness is insincerity and good breeding is lying. One important aspect of the corruption of language, then, is the *professional* insincerity of its use by those most dependent on and skilled in its arts—writers, politicians, and polite speakers as well as the learned professions. The effect is not only to remove particular words and phrases from the vocabulary of truth but also to bring all direct professions of virtue or merit into disrepute. "The Difficulty," says Fielding in the case of claimants to patriotism, "is the same in this as in other Virtues, to distinguish Truth from Falshood and Pretence. This is indeed an Art, which requires . . . great Attention, as well as Penetration. . . . Hence the Hypocrite finds it so easy to impose on Mankind. The thinnest Disguise is sufficient to hide the grossest Affectation; and Men have little more to do, than to declare they are what they desire to be thought."[125]

[124]Baker ed., p. 40.
[125]*True Patriot*, Nov. 12, 1745.

It is no news, of course, that Fielding was preoccupied with hypocrisy. All of his heroes (with the exception of the anti-hero, Jonathan Wild) are in one way or another the victims of this vice, and not just once but many times over. But hypocrisy works primarily through language, exploiting it, perverting it from its true purpose as the medium of truth and contaminating it with the odor of deceit. " 'Tis a phrase often apply'd to a man, when speaking, that *he speaks his MIND,*" wrote Fielding's friend James Harris in *Hermes, or a Philosophical Inquiry concerning Language and Universal Grammar* (1751); "as much as to say, that his Speech or Discourse is *a publishing of some Energie or Motive of his Soul.* So it indeed is in every one that speaks, excepting the Dissembler or Hypocrite; and he too, as far as possible, affects the appearance."[126] To Fielding's way of thinking, however, the affecting of the appearance had become so universal that speaking one's mind no longer seemed an effective way of publishing the energy or motive of the soul, and even less could one trust the declarations of others. Summing up his hero's philosophy at the end of *Jonathan Wild,* the narrator reports:

The character which he most valued himself upon, and which he principally honored in others, was that of hypocrisy, . . . for which reason, he said, there was little greatness to be expected in a man who acknowledged his vices, but always much to be hoped from him who professed great virtues: wherefore, though he would always shun the person whom he discovered guilty of a good action, yet he was never deterred by a good character, which was more commonly the effect of profession than of action; for which reason he himself was always very liberal of honest professions, and had as much virtue and goodness in his mouth as a saint. (II, 202)

One of Fielding's objections to *Pamela* is that the vaunted "virtue" of the heroine rests largely on her own professions. She too has as much virtue and goodness in her mouth as a saint, but her actions, as his own *Shamela* demonstrates, the sheer facts of her prolonged resistance to seduction, might as easily and perhaps more plausibly be those of a sinner and a hypocrite. "Richardson accepts nominal virtue and vice as the reality,"

[126]P. 15.

H. V. D. Dyson and John Butt point out, "and makes play with the names of moral qualities rather than the qualities themselves."[127] Similarly Colley Cibber, in his *Apology*, had claimed all virtues but chastity (an omission for which Pamela more than compensated), and it is this fact rather than, as has been suggested, Fielding's mistaken belief that Cibber was the author of *Pamela*, which explains why the title of Fielding's burlesque is *An Apology for the Life of Mrs. Shamela Andrews* and why the supposed author is called "Conny Keyber." When a constable in *Joseph Andrews* with the revealing name of Tom Suckbribe is suspected of having aided a prisoner to escape, Fielding as narrator expresses a personal confidence in the man's innocence because he has been assured of it, he says ironically, "by those who received their informations from his own mouth, which, in the opinion of some moderns, is the best, and indeed only, evidence" (I, 85).

Pamela and Cibber, as Fielding reads their characters between the lines of their respective narratives, are both guilty of affectation. But whereas Pamela is a thoroughgoing hypocrite, Cibber is merely an ostentatious ass. "Affectation," Fielding explains in the Preface to *Joseph Andrews*, "proceeds from one of these two causes, vanity or hypocrisy: for as vanity puts us on affecting false characters, in order to purchase applause, so hypocrisy sets us on an endeavor to avoid censure, by concealing our vices under an appearance of their opposite virtues" (I, 22). Yet both causes result in the distortion of truth and the perversion of language, and Fielding's good characters, it will be observed, are not much more trustworthy as witnesses to their own merits and motives than are his villains. Parson Adams' professions of stoicism are forgotten the moment he hears (mistakenly) that his youngest son has been drowned. In an earlier chapter, moreover, Adams generalizes about the futility of conjectural disputes and then immediately gets embroiled in one himself, and in another he betrays vanity concerning one of his sermons in which, he professes, "I have never been a greater enemy to any passion than that silly one of vanity" (I, 174, 243, 350–52). Tom Jones's account to Partridge of the adventures leading to his expulsion

---

[127] *Augustans and Romantics* (London: Cresset Press, 1950), pp. 62–63.

from Squire Allworthy's house, though closer to the truth than the version of the same adventures which Blifil had related to Allworthy, falsely suggests that Jones's behavior had been entirely blameless. For "every thing now appeared in such favorable colors to Jones, that malice itself would have found it no easy matter to fix any blame on him. Not that Jones desired to conceal or to disguise the truth; . . . but, in reality, so it happened, and so it always will happen; for let a man be never so honest, the account of his own conduct will, in spite of himself, be so very favorable that his vices will become purified through his lips, and, like foul liquors well strained, will leave all their foulness behind. For though the facts themselves may appear, yet so different will be the motives, circumstances, and consequences, when a man tells his own story, and when his enemy tells it, that we scarce can recognize the facts to be one and the same" (IV, 81).

Even an honest man, then—as much as the hypocritical Lawyer Dowling later in the same novel—may "convey a lie in the words of truth" (V, 334), and this fact of the *subjective* element in language was another cause of its perversion, another instance of the contamination of the words of truth. "A man must take heed of words," warned Hobbes, "which besides the signification of what we imagine of their nature, have a signification also of the nature, disposition, and interest of the speaker";[128] and Locke placed verbal testimony a poor second to personal experience because the former can be so easily distorted by "passion, interest, inadvertency, mistake, . . . and a thousand odd . . . capricios [of] men's minds."[129] The subjectivity of the speaker or writer is not, strictly speaking, an imperfection of language. But insofar as it is reflected in language and perverts it from its proper function as the medium of truth, it must be taken into account.

Nor is subjectivity a problem only in a man's "account of his own conduct." Fielding's recognition, in the passage just quoted from *Tom Jones*, that the enemy's version of the same facts will be distorted too implies further that *any* version may reflect the bias of the speaker and so miss objective truth. Thus the third

[128]*Leviathan*, Lindsay ed., pp. 30–31.
[129]*An Essay Concerning Human Understanding*, Bk. IV, Ch. xvi, Sec. 11.

target of his satire in *Shamela*, after Richardson's *Pamela* and Cibber's *Apology*, is Conyers Middleton's *Life of Cicero* (1741).[130] Middleton, according to Lord Macaulay, was "an idolater . . . composing a lying legend in honor of St. Tully. . . . Actions for which Cicero himself, the most eloquent and skillful of advocates, could contrive no excuses, actions which in his confidential correspondence he mentioned with remorse and shame, are represented by his biographer as wise, virtuous, heroic."[131] We need look no further than this for Fielding's reasons for attacking him. Middleton was, like the narrator of *Jonathan Wild*, a whitewashing biographer, and the fact that his subject was a man whom Fielding admired did not make the author any less guilty as a corruptor and discreditor of the language. But again even basically honest speakers can be guilty of the same kind of faults. When Colonel James in *Amelia* tells Sergeant Atkinson his intention to let Booth stay in jail so that the colonel may pursue Amelia without interference, Atkinson relates the story to his wife and she to Amelia: "And as the sergeant had painted the matter rather in stronger colors than the colonel, so Mrs. Atkinson again a little improved on the sergeant. Neither of these good people, perhaps, intended to aggravate any circumstance; but such is, I believe, the unavoidable consequence of all reports" (VII, 107).

Rarely, in fact, does Fielding allow any profession or report, however sympathetic the character who delivers it, to pass unchallenged. It is not surprising, therefore, that he is equally conscious of the possibility of subjective bias in his own narrations. In the *Voyage to Lisbon* he describes, with some indignation, how he chased from his cabin a flunky officer of the ship who had rudely interrupted himself and his wife at dinner. But he also reports the officer's version of the incident as related later to the captain. The officer, whose name is Honest Tom, "hastily began his narrative, and faithfully related what had happened . . . ; we say faithfully, tho' . . . it may be suspected that Tom chose to add, perhaps, only five or six immaterial circumstances, as is always, I believe, the case, and may possibly have been done by me in relating this very story, though it happened not many hours ago" (XVI, 303–4).

[130]See Baker's Introduction, pp. xxiv–xxvii.
[131]*Lord Bacon, The Complete Works of Macaulay* (New York: Putnam's, 1898), 14: 6.

The problem is different, of course, in fictional narratives, but the principle, if the author is a serious one, is the same. For though his object is general truth rather than particular, his success depends on the degree to which he convinces his readers of his own sincerity and of the objective validity of his judgments. Richardson's interpretation of Pamela's "virtue" would not, to Fielding's mind, have been any more convincing if he had proposed it in his own person rather than through the protestations of his heroine because it would still have rested, like Middleton's interpretation of Cicero, primarily on verbal professions concerning motives never really submitted to the test of objective action. Thus *Joseph Andrews* is not a parody of *Pamela*, nor is it likely that Fielding began it as such. For if he had been interested in burlesquing Richardson's novel he would certainly not have slighted (as he did not in *Shamela*) its most imitable feature, the epistolary form. It is rather an *alternative* to *Pamela*, exhibiting through action the same kind of virtue which in Richardson remained largely nominal and hence psychologically unconvincing.

"The only Ways by which we can come at any Knowledge of what passes in the Minds of others," Fielding writes in the *Champion* for December 11, 1739, "are their Words and Actions; the latter of which, hath by the wiser Part of Mankind been chiefly depended on, as the surer and more infallible Guide," and this introduces a letter from a self-acknowledged hypocrite who boasts of his success in misleading the world by the "Expense of a little verbal Piety" and who, though he does not give himself away by signing the letter, concludes, "I am Sir, (Tho' I care not if you was hang'd.) Your most obedient humble Servant." And again, in *An Essay on the Knowledge of the Characters of Men* (published in the *Miscellanies* of 1743):

Surely, the actions of men seem to be the justest interpreters of their thoughts, and the truest standards by which we may judge them. . . . And indeed, this is so certain a method of acquiring the knowledge I contend for, that, at first appearance, it seems absolutely perfect, and to want no manner of assistance. There are, however, two causes of our mistakes on this head; and which lead us into forming very erroneous judgments of men, even while their actions stare us in the face, and, as it were, hold a candle to us, by which we may see into

them. The first of these is, when we take their own words against their
actions. . . . This error is infinitely more common than its extreme
absurdity would persuade us was possible. And many a credulous
person hath been ruined by trusting to the assertions of another, who
must have preserved himself, had he placed a wiser confidence in his
actions. The second error is still more general. This is when we take
the colour of a man's actions, not from their own visible tendency, but
from his public character: when we believe what others say of him, in
opposition to what we see him do. . . . I will venture to affirm, that I
have known some of the best sort of men in the world, (to use the
vulgar phrase) who would not have scrupled cutting a friend's throat;
and a fellow, whom no man should be seen to speak to, capable of the
highest acts of friendship and benevolence. (XIV, 289–90)

There can be no question, then, that Fielding saw the problem
of the valid judgment of human character, and hence of literary
narration, as in part at least a matter of language and its perversions. He could not, as a writer, repudiate language, however
much he distrusted it. But living in "the world of common men,
and not of philosophers"—the world of hack authors, politicians,
and polite society, of doctors, lawyers, and clergymen, and of
countless hypocrites and false witnesses in all orders of life—he
was aware that truth, having to be expressed through language,
was susceptible to all kinds of distortions and hazards both of
medium (the imperfections and corruptions of the language
itself) and of agent (the "interest," bias, ignorance, insincerity,
or vanity of the speaker or writer). He recognized, therefore, that
the serious writer must devise means to make the truths he would
express independent of these hazards, or at least to create the
illusion of such independence; to *insulate* truth from the corruptions of medium and agent through which, in an imperfect
world, it must necessarily pass. How Fielding met this challenge
in his own writings will be the subject of the following chapters.

Chapter IV
IRONY AND ACTION

"The very best Advocate a good Cause can have," says the Gentleman of Fielding's *Dialogue between a Gentleman of London and an Honest Alderman,* "is plain-spoken Truth." But the communication of truth in plain, unequivocal words, an ideal that Fielding shared with the whole seventeenth- and eighteenth-century movement of language reform, was not, he knew, a simple matter. The Gentleman himself discovers that even the plain statement of fact that the Alderman's candidate is a "*known* Jacobite" fails of its purpose when the Alderman dismisses the term Jacobite as "a mere Bugbear," and refuses to be imposed on by such "empty Sounds" because of his distrust of political professions: "The Court, my Friend, has long cheated us with Names." Not only is the plain word Jacobite without a clear and distinct agreed meaning (the Alderman insists that he is himself a "Jacobite upon republican Principles"),[1] but all direct professions of truths are suspect of insincerity.

The culminating triumph of the Augustan plain style after nearly a century of linguistic criticism and reform over the baroque rhetoric of the "former Age" had in a sense merely exposed the basic problems of communication in language more nakedly. "The clarity of the new style," as Martin Price has observed, "makes for a sharp awareness of the oppositions of terms and of the latent implications in a general term. . . . Terms were now to be scrutinized carefully for both their sincerity and their practical consequences."[2] Price's point is that the achievement of the plain style in the early eighteenth century cleared the way for the development of Augustan irony, created the necessary conditions in which the ironic art of a Swift could flourish as it

[1] Pp. 7, 73.
[2] *Swift's Rhetorical Art,* pp. 13–14.

could not have done in the time of Jeremy Taylor and Sir Thomas Browne. "Irony had come in with the plain prose style," as Saintsbury pointed out even earlier, "without which it is almost impossible,"[3] and Ian Watt, more recently, has maintained that "eighteenth-century irony both required and stimulated the development of a kind of prose perspicuous enough for its double meanings to be sufficiently transparent." Watt, like Price, notes that one consequence of the plain style is the prominence it gives to the general term and observes that "the use of abstract words in itself often creates an ironical effect . . . whether intended or not." But neither he nor the other critics who have recognized the connection between the development of the plain style and the rise of irony have sufficiently emphasized that as well as being an exploitation of the resources of the new style, irony was also, in writers like Swift and Pope and Fielding at least, sometimes a *critique* of that style—or rather, of the imperfections and abuses of language which the plain style brought into inescapable prominence.

Watt's notion that the "generalizing tendency of the eighteenth-century vocabulary" was itself "ironigenic"[4] is merely another way, in fact, of describing the process which Fielding and his contemporaries called the corruption of language. Shaftesbury, complaining of the "prostitute" manner of the modern encomium, declared that "in reality the Nerve and Sinew of modern *Panegyrick* lies in a dull kind of Satir; which the Author, it's true, intends shou'd turn to the Advantage of his Subject; but which, if I mistake not, will appear to have a very Contrary effect."[5] And Pope, who argued that as a result of "this prostitution" the serious author "can find no Terms . . . but what have already been used, and rendered suspected" and that "even Truth itself . . . will appear a Cheat by being so drest like one,"[6] turned the same principle to positive advantage in *The Art of Sinking in Poetry* by making it the basis of a mock rhetoric which was really a program of resistance to the ironigenic corruption of

[3]George Saintsbury, *The English Novel* (London: Dent, 1913), p. 104.
[4]Ian Watt, "The Ironic Tradition in Augustan Prose from Swift to Johnson," *Restoration and Augustan Prose*, pp. 24–28.
[5]*Characteristicks*, 1: 226. I am indebted to Aubrey L. Williams for calling attention to this passage and its relevance to Augustan satire, in *Pope's Dunciad*, p. 13.
[6]*Prose Works*, 1: 76–77.

language. The principle he taught, as William B. Coley has excellently expressed it, was "to beat dulness at its own game, to put on more leads and outsink it, to formalize its imperfection."[7]

Fielding, as we have seen, was also concerned lest the fawning panegyrists of his day should "prevent the very use of praise," and the examples he offers in *Joseph Andrews* of Colley Cibber's powers to "metamorphize and distort . . . the English language" by making "cowardice brave, avarice generous, pride humble, and cruelty tender-hearted" (I, 46) are not much different from those supplied by Locke to illustrate the "abuse of words," nor from those cited by Pope in *The Art of Sinking* to demonstrate his ironigenic formula for converting "Vices into their bordering Virtues."[8] Or again, in *Love in Several Masques*, Lady Matchless tells Wisemore that in high society "Merit is demerit, constancy dulness" (VIII, 65). The ironigenic effect of corrupt language, in fact, is sometimes evident even to Fielding's characters themselves. "To be called a coxcomb by a woman," says a character in *The Temple Beau*, "is as sure a sign of sense, as to be called rogue by a courtier is of honesty. . . . I rejoice in the irony" (VIII, 108).

The ironic manner which is a hallmark of Fielding's style is not, then, as Austin Dobson once said, "his natural speech"[9] so much as a deliberate response to the corrupt state of the medium in which he had to work, an attempt, in the best Augustan tradition, "to formalize its imperfection." Irony, for Fielding, is a means of coming to terms with the corrupt language of his day, a way of accommodating it to the ideal of plain-spoken truth. To a certain extent, of course, as the above discussion has suggested, this is true of the other great ironists of the age as well, and it can be seen as one of the factors underlying the use of verbal irony in any age. As G. G. Sedgewick has remarked, irony "is, so to speak, language mocking itself."[10] But to a much greater degree than any of his predecessors or contemporaries, Fielding is

---

[7] "The Background of Fielding's Laughter," *ELH*, 26 (1959): 244.

[8] See above, pp. 45–46. Cf. also Thomas Hobbes's examples of "abuse": "For one calleth *Wisdome*, what another calleth *feare*; and one *cruelty*, what another *justice*; one *prodigality*, what another *magnanimity*; and one *gravity*, what another *stupidity*." *Leviathan*, Lindsay ed., p. 31.

[9] Editor's Introduction, *The Journal of a Voyage to Lisbon*, Henley ed., 16: 176.

[10] *Of Irony, Especially in Drama* ("University of Toronto Studies: Philology and Literature Series," No. 10 [Toronto: University of Toronto Press, 1935]), p. 12.

conscious of this function of his irony. Not always, of course, is it overtly an irony of corrupt language, and not every word he uses ironically is necessarily a corrupted one. But more than Swift or Pope, or Lucian or Cervantes, or any of the other masters of irony to whom he acknowledges a debt, he tends to treat the ironic term as a "given" quantity, a product of social and linguistic forces beyond his control, and more than any of the others he works with a recurring set of terms that can be identified as his ironic vocabulary.

"The satiric method Fielding takes from Swift," says Professor McKillop, "is to set up and isolate an absolute standard denoted by noble words which are then deprived of content or taken to mean the opposite of themselves."[11] But even when he is imitating Swift quite frankly, as for example in a paper in the *Covent-Garden Journal* No. 11 modeled on *A Modest Proposal*, there is evidence that he is more concerned than Swift was with the function of irony as critique and purification of language. The essay, a "projection" for providing for the London poor, opens in a true Swiftian vein with the observation that Dean Swift's scheme, however "proper and humane" it might be in Ireland, would not work in London because "here, as the Children of our Poor are very little better than a Composition of Gin, to force their Parents to eat them, would in Reality be to force them to poison themselves." But when he gets to his own proposal, a plan for the revival of human sacrifice, Fielding slips into a kind of irony that is not Swiftian at all. There is historical precedent for his scheme, he argues, because originally "these Sacrifices were no other than an Invention of Politicians to *provide for*, or rather to remove those redundant Members in every Society, for which the better (that is the richer) Sort had no Manner of Use, and who were consequently in the Language of the Law *become chargeable*." And in imitation of Swift's concluding assurance that he has "no other motive than the public good of my country, by advancing our trade, providing for infants, relieving the poor, and giving some pleasure to the rich," Fielding ends with the claim that his proposal "is for the Good of the Nation *in general*; that is to say, for the richer Part."

[11]Alan Dugald McKillop, *The Early Masters of English Fiction* (Lawrence: University of Kansas Press, 1956), p. 116.

Both writers exploit the ironic potential of political clichés such as "providing for the poor" and "the public good" and both spell out the kind of brutal particulars these can be made to cover. But if Fielding goes further and explicitly "defines" the ironic term, "translates" it into its corrupt "real meaning," it is not entirely because he lacks Swift's subtlety and cannot resist the temptation of explaining a joke. He also wants to call attention, in a way Swift seldom finds necessary or desirable, to the *real* corruptions of speech of which his ironies are mocking imitations. Swift, it is true, sometimes focuses on the strictly linguistic implications of his irony too, most notably perhaps in *An Argument against the Abolishing of Christianity*, where nominalism is made the central issue; in the ironic definition of the "true critic" in *A Tale of a Tub*; and in the sections of *Gulliver's Travels* where Gulliver's translations from a corrupt English into the plain and "significant" language of the Houyhnhnms give the lie to such hollow abstractions as "Power, Government, War, Law, Punishment, and a Thousand other Things [which] had no Term wherein that Language could express them."[12] But even in these and similar instances Swift is not as ready as Fielding is to make the corruption of language itself the main rationale of his irony.

Swift's irony, it may be freely admitted, is more profound and more complex than Fielding's, more deeply rooted in a philosophical awareness of the disparity between the ideal values implicit in a phrase like "the public good" and the grim reality it is made to stand for. Its source, finally, is his sense of the corruption not of language but of human nature, as represented, usually, by a satiric *persona* whose abuse of words is merely one aspect of a larger projection of evil or stupidity, a revelation of character which is in turn a revelation of human nature. What "the public good" means to the *persona* of *A Modest Proposal* cannot be defined in a parenthetical aside because it is too integral a part of a whole moral and psychological conception of character. It is ironic not so much because it is corrupt in itself but because its user is corrupt.

To the extent, of course, that Fielding makes use of fully

developed satiric *personae* or characters (as in *Jonathan Wild* and in the early numbers of the *Jacobite's Journal*, before he abandoned the John Trot-plaid mask), he too conceives of the ironic speaker as a vicious or stupid personage. But the creator of Parson Adams and Squire Allworthy, though he was fully alive to the social causes and effects of corrupt language, did not see degenerate human nature as its ultimate source. He tends to look on the corruption of words as a condition of language itself which the serious writer must cope with as best he can. If one is to achieve the ideal of plain-spoken truth he must reclaim the words of truth—particularly the abstractions which according to Locke give form and coherency to intangible values—from the erosions of specialization and the contaminations of insincerity. "Better" is defined as "richer" in the Projection for the London Poor essay not just because it fits Fielding's immediate satiric purpose to so define it but because he was apparently convinced, as we have seen earlier, that this (or some other purely social reduction of an originally moral term) was what the word was actually coming to mean in popular usage, and "the Good of the Nation" (or variant forms of the cliché) has a similar ironic career that can be traced throughout his works.[13]

Even the moral inversions of Fielding's most Swiftian *persona*, the fawning, hero-worshipping narrator of *Jonathan Wild*, are presented primarily as verbal confusions, and both the narrator and the "great" characters he admires are conscious of their language in a way that would be grossly out of character in Swift. They are constantly defining and commenting on their terms, and the whole vocabulary of political clichés and polite euphemisms which make up the ironic language of the book is merged and identified with the underworld cant which has to be glossed for the benefit of uninitiated readers. Just as the term "prig" must be translated into "plain English" ("thief") for the sake of those readers whom the narrator contemptuously refers to as "the vulgar" (i.e., honest men), so must terms like "greatness," "great man," "honor," "liberty," and "love" be translated. The debtors who fall under Wild's influence in Newgate, reports the

[13]See *Jonathan Wild*, Bk. I, Ch. 12. Henley ed., 2: 39; *A Journey from This World to the Next*, Bk. I, Ch. 7. Henley ed., 2: 244; and the Introduction to *A Voyage to Lisbon*, Henley ed., 16: 189.

narrator, "now grew so great, *i.e.*, corrupted in their morals, that they spoke with the utmost contempt of what the vulgar call honesty. The greatest character among them was that of a pick-pocket, or, in truer language, a *file*." And it is Jonathan Wild's own awareness that "we have no name to express it by in our Cant Dictionary" which causes him to appropriate and define for his cohorts that "word of such sovereign use and virtue, . . . honor" (II, 42, 188–89).

Jonathan Wild, which is the most purely ironic of Fielding's major works, is also, significantly, the most language conscious. But *Joseph Andrews* and *Tom Jones* also abound in turns of phrase like "that is to say," "what is called," "to wit," "*viz.*," "or rather," "as it is generally expressed," "in other words," "in common phrase," "in short," "in plainer words," "in a word," and (most ubiquitously of all, perhaps) "to say the truth" and "in plain English"—the net effect of which is to make the reader aware of the language of narration *as language* and to keep him constantly alert to the meanings of words.

It would be no great exaggeration, in fact, to maintain that the meaning of words is a central preoccupation in nearly all of Fielding's works—even those which are entirely non-ironic. The most interesting of his early poems printed in the *Miscellanies* of 1743 (*Of True Greatness, Of Good Nature, Liberty*) are verse essays in definition of some of the words and concepts which were to be so important to him throughout his career and which were also destined—no doubt for this very reason—to become among the most familiar terms of his ironic vocabulary. The prose essays in the same collection are also much concerned with the meanings of words central to his system of thought. *An Essay on Conversation* examines the meanings of "conversation" and "good breeding," *An Essay on the Knowledge of the Characters of Men* contains the famous definition of hypocrisy, *Of the Remedies of Afflictions for the Loss of Our Friends* focuses on such key words as virtue, religion, and philosophy, and even the burlesque exercise *On Nothing* is framed as an essay in definition.

There are more full-length essays in definition in the *Covent-Garden Journal* than in the political journals, but it is remarkable how many of even the earlier papers also take off from analyses of words. The whole of the *True Patriot*, in fact, can be looked upon as an extended definition of its title, a purpose Fielding makes explicit in the second number. His aim, he announces, "however the Word *Patriot* hath been abused, or whatever Odium it may have thence contracted among the honest Part of Mankind," is to restore the word to its original meaning and dignity. We have already examined the background of Fielding's distrust of this political term and considered some examples of his ironic use of the word in its abused senses. But this essay is also interesting as a statement of his philosophy of definition. "The Difficulty," he explains, "is the same in this as in other Virtues, to distinguish Truth from Falshood and Pretence," and the purpose of the journal is "to arm my Countrymen . . . by lending him [*sic*] some Assistance to discover the true Patriot from the false."

Nearly all of Fielding's definitions assume a similar difficulty and serve a similar purpose. Always he is concerned with sets of contrary ideas or values which have become so confused in popular usage that they are both expressed by a single word, and always he is involved in an attempt to distinguish the "true" (or "original") meaning from the "false" (or "corrupt") meaning. Definition thus becomes a negative as well as a positive process, and is thus merely a special case of judgment, a term which Fielding, in a later *True Patriot* essay, defines as "no other than the Distinction of Right from Wrong; or as Mr. *Lock* hath more accurately describ'd it, 'The separating carefully Ideas wherein can be found the least Difference, thereby to avoid being misled by Similitude, and by Affinity to take one Thing for another.' "[14] The definitions of conversation and good breeding in *An Essay on Conversation* are constructed on a similar true vs. false pattern, as are—to cite only some of the more notable examples—the essay on good nature in the *Champion* for March 27, 1740, the analyses of the false sublime in the Preface to *The Tragedy of Tragedies* and the *Champion* for April 29, 1740, the observations on the true ridiculous in the Preface to *Joseph Andrews*, and the essays on wit and humor in the *Covent-Garden Journal* Nos. 18 and 19.

[14] *True Patriot*, Dec. 24, 1745. *An Essay Concerning Human Understanding*, Bk. II, Ch. xi, Sec. 2. Fielding misquotes slightly. Locke wrote, ". . . in separating carefully, one from another, ideas . . .," etc.

There was nothing unique or original, of course, in Fielding's use of the true-false formula of definition. What is interesting is his extension of the method to his dramatic and narrative works, wherein the same kind of negative purification of words is achieved through the use of irony even while their positive "true meanings" are being built up by means of dramatic exemplification. For at its most characteristic, Fielding's irony also assumes the confusion within a single word of jarring contrary senses and also seeks to effect a separation of the true meaning from the false. This is why he so often makes the negative meaning of his ironic term explicit by translating it into "plain English." The translation, like the negative definition, empties the word of its alien denotations and exposes it as a mere honorific husk, and the positive meaning is simply the denotation which the reader supplies (often, of course, with Fielding's guidance) to account for the honorific connotations and fill the emptiness. The ironic definition, translating the sanctifying abstraction into its plain English "real meaning," is in reality an act of purification, a surgical separation of the diseased growth of corruption from the healthy tissue of "original idea." Moreover, just as in his essays it is naturally the key words of the subject which are singled out for definition, so in the dramatic and narrative works it is always the words representative of central thematic values that are subjected to the severest ironic exploitation. Often, indeed, as we have remarked before, they are the same words, and Fielding's ironic vocabulary is merely his serious vocabulary turned inside out.

But before we examine the relationships of irony and theme in the novels, we would do well to consider Fielding's plays, particularly the comedies. For though his dramatic burlesques and satires are rich in satiric attacks on the corrupters of language, it is in his more serious comedies of manners that we see him for the first time actually involved in the attempt to purify by irony the very words which he wants to carry the main burden of thematic import. Nearly all of the comedies, in fact, can be read, in part at least, as dramatic essays in definition of abstract social and moral virtues, and their plots frequently turn on questions of words and their meanings. Again, as in the periodical essays, true and false meanings of the same words are brought into conflict, and negative or corrupt senses are exposed through the unmasking of hypocritical pretenders to the virtues in question or through the disabusing of characters honestly misled by corruptive specialization or nominalism.

The most obvious example, perhaps, is *The Fathers, or The Good Natured Man*, which, as the subtitle indicates, is an attempt to define in dramatic terms Fielding's central concept of good nature. But though he is concerned, as always, with the concept that exists independently of the word used to express it, he also recognizes the practical necessity of repairing any split between concepts and the words which, according to Locke, "preserve essences" of abstract ideas "and give them their lasting duration." In his formal essay on the same term in the *Champion* for March 27, 1740, he defines good nature as "a Delight in the Happiness of Mankind, and a Concern at their Misery, with a Desire, as much as possible, to procure the former, and avert the latter; and this, with a constant Regard to Desert." But he also emphasizes that it "is not that Weakness, which, without Distinction, affects both the Virtuous and the Base," nor is it "that Cowardice which prevents us from repelling or resenting an Injury." Furthermore, "it is impossible for a Fool, who hath no distinguishing Faculty, to be good-natured." Clearly it is these false meanings of the term that Fielding believed were contaminating the name of good nature and therefore threatening to discredit the concept itself. Indeed John Hughes (whose ambition, like Fielding's, was "in the Course of my Writings, to restore, as well I was able, the proper Ideas of Things") was already insisting in the *Spectator* for November 1, 1712, that "good-nature" had been "rendered Suspicious, and in danger of being transferred from its original Sense, to so distant an Idea as that of *Folly*."[15]

In *The Fathers* Boncour is the good-natured man in the true sense, the kindly father whose generous indulgence of his son and daughter is contrasted with the tyrannical severity of Old Valence toward his children and proved to be the sounder system. For Old Valence good nature is a weakness, and for his son, Young Valence, a sort of Blifil-figure who conceals his selfish will under

[15]Everyman ed., 4: 156.

the hypocritical pose of unquestioning obedience, it is a form of cowardice. But it is Boncour's brother Sir George who is the harshest critic of good nature, because, though a good man himself, he honestly confuses good nature with folly and suspects that it is only the honorific ring of the word which prevents his brother from recognizing this folly for what it is: "Good nature! Damn the word; I hate it" (XII, 199). But though Boncour's good nature is not represented as perfect (his overindulgence of his wife, which is not corrected till the end of the play, is an instance of how the impulse of generosity, when the "distinguishing Faculty" is relaxed, may indeed degenerate into folly), the working out of the plot demonstrates that it is a genuine and practicable virtue, not to be confused with folly or weakness or cowardice, and in the end even Sir George is convinced that the word and the idea it represents are worthy of respect.

The special problem to which *The Fathers* addresses itself, to recall again Fielding's paraphrase of Locke's theory of judgment, is that of "separating carefully Ideas wherein can be found the least Difference, thereby to avoid being misled by Similitude, and by Affinity to take one Thing for another," or, in Pope's phrase, of distinguishing "Vices from their bordering Virtues."[16] But the problem is a relatively simple one here because though the characters in the play represent different attitudes toward good nature, none of them apart from Boncour (and perhaps his son and daughter) claim to possess the virtue themselves. The sentimental plot is a single-minded testing of the concept of good nature as personified by one man. There is no complicating confusion of pretended or merely nominal good nature in others. But in Fielding's other comedies the situation is usually more complex. Not only do their Congrevean plots of gallantry and intrigue in fashionable society involve a wider range of abstract virtues (love, honor, good breeding, virtue, etc.) to be dramatically defined and separated from their bordering vices (lust, hypocritical regard for appearances, flattery, prudishness, etc.), but also a broader scope for the exhibition of such abuses of language as insincerity, hollow professions, and cynical nominalism.

---

[16]One of Pope's own examples concerns the conversion of "Intemperance into Good Nature." See above, p. 45.

Fielding's first play, for example, *Love in Several Masques*, is an examination of "love" in high society, but such related terms and concepts as "right," "merit," "constancy," "virtue," "modesty," "good breeding," and "honor" are also brought under review, and the key word "love" itself is submitted to a much more rigorous regime of dramatic definition and ironic purification than Fielding found necessary in the case of good nature. Not only does the play reject the prudish notion of one character that love is an "indecent passion" and the cynical view of another that it is "an out-of-fashion Saxon word, which no polite person understands" (VIII, 35, 65), but before the title of true love can be finally settled on the virtuous alliance of the hero and heroine, the "several masques" of love must be torn off such hypocritical claimants of the title as lust, dalliance, and fortune-hunting. The play is a defense not merely of the concept of virtuous and honorable love between the sexes but of the words which are essential to its preservation as a vital social and moral ideal.

The words to which Fielding devotes most attention in his comedies, however, and which he would seem to be most concerned to rescue from the bad company of degrading associations and restore to their rightful meanings, are "honor" and "virtue." His second play, *The Temple Beau*, is particularly concerned with the separation of true honor as a noble ideal of Christian morality from the false honor of masculine pride and feminine vanity. Challenged to a duel in the name of honor by Valentine, his rival in love, Veromil protests that to accept would be to act against religion. "He that has not honour wears but the mask of piety," Valentine taunts. But Veromil, stating what is clearly Fielding's own view of the matter, replies, "You speak the meaning of a libertine age; the heart that throws off the face of religion wears but the mask of honour." And if Valentine represents a corrupt specialization of the word (the kind of reductionism that Fielding hit in the Glossary by defining honor as "dueling"), other characters in the play stand for its contamination by hypocrisy and cynical nominalism. Lady Gravely, for example, outwardly prudish but secretly lascivious, agrees to keep a secret so long as it "is not contrary to virtue and honour," and her sister, the cynical coquette Lady Lucy Pedant, replies, "Nay, but I am afraid that you refine too much on those words" (VIII, 155, 162).

Fielding, however, continued to refine on them throughout his career. *Miss Lucy in Town* explores the relationship of virtue and honor to social degree, concluding that the "noblest birth without these is but splendid infamy; and a footman with these qualities, is a man of honour" (XII, 63). *The Modern Husband* distinguishes between virtue and honor on the one hand and mere reputation on the other, and *The Universal Gallant* demonstrates that an "honourable passion" is not a contradiction in terms. The latter play is particularly interesting because the hero Gaylove, like Tom Jones, is himself torn between conflicting senses of the word, and his actions are in part motivated, like Jones's, by the semantic confusion. A reformed rake returned to London after two years' retirement in the country, he is resolved to win Clarinda, the lady who had earlier spurned him, by proving that his conduct is now strictly "honourable." He therefore repudiates the cynical view of the foppish Captain Sparkish that "in my sense of the word dishonourable, . . . nothing dishonourable can pass between man and woman." But he falls prey to a more insidious corruption of the term as used by his rakish friend Mondish, who tells Gaylove that Mrs. Raffler is in love with him and convinces him that it would be "dishonourable" for Gaylove to refuse her, despite his "honourable engagement" to Clarinda. For Mondish honor is simply the arbitrary rules of gallantry, for Captain Sparkish it is a code of arms irrelevant to sexual morality, for Mrs. Raffler it is appearance or reputation, and for Lady Raffler it is prudishness. The irony which thus surrounds the word and makes it suspect through most of the play is sharpened by the fact that the dialogue is peppered with such hollow oaths and empty forms as "upon my honour," "do me the honour," and "I have not had the honour," which, in context, are often heavy with innuendo, as for example when a jealous husband says of his wife's secret lover, "I think he does us the honour of making this house his own," and the lover replies, "I have indeed, sir, lately done myself that honour" (XI, 90, 91, 109, 117). Only for Clarinda is honor an active and universal principle of moral conduct, but it is this positive meaning of the word which the irony assumes as its standard and which is affirmed at the end after Gaylove has painfully extricated himself from the web of contradictory false meanings and is able at last to realize with Clarinda the true honor of faithful and lawful love.

It would appear, then, that it was in his plays that Fielding first began to exploit the ironigenic potentialities of corrupt language as a means of isolating thematic concepts to be defined through dramatic action. The very words which must carry the heaviest thematic freight are systematically turned inside out, not in order to proclaim cynically, in the manner of Mandeville, that emptiness is their natural condition, nor to measure, in the manner of Swift, the impassable distance between the reality and the ideal, but to create a vacuum of meaning which cries out to be filled. Irony, which depends on our recognition of incongruity between the honorific word and its ignoble application, or between the virtuous profession and the vicious act, thus becomes a kind of negative test of truth. For only when the word is united with its "proper idea," only, that is, when a meaning is provided that fulfills the word's implicit promise and accounts for its dignity of connotation, will the ironic alarm fail to sound.

But the positive definition, the reunification of the word with its "proper idea," is effected primarily through the dramatic action itself, by the exhibition in practice of the idea the word properly stands for. Locke, like most other reformers of language before and since, had urged among his "Remedies of the Imperfections and Abuses of Words" the use of examples either in support or in lieu of certain kinds of definition. But according to the author of the *Essay Concerning Human Understanding*, moral terms, as mixed modes or abstractions, could be rendered fully clear and distinct only by analytical definitions, for "they being combinations of several ideas that the mind of man has arbitrarily put together, without reference to any archetypes," the use of examples to represent them is impossible. Locke, naturally, was thinking in terms of the formal philosophical treatise whereas Fielding was writing imaginative literature dealing with the world of "common men and not of philosophers." But also, as we have seen, Fielding did not in any case share Locke's nominalist disbelief in the "real" existence of abstract ideas, and in fact he often treated moral abstractions as though they were simple ideas which could be communicated, as Locke phrased it, "by presenting to [the hearer's or reader's] senses that subject which may produce [the idea] in his mind, and make him actually have the idea that word stands for."[17]

In Fielding's actual practice, of course, the reader's recognition of this proper idea and hence of ironic deviations from it depends in part on his sharing the author's sense of the traditional values of words to begin with. But as a critic and purifier of the language Fielding also seeks, through the objective representation of the idea, to invoke it direct in the reader's mind and thus to invite him to discover for himself that this, rather than any of the corrupt alternate senses provided by the ironic definitions, is the true meaning of the word and the only one which can support its dignified connotations. "Honor," for example, in *Miss Lucy in Town*, though never defined in formal terms, is shown to reside not in pride of station or in worldly fame but rather in the kind of moral superiority displayed by the footman Thomas in contrast to Lord Bawble—just as true "nobility" in *Amelia* is dramatically defined as the moral superiority of Sergeant Atkinson to the "noble lord."

The "good natured reader" Fielding habitually addresses in the novels is not one who necessarily agrees in advance that words like "honor" and "nobility" are primarily moral rather than social terms, but one whose inner experience of the dramatized ideas of honor and nobility will dispose him to recognize this crucial distinction once it has been pointed out to him. Fielding does not insist that such ideas are "innate in the mind." But he is closer to Shaftesbury than to Locke in his belief in an innate potential of moral sympathy to which one can appeal directly through examples when the words that traditionally represent the moral ideas in question are too corrupt to be depended upon.

His expectation seems to be that this experiential exposure to the idea, in combination with the purification by irony of the word, will make possible a reunification of word and idea that will restore the word to the vocabulary of truth and rescue the idea from a contaminating confusion with its bordering vices. Tom Jones, for example, "loves" both Molly Seagrim and Sophia, and both he and the author, in the early chapters of the novel, apply the word indiscriminately to both relationships.

[17] *An Essay Concerning Human Understanding*, Bk. III, Ch. xi, Secs. 14, 15.

But in Chapter V of Book V, when Jones discovers Square crouched behind the draped rug in Molly's loft and Fielding, by way of explanation, reports that Molly, though she indeed "loved" Jones, also "loved" Square and that Square "loved" her (not to mention that she had formerly been "loved" by a certain "country gallant" who had still earlier been the "lover" of her sister Betty), the word "love" emerges from the chapter so charged with irony that its cynical ironic sense threatens to insinuate itself into our understanding of Jones's "love" for Sophia as well. But the title of the next chapter, in which Jones declares his feeling for Sophia in a scene as tender as the ones involving Molly are coarse, announces that by comparing this chapter with the former "THE READER MAY POSSIBLY CORRECT SOME ABUSE WHICH HE HATH FORMERLY BEEN GUILTY OF IN THE APPLICATION OF THE WORD LOVE."

It is not, however, till the prefatory chapter of the next book, "OF LOVE," that Fielding pauses long enough to offer an extended commentary on the distinction between the two kinds of love which has already been exemplified in the dramatic action: "What is commonly called love, namely, the desire of satisfying a voracious appetite with a certain quantity of delicate white human flesh, is by no means that passion for which I here contend" (though genuine love between the sexes is not inconsistent with that "appetite"), true love being instead that "benevolent disposition," present in many, but not all human breasts, "which is gratified by contributing to the happiness of others," and "if we will not call such a disposition love, we have no name for it." But on those readers who deny the existence of love or who continue to equate it with lust he refuses to waste more time. He is addressing only those who, because they have themselves the capacity to experience it, will respond to its "exemplification." For "to treat of the effects of love" to those who lack this capacity would be "as absurd as to discourse on colors to a man born blind, since possibly your idea of love may be as absurd as that which we are told such blind man [*sic*] once entertained of the color scarlet; that color seemed to him to be very much like the sound of a trumpet: and love probably may, in your opinion, very greatly resemble a dish of soup, or a sirloin of roast beef" (III, 271–73).

Like so many of Fielding's remarks on language, the example of the blind man comes from Book III of Locke's *Essay Concerning Human Understanding*, where it is used, however, to illustrate the proposition that *simple* ideas, such as of color, cannot be defined or even communicated unless the hearer has himself experienced them as sensations.[18] But Fielding goes beyond Locke and implies that a formal definition is equally futile in the case of a *complex* idea like love if that idea does not rest on an experiential base, and it was perhaps for this reason that he had earlier insisted he was himself "greatly in love with Sophia" and that "many of our readers will probably be in love [with her] too before we part" (III, 141). We have seen that he was more conscious than Locke of the emotional content of words, and if he distrusted the philosopher's rationalistic method of definition it was not only because that method treated moral concepts as "nominal essences" but also because it seemed to neglect entirely their true essence of human feeling. This true essence, Fielding seems to have felt, could not be fully conveyed by formal definition but only, like the essence of a simple idea in Locke, through "exemplification."

Fielding's sense of the inadequacy of the purely rationalistic definition of a moral term is best seen, however, in connection not with "love" but with "honor," a word which in *Tom Jones*, as in the plays, is subjected to a merciless series of ironic tests even while it is being seriously urged as a central term of the novel's theme. Honor is one of the indispensable virtues which Jones must achieve before he can rightfully claim his inheritance as a true gentleman, and it therefore has to be carefully defined, chiefly in terms of his actions, and distinguished from the many species of false honor which have corrupted and confused its name. The question of the meaning of the word is first raised early in the novel when Jones, caught poaching on Squire Western's estate, admits his own guilt but in order to protect Black George declares untruthfully that he was alone. He "scorned a lie as much as anyone," he explains later, when the truth (thanks to Blifil) comes out, but having promised the gamekeeper not to betray him, "he thought his honor engaged."

[18]Bk. III, Ch. iv, Sec. 11.

Squire Allworthy punishes Jones for lying and then quickly forgives him because he sees that his motive was "a mistaken point of honor." But this sets Thwackum and Square off on a dispute over the meaning of that term. Locke's rationalistic theory of definition is recalled at the outset through Square's insistence that "it was impossible to discourse philosophically concerning words till their meaning was first established." Thwackum, rising to the challenge, thereupon defines honor as "that mode of Divine grace which is . . . dependent upon . . . religion," by which he means "the Christian religion; and not only the Christian religion, but the Protestant religion; and not only the Protestant religion, but the Church of England." Square, not to be outdone, asserts that honor is "founded on the unalterable rule of right, and the eternal fitness of things" (III, 113, 115–16, 119). Both however agree that "true honor cannot support an untruth" and thus that Jones could not have acted from an honorable motive.

Thwackum's definition, as his progressive narrowing of the term's application comically suggests, is an example of corruptive "specialization," and Square merely carries the process of degeneration to its logical conclusion by speaking, as Thwackum says later, a "jargon of words, which means nothing" (III, 153). But Fielding's more serious objection to such definitions can be glimpsed in Squire Allworthy's impatient interruption, "very coldly" spoken, to the effect that "they had both mistaken his meaning; for that he had said nothing of true honor," and in Fielding's earlier observation that the two disputants really agreed on only one point, "which was, in all their discourses on morality never to mention the word goodness" (III, 114, 116). Their definitions miss the essence of honor not only because of their bigotry and pedantry and hypocrisy but also because neither of them has ever felt in his own breast the intrinsic quality of goodness on which all moral ideas must rest. Even a "ruffian," as Shaftesbury explains in a passage which anticipates Fielding's example, "who out of a sense of Fidelity and Honour of any kind, refuses to discover his Associates, . . . has certainly some Principle of Virtue, however he may misapply it."[19]

[19]*Characteristicks*, 2: 39.

But this "Principle of Virtue," since it is of its nature irreducibly experiential, is precisely what their formal definitions of honor—and, Fielding seems to imply, *any* formal definition—fail to register. "There are a sort of persons," he says later, "who, as Prior excellently well remarks, direct their conduct by something

> Beyond the fix'd and settled rules
> Of vice and virtue in the schools,
> Beyond the letter of the law."
>
> (V, 187)[20]

And this "something"—call it "goodness" or "good nature" or a "Principle of Virtue"—must be "presented to our Understanding," as Shaftesbury said, in the same way that "the common subjects of *Sense*, . . . Shapes, Motions, Colours, and Proportions, are presented to our Eye"—through "*Behavior* and *Action*."[21]

Tom Jones's rudimentary sense of honor survives the influence of Thwackum and Square and is proof against the even narrower usage of the soldiers he meets in Books VII and IX who identify it with the code of dueling and so "contaminate the name of honor by assuming it" (IV, 163); and unlike his two tutors, he is able to tell Nightingale that "the very best and truest honor . . . is goodness" and persuade him to act accordingly when his London friend comes to him as "a man of honor" for advice about whether he can "think of . . . an alliance with honor" with a girl whom he has seduced (V, 123–25). But Jones himself is not freed from the corruptive effects of false applications of the word until the end of the story. Significantly, since honor as a social value is an aristocratic term, it is the high-life scenes of the later books of the novel which submit the word to its most rigorous test. Jones's confusion over the "mistaken point of honor" in the Black George poaching incident was comparatively innocent, but there is no reason to believe that Fielding in any way condones his hero's involvement with Lady Bellaston or sees it as anything but a sordid and dishonorable alliance. Jones himself is concerned when he meets Sophia at Lady Bellaston's house that she will learn of "the ignominious circumstance of [his]

---

[20]The quotation is from Prior's "Paulo Purganti and His Wife."
[21]*Characteristicks*, 2: 29.

having been kept." But like Gaylove in *The Universal Gallant*, he has become so blinded by the false code of gallantry that he finds himself faced with the dilemma of trying to behave honorably in dishonorable circumstances, and it is the tortuous complications and contradictions of this paradox which expose the confusion of values inherent in the corrupted word: "As his necessity obliged him to accept [Lady Bellaston's money], so his honor, he concluded, forced him to pay the price" (V, 74, 82–83).

The appearance of Sophia in London intensifies Jones's moral and semantic dilemma by reminding him of his *truly* honorable obligation to her. But as with "love" earlier in the novel, Jones's sense of honor with regard to Sophia has to be distinguished, both for his sake and for the reader's, from the false honor of his relationship to Lady Bellaston. The issue is brought to its ironic head when Lady Bellaston comes to Jones's rooms and, berating him for his coldness, accuses him of having "betrayed my honor." Jones insists that "If there be honor in man," he has done nothing to merit her anger, but before he can go further Mrs. Honour (who is a kind of grotesque personification of the corrupt word and its ironic potential) arrives to deliver a message from Sophia and a coarse polemic of her own against Lady Bellaston, who is concealed within easy earshot. Protesting that he will not listen to slander against "a lady of such honor," Jones gets rid of Sophia's maid only to have to face renewed charges from Lady Bellaston that he is responsible for her ruin: "my reputation, my honor—gone forever!" She demands, in recompense for her "sacrifice," that he show her Sophia's letter, but Jones's reply reintroduces the word at its true value and so equates his conflict between true and false honor with his choice between Sophia and Lady Bellaston: "And can your ladyship . . . ask of me what I must part with my honor before I grant?" (V, 97–99).

But though the following chapters show him guiding Nightingale to a proper understanding of the word and its inseparability from goodness, Jones is still not able to extricate himself from his own web of moral and semantic confusion. Nightingale's plain-spoken account of Lady Bellaston's history, which "contained many particulars highly to her dishonor" hitherto unknown to Jones, convinces him at last that it is he rather than she who has been debauched, and that his only real obligation is to Sophia, his "honorable mistress." He is uneasy, however, about the "handsome pretence" he seizes to break off the affair. Lady Bellaston, as he had expected, indignantly refuses his proposal of marriage, thus delivering him from any further obligation to her. But "there was in this scheme too much of fallacy to satisfy one who utterly detested every species of falsehood or dishonesty; nor would he, indeed, have submitted to put it in practice, had he not been involved in a distressful situation, where he was obliged to be guilty of some dishonor, either to one lady or the other" (V, 181–85). And significantly, it is this same letter of proposal, with its insincere appeals to Lady Bellaston's "honor, . . . as dear to me as my own," that later falls into Sophia's hands and convinces her that Jones had betrayed her not out of mere weakness, which she could have forgiven, but out of conscious duplicity.

The difficulty here is not, as in the Black George incident, a matter of an overly generous impulse of loyalty but of a false allegiance to a corrupt code of gallantry, and the consequence is not just a "mistaken point of honor" but a positively dishonorable act which continues, justly in Fielding's view, to haunt Jones until he has succeeded in demonstrating to even such a discriminating sensibility as Sophia's that he has since conducted himself by a more infallible standard. What that standard is, is suggested when he receives a letter of proposal himself from the wealthy and attractive widow Arabella Hunt. In view of his desperate financial condition and the apparent hopelessness of his situation with Sophia, he is strongly tempted to accept, persuading himself for a moment that this course would be best not only for himself but also for Sophia. "He had almost determined to be false to her from a high point of honor." But the falseness of this "refinement," however compatible it might be with the rationalistic definitions of "honor" of a Thwackum or a Square or with the "fix'd and settled rules / Of vice and virtue in the schools," is brought home to Jones by its incompatibility with "the voice of nature, which cried in his heart that such friendship [to Sophia] was treason to love" (V, 193). Only when Jones has learned to obey the voice of nature, the innate moral sense, and to act upon it under the guidance of the "distinguishing

Faculty" of prudence that Fielding insists is essential to good nature, does he achieve true honor.

In part, Fielding's insistence on the test of action is the consequence of a Miltonic distrust of cloistered virtues. Good nature, he declares in *Tom Jones*, "is an active principle, and doth not content itself with knowledge or belief only" (III, 164). And later, taking exception to the idea that "virtue is the certain road to happiness . . . in this world" (to which Fielding has but one objection: "namely, that it is not true"), he distinguishes between passive and active virtue in a manner which makes it clear that in his opinion only the latter genuinely deserves the name. If the moralists who have preached this "comfortable doctrine . . . mean the exercise of those cardinal virtues which like good housewives stay at home, and mind only the business of their own family," he concedes that happiness may well be the result —though "I could almost wish . . . to call [this] rather by the name of wisdom than by that of virtue." But "if by virtue is meant (as I almost think it ought) a certain relative quality, which is always busying itself without-doors, and seems as much interested in pursuing the good of others as its own, I cannot so easily agree" (V, 141).

In *Joseph Andrews* it is precisely this comfortable doctrine of "Virtue Rewarded" (as Richardson's subtitle to *Pamela* has it) that provides Fielding with an ironic point of departure for a thoroughgoing redefinition of the word "virtue." Not only is Joseph *not* rewarded for the same kind of virtue which had made Pamela's fortune: he positively suffers as a result of it; and the pointed artificiality of the novel's happy ending, far from being a flaw, drives home the moral that there is no necessary cause-and-effect connection between virtue and worldly happiness or prosperity.

But Fielding is also critical of Richardson's use of the word "virtue" in the reductionist and fundamentally passive sense of chastity. Fielding does not deny that chastity is a virtue, and his substitution of male for female chastity is not the cynical joke that it has so often been taken for. It rather raises the question of whether passive virtue of the kind that Joseph exhibits in the early chapters of the novel, before he is turned "without-doors" and forced to take an active and manly role in the world, is really the essential stuff, the *virtus* in the original sense which we may be sure was never far from Fielding's mind, out of which heroes are made; and if Joseph is a clown rather than a hero in these early chapters this is the reason. There is nothing inherently comic in his resistance of Lady Booby's attempts to seduce him. What is ridiculous are his naively pompous protestations, conspicuously derived from Pamela, of his *virtue*. When Lady Booby coyly asks him whether his passions might be inflamed if she were to kiss him, he stuffily replies, "Madam, . . . if they were I hope I should be able to control them without suffering them to get the better of my virtue." "Your virtue!" cries Lady Booby, after a moment of stunned silence. "Did ever mortal hear of a man's virtue? Did even the greatest or the gravest men pretend to any of this kind? . . . And can a boy, a stripling, have the confidence to talk of his virtue?" "Madam," says Joseph, "that boy is the brother of Pamela, and would be ashamed that the chastity of his family, which is preserved in her, should be stained in him" (I, 50–51).

Such rhetoric from a Pamela, given the traditionally passive role of heroines, might pass without challenge. But spoken by a man whom the author has taken pains to designate as "our hero," it is exposed as a corruptive specialization of language. To equate virtue with chastity, as Richardson had in effect done by resting Pamela's claims to heroic stature and moral excellence almost exclusively on her resistance to seduction, was to reduce a great moral principle to a single punctilio. What Fielding does in the opening section of *Joseph Andrews* is to put this specialized usage to the test by simply applying it to a man. The result, as with his other adoptions of corrupt words, is irony. The Richardsonian denotation of chastity is absurdly out of proportion to the grandiose connotations the word "virtue" is given in Joseph's heroic speeches, and the stage is set for the positive definition by action which will restore the balance.

Joseph himself, of course, is not aware that his adventures are in part a quest for the meaning of true virtue. But almost from the moment he is turned out of Lady Booby's house he finds himself in a world in which passive virtue appears either irrelevant or hypocritical and in which he is dependent for both his physical survival and his self-respect on active virtue. His very first adventure on the road leaves him naked and bleeding in a ditch, the victim of robbery and violence, and in vital need of aid. But the respectable persons in the coach who discover him are not disposed to give it. The old gentleman fears for their own safety, the lawyer is afraid they may be suspected of some part in the crime, the coachman thinks only of Joseph's inability to pay his fare, and the lady refuses to ride in the same coach with a naked man—a manifestation of passive "virtue" that she shares with Joseph himself, who is "so perfectly modest" that he refuses to enter unless he is "furnished with sufficient covering to prevent giving the least offence to decency." But when the others fail to meet even this minimal condition of active virtue, "the postilion (a lad who hath been since transported for robbing a henroost) . . . voluntarily stript off a great-coat, his only garment, at the same time swearing a great oath (for which he was rebuked by the passengers), 'That he would rather ride in his shirt all his life than suffer a fellow-creature to lie in so miserable a condition'" (I, 63–65). Judged by the conventional standards of passive virtue, the postilion, who, as Fielding emphasizes in his parenthetical asides, is capable of bad as well as good acts and who has none of the sense of verbal propriety and respect for appearances of the other passengers, would seem the least likely candidate for an exemplar of true virtue. But he alone *acts*, and from this point on in the novel it is action, as opposed to passive belief or mere verbal profession, which defines the positive meaning of virtue.

Even chastity is relegated to a secondary level of importance on this active scale of values, for though Joseph never for a moment wavers, Fielding gives us in Mrs. Tow-wouse's maid Betty a character who, despite her conspicuous lack of chastity, nevertheless emerges, like the postilion, as more virtuous in the larger sense of the word than those who look down on her. "My be-betters are wo-worse than me," she sobs when Mrs. Tow-wouse discovers her in bed with her husband, and though it is certainly Mrs. Tow-wouse who is the injured party here (Is this, she asks, "the reward of my virtue?") Betty's paradoxical statement of her relationship to her "betters" forces us to see this word, as elsewhere in Fielding, in its moral as well as its social sense and strikes us as basically just. For of all the people at the inn where Joseph lies sick and penniless, she alone is generous in action, first admitting him to a room despite his inability to pay, and then, despite Mrs. Tow-wouse's grumbling pronouncement that "common charity teaches us to provide for ourselves, and our families," bringing him "a shirt from the hostler, who was one of her sweethearts" (I, 68, 97–98). Fielding does not condone Betty's promiscuity, but his mention of the source of the shirt in the same sentence which records her generosity sets it in its proper perspective. It is not chastity which is the quintessential virtue but charity.

And of course it is Parson Adams, whose first words, almost, in the novel are a reminder to the surgeon attending Joseph that "it was the duty of men of all professions to apply their skill gratis for the relief of the poor and necessitous" (I, 74), and whose first act, upon discovering Joseph at the inn, is to postpone his journey to London until Joseph's health is restored and to offer him the nine shillings and threepence halfpenny in his pocket, who is the personification of charity. He is also, as the more traditional formulation has it, the incarnation of good nature. But his pastoral office allows Fielding to develop the positive definition of virtue in specifically Christian terms. Good nature, as Martin Battestin has observed, "is finally subsumed within a larger, more exalted concept. It is the natural predisposition to charity, which is the end of morality—and to Fielding a distinctively Christian virtue."[22]

The theological basis of Fielding's emphasis on charity as the archetypal Christian virtue—derived, as Battestin has shown, from the latitudinarian divines—is established in Adams' debate with Mr. Barnabas on Methodism, in which he denounces Whitefield's "detestable doctrine of faith against good works." For Adams the only test of the true Christian is virtue in action, and virtue in action is charity. When Parson Trulliber, refusing to lend his destitute fellow clergyman the fourteen shillings he has asked for, self-righteously tells Adams, "I know what charity is better than to give to vagabonds," Adams answers, "I am sorry . . . that you do know what charity is, since you practice it no better; I must tell you, if you trust to your knowledge for your

[22]Introduction, *Joseph Andrews and Shamela*, ed. Martin C. Battestin (Boston: Houghton Mifflin, 1961), p. xxviii.

justification you will find yourself deceived, though you should add faith to it, without good works. . . . Whoever . . . is void of charity, I make no scruple of pronouncing that he is no Christian" (I, 96, 192–93).

But Parson Trulliber is not the only character in the novel whose use of "charity" in a corrupt sense works to purify the word by irony even while Fielding is defining it positively through the benevolent actions of such characters as Adams himself, the postilion, Betty, and the peddler who gives Adams the six shillings and sixpence he has in his pocket just as Adams is lamenting that "it was possible, in a country professing Christianity, for a wretch to starve in the midst of his fellow-creatures who abounded." The lawyer's laughing declaration, in the face of Joseph's distress, that "charity began at home," Mrs. Towwouse's morose insistence that it "teaches us to provide for ourselves," the lavish professions of charitable intentions, never fulfilled, by the gentleman at the inn, the "honest elderly man" (I, 64, 68, 198–204, 232–33) in Mr. Wilson's story who urges Wilson to challenge a rival and offers, "out of pure charity," to arrange the duel ("A very charitable person, truly!" cries Adams) —these and other appearances of the word in compromising contexts sustain the ironic counterpoint of word and action which is central to Fielding's method of dramatic definition.

But it is Adams' dispute with the miserly Peter Pounce near the end of the novel that brings the positive definition of charity into its sharpest confrontation with the negative corruptions of the word. "You and I," Peter tells Adams, "have different notions of charity. I own, as it is generally used, I do not like the word, nor do I think it becomes one of us gentlemen; it is a mean parson-like quality; though I would not infer many parsons have it neither." "Sir," says Adams, "my definition of charity is, a generous disposition to relieve the distressed." "There is something in that definition," answers Peter, "which I like well enough; it is, as you say, a disposition, and does not so much consist in the act as in the disposition to do it" (I, 310). But as Martin Battestin points out, the original definition, as it appears in a sermon by Isaac Barrow (one of the same "Divines and moral Writers" who represent the standard of proper meaning in the "Modern Glossary" paper), adds that "we should really express that disposition in our practice;"[23] and in a similar dispute with Captain Blifil in *Tom Jones*, Squire Allworthy admits that he is not learned enough in biblical Greek to answer the captain's arguments "as to the true sense of the word which is translated charity; but that he had always thought it was interpreted to consist in action" (III, 83).

The central moral term which Fielding sets out to purify and define in *Tom Jones*, however, is not "charity" or "virtue," nor is it "honor" or "good nature." It is "prudence." But since the process of ironic purification and positive definition of "prudence" in *Tom Jones* is at once the most interesting and the most misunderstood of Fielding's exploitations of the ironigenic corruption of language, it had best be treated in a separate chapter.

[23]*Ibid.*, p. xxvii.

Chapter V
"THE SERPENT AND THE DOVE": "PRUDENCE" IN *TOM JONES*

========

In the Dedication to *Tom Jones*, Fielding declares that his purpose is not merely "to recommend goodness and innocence" but also to "inculcate that virtue and innocence can scarce ever be injured but by indiscretion; and that it is this alone which often betrays them into the snares that deceit and villainy spread for them" (III, 12). But the operative term of this moral theme in the novel proper—and the word which, accordingly, is subjected to the most grueling regimen of ironic decontamination as a corruption of language—is "prudence." But also, as always in Fielding, the negative purification by irony operates in collaboration with a positive definition, by precept and example, of the "proper and original" moral meaning of the word.

In *Joseph Andrews* Fielding is concerned with the definition of virtue as the expression, in the active form of charity, of instinctive good nature, and the assumption is that this active virtue, though it may not be rewarded in the Richardsonian material sense, is sufficient unto itself and its own reward. Even the good nature of a Parson Adams, constantly teetering on the brink of folly, is somehow proof against the manifold evils of the world. But the moral system of *Tom Jones* is more complex:

It is not enough that your designs, nay, that your actions, are intrinsically good; you must take care they shall appear so. If your inside be never so beautiful, you must preserve a fair outside also. This must be constantly looked to, or malice and envy will take care to blacken it so, that the sagacity and goodness of an Allworthy will not be able to see through it, and to discern the beauties within. Let this, my young readers, be your constant maxim, that no man can be good enough to enable him to neglect the rules of prudence; nor will Virtue herself look beautiful unless she be bedecked with the outward ornaments of decency and decorum. And this precept, my worthy

disciples, if you read with due attention, you will, I hope, find sufficiently enforced by examples in the following pages. (III, 131–32)

It is Jones's neglect of this principle, in his failure to make his
outward actions mirror his inner goodness,[1] which accounts for
his progressive loss of the sympathy and respect of his true
friends from the time he tells the lie to protect Black George (and
gives Blifil his first opportunity to discredit him with Allworthy)
to the lowest point of his fortunes when he is jailed as a murderer,
believes himself guilty of incest, and receives a letter from Sophia
renouncing him for his letter of proposal to Lady Bellaston—all
of which calamities, as Fielding remarks, are "owing to his
imprudence" (V, 247–48).

Allworthy himself after his reconciliation with Jones, wonders
at the dangers to which "imprudence alone may subject virtue,"
and distinguishes between "those faults which candor may con-
strue into imprudence, and those which can be deduced from
villainy only," which seems to imply that all of Jones's faults,
including even the·shameful alliance with Lady Bellaston, are
basically the result of his imprudence. For true prudence will
always counsel virtue, not out of crass self-interest and mere
attention to appearances but because prudence is the guardian
of innocence. This does not mean, however, that Fielding excuses
Jones's faults as inconsequential or implies that they are not
vices. Like Jones himself, who tells Allworthy that "I have not
been punished more than I have deserved," he sees that his hero
has committed "follies and vices more than enough to repent and
to be ashamed of" (V, 346–47). All he is asking us to recognize
is that these vices proceed, *in Jones's case*, not from a wicked
nature but from a defective wisdom. But imprudence is dangerous because others, not privy to the minds and motives of the

---

[1]Cf. the *Champion* for Nov. 22, 1739: "I would . . . by no Means recommend to Mankind to cultivate Deceit, or endeavour to appear what they are not. . . . I would only
convince my Readers, *That it is not enough to have Virtue, without we also take Care to
preserve, by a certain Decency and Dignity of Behaviour, the outward Appearance of it
also.*" Elsewhere, however, Fielding seems to disallow to true virtue even thus much of
"ostentation." "There is nothing so oppugnant to True Virtue, and true Understanding," he wrote in the *True Patriot* for June 10, 1746, "as Ostentation. The innate Dignity
which always attends these, will not stoop to mean and laborious Acts to inform others
of what they conceive must be sufficiently apparent to them. Cunning, on the contrary,
is eternally teaching the Counterfeits of all three a thousand little painful Tricks, to
represent Falsehood as Truth, and to gain a Belief and Admiration by Imposition."

actor, must judge him only by his *actions*, which, in Jones's case, seem to argue precisely the kind of wicked nature he does not have. When the wicked Lord Fellamar, upon seeing Sophia for the first time after having made a violent attempt on her virtue, delivers himself of "many declarations of the most pure and ardent passion," Sophia says, "My lord, you must be yourself conscious whether your former behavior to me hath been consistent with the professions you now make" (V, 279). But even after the letter of proposal and other matters have been explained, Sophia, judging Jones by the same standard, has difficulty believing his renewed declarations of "the purest passion" as well: "Indeed, you have acted strangely. Can I believe the passion you have professed to me to be sincere?" And when he argues that he has repented and reformed, she replies, "Sincere repentance, Mr. Jones, . . . will obtain the pardon of the sinner, but it is from One who is a perfect judge of that sincerity. A human mind may be imposed on; nor is there any infallible method to prevent it" (V, 361–62).

This is the human condition of judgment which makes prudence necessary for the good man. It is not enough to have basically good motives; prudence must see to it that one's actions *appear* good as well (or at least that they do not appear positively evil) or else suffer the situation of Jones in relation to Sophia: "guilty as I am, my guilt unfortunately appears to her in ten times blacker than the real colors" (V, 349). The "real colors" here represent the extent of Jones's vice; the appearance to Sophia represents the extent of his imprudence.

So far as worldly rewards and punishments are concerned, then, it is not so much virtue or vice which determine them as prudence or imprudence. Sophia's original estrangement from Jones is not so much the consequence of his sexual adventure with Mrs. Waters at the inn in Upton (which again she is willing to forgive) as of his loose tongue and his imprudent trust in Partridge, which result in Sophia's name being dragged publicly through the whole sordid affair and which cause Jones to appear in the character of a rake vulgarly boasting of his success with the ladies. Some readers, Fielding says, may consider the calamity of Sophia's flight from Upton and her renunciation of Jones "a just punishment for his wickedness with regard to women," and others "may comfort themselves in their vices by flattering their own hearts that the characters of men are rather owing to accident than to virtue." But the moral which Fielding himself discovers "would alike contradict both these conclusions, and would show that these incidents contribute only to confirm the great, useful, and uncommon doctrine, which it is the purpose of this whole work to inculcate" (IV, 336–37)—namely, the necessity of prudence.

Jones's reconciliation with Sophia is not effected by his renewed professions of love and virtue, then, but by the new evidence supplied by his London friends—Nightingale, Nancy, and Mrs. Miller—of the benevolent actions which reveal his true goodness of heart. He is still "guilty of a great indiscretion" (V, 361), as he tells Sophia himself, in the matter of the letter to Lady Bellaston, but with this exception (which is complicated, as we have seen, by his dilemma of trying to extricate himself honorably from a dishonorable situation) Jones's actions demonstrate that he has at last acquired the prudence of outward behavior that is the necessary complement of his intrinsic good nature.

But it is not Jones, of course, who is the exemplar of prudence in the novel. He acquires prudence in the end, but through the greater part of the story he is rather the representative of imprudence. Nor can Squire Allworthy be considered the ideal prudent man. He is never so wildly imprudent as Jones, but he too has a "blamable want of caution and diffidence in the veracity of others" (IV, 89) and his good nature is too easily imposed on by the pious professions of such as Thwackum and Square and Blifil. "Thus is the prudence of the best of heads often defeated by the tenderness of the best of hearts" (V, 229), Fielding remarks when Allworthy allows Blifil to persuade him, against his better judgment, to let him continue his suit to Sophia. There are only two ways, he explains, by which men become possessed of the "caution and diffidence" of prudence: "The one is from long experience, and the other is from nature; which last . . . is infinitely the better of the two, not only as we are masters of it much earlier in life, but as it is much more infallible and conclusive. . . . As Jones had not this gift from nature, he was too young to have gained it by experience; for at the diffident wisdom which is to be acquired this way, we seldom arrive till very late in life" (IV, 89). Allworthy is presumably an example of one who, like Jones, lacks the natural gift of prudence and, having to learn it from experience, remains fallible.

But there is one character in the novel who, while not absolutely infallible in the matter of prudence, comes as close to the mark as Fielding probably believes possible in an imperfect world. It is Sophia (as her name is surely intended to suggest) rather than Allworthy who is the model of the kind of prudence he is recommending in *Tom Jones*, and thus she is a more important character in the thematic scheme of the novel than has generally been recognized. She is thoroughly good and innocent, but unlike Allworthy and Jones she sees through Blifil from the very beginning. When, jealous of her preference for Jones, he maliciously releases her pet bird and then defends the act by pleading the cruelty of the bird's confinement and its natural right to liberty (an argument Fielding neatly refutes by having the bird carried off by a hawk the moment it is freed), no one except Sophia, who imputes the "action of Master Blifil to his anger" (III, 150), sees the true inner motive behind the outward act. Although Jones and Squire Western agree in condemning Blifil, neither is concerned with his motive so much as with the act itself: it caused pain to Sophia; therefore it must be wrong. Thwackum and Square, of course, defend the motive as well as the act, Thwackum by arguing that Blifil's behavior proceeded from "a Christian motive" and Square that it was according to "the law of nature," and even Allworthy, though he is "sorry for what his nephew had done," believes that "he acted rather from a generous than unworthy motive. . . . (For as to that malicious purpose which Sophia suspected, it never once entered into the head of Mr. Allworthy)" (III, 153–54). Sophia alone, apparently, has the gift of prudence from nature: "She honored Tom Jones, and scorned Master Blifil, almost as soon as she knew the meaning of those two words" (III, 157), and when Blifil begins to call on her as a suitor, with the blessing of both Squire Allworthy and her father, Sophia again is the only one who recognizes his true motive—the prospect of inheriting Squire Western's fortune. "For simplicity, when set on its guard," Fielding explains, "is often a match for cunning" (III, 352).

Earlier he had defined "simplicity," as applied to Sophia, as meaning not that she was "silly" (which is how the word is "generally understood"), but that she lacked "that useful art which females convert to so many good purposes in life, and which, as it rather arises from the heart than from the head, is often the property of the silliest of women" (III, 344). Sophia is not without "art," but it is the good art of genuine prudence and arises not from her heart, which is pure and innocent, but from her head, which must, in the interests of virtue, sometimes borrow the cunning of the vicious. Thus when Sophia, determined to flee to London rather than be forced into marriage with the man whom she alone recognizes as a villain, prepares her escape by first tricking her Aunt Western into turning Mrs. Honour out of the house, Fielding observes that Sophia "indeed succeeded admirably well in her deceit, considering it was the first she had ever practised. And, to say the truth, I have often concluded that the honest part of mankind would be much too hard for the knavish, if they could bring themselves to incur the guilt, or thought it worth their while to take the trouble" (IV, 17).

Fielding's use of the words "deceit" and "guilt" is not ironic in the usual sense, but it would seem to reflect his sense of the inadequacy of absolute moral categories in the world of "common men and not of philosophers" and his appreciation of the complexity of a morality "Beyond the fix'd and settled rules / Of vice and virtue in the schools, / Beyond the letter of the law." Only the stay-at-home, passive virtue which never busies itself "without-doors" can afford to disdain the necessity for beating the knavish at their own game. Once Sophia resolves to leave home and make her own way in the world, her virtue, like Joseph Andrews', becomes the "certain relative quality" which Fielding plainly regards as *true* virtue, and this active virtue requires an active prudence for its protection. When he tells us later that Sophia is guilty of what "may be called a kind of dishonesty" (IV, 283) in suppressing all reference to Jones from the account she gives to her cousin Harriet Fitzpatrick of her flight, he is really commending her for the very kind of prudence which Jones, with his naive trust in the good faith of others, so conspicuously lacks. In the next book, in fact, when Lawyer Dowling (Blifil's secret confederate) asks Jones to tell *his* story, Fielding explicitly points up the contrast between his hero and heroine by observing that "Jones, who in the compliance of his disposition (though not in his prudence) a little resembled his lovely Sophia, was easily prevailed on to satisfy Mr. Dowling's curiosity" (IV, 344).

But the crucial distinction between "deceit" in defense of virtue, which is prudence, and deceit in defense of vice, which is hypocrisy—the separation, in short, of the virtue from its bordering vice—is effected in Fielding's account of the arrival in London of Sophia and Mrs. Fitzpatrick. Sophia's cousin had also told Sophia her story, so similar in outward circumstances to Sophia's, of her flight from a tyrannical husband, and in fact it is because of "the apparent openness and explicit sincerity of the other lady" (IV, 283) that he pretends to be embarrassed by Sophia's "dishonest" omission of Jones from her own narrative. But when Mrs. Fitzpatrick is met at the inn by a "friend," a nobleman who was not mentioned in her story but is obviously her lover ("as the lady did not think it material enough to relate to her friend," says Fielding coyly, "we would not at that time impart it to the reader [or] . . . interrupt her narrative by giving a hint of what seemed to her of too little importance to be mentioned") (IV, 288–89) he clearly intends the surface parallels between the situations of Sophia and Mrs. Fitzpatrick to accentuate the vital difference between prudence and hypocrisy in relation to their inner motives. Mrs. Fitzpatrick, continuing to play the role of virtue in Sophia's presence, "would by no means consent to accept a bed in the mansion of the peer," and Fielding, in one of the richest ironic passages of the novel, comments: "The most formal appearance of virtue, when it is only an appearance, may, perhaps, in very abstracted considerations, seem to be rather less commendable than virtue itself without this formality; but it will, however, be always more commended; and this, I believe, will be granted by all, that it is necessary, unless in some very particular cases, for every woman to support either the one or the other" (IV, 295–96).

Fielding is clearly rejecting here the notion that prudence is *mere* attention to appearance. Mrs. Fitzpatrick is one of the prime examples of this kind of false prudence—which is really the bordering vice of hypocrisy—and is contrasted with Sophia in this respect throughout, just as Jones's imprudence is played against Sophia's prudence in the alternating books which detail their roughly parallel adventures on the road and in London. [But the most difficult distinction Fielding must make in defining the nature of true prudence is to show that Sophia's gift of penetrating false appearances is not the kind of cynical distrust of human nature which makes Mrs. Western and Lady Bellaston, for example, so eternally suspicious of other people's motives.

Fielding's other exemplary characters—Parson Adams, Joseph Andrews (in the beginning at least), Squire Allworthy, even Amelia and Dr. Harrison—are victimized by hypocrites because their own goodness makes them in one degree or another blind to the wickedness of others. Their innocence, in fact, is in part at least defined by their lack of suspicion. So in making Sophia the model of prudence, Fielding takes great pains to assure us that her shrewdness is a matter of a natural sagacity of mind which in no way compromises her basic innocence and goodness of heart. When she begins to entertain doubts that Mrs. Fitzpatrick is all she professes to be, he asks us not to "fix the odious character of suspicion on Sophia . . . till we have first suggested a word or two . . . touching suspicion in general." There are, he says, "two degrees" of suspicion. The first is "from the heart" and "seems to denote some previous inward impulse" which "often forms its own objects; sees what is not, and always more than really exists." It "observes not only upon the actions, but upon the words and looks of men; and, as it proceeds from the heart of the observer, so it drives into the heart of the observed." But because this kind of suspicion often projects its own guilt on others, it causes "many sad mischiefs and most grievous heartaches to innocence and virtue" and is therefore "a very pernicious evil in itself." But there is "a second degree of this quality" which "seems to arise from the head. This is, indeed, no other than the faculty of seeing what is before your eyes, and of drawing conclusions from what you see." It judges men, in short, by their actions; and if it is therefore not infallible, since even actions are sometimes misleading, the fault, as in the case of Sophia's mistaken judgment of Jones, is usually not with the prudence of the beholder but with the imprudence of the actor. This kind of suspicion is "altogether as bitter an enemy to guilt as the former is to innocence," and "to confess the truth, of this degree of suspicion I believe Sophia was guilty" (IV, 296–97).

Fielding's confidence in Sophia's purity of soul, then, allows him to excuse her a measure of deceit in the prudent interests of arming her virtue against the more practiced and cynical cunning of Mrs. Western and Lady Bellaston. When she encounters Jones in the latter's house, she prudently pretends not to know him, and when Lady Bellaston (who, thanks to Mrs. Honour's indiscretion, knows all about their relationship), enjoying her discomfiture, suggests that it is he, Sophia, "affecting a laugh," sticks to her story, even when Lady Bellaston says, "I . . . almost question whether you have dealt ingenuously with me." There is no doubt that Fielding sees Sophia's deception as entirely justified, but she herself, he tells us, "was not perfectly easy under this first practice of deceit [actually it is her second at least]: upon which . . . she reflected with the highest uneasiness and conscious shame," and in fact it is by means of her uneasiness and shame that he convinces us that her basic innocence remains intact, "for the frame of her mind was too delicate to bear the thought of having been guilty of a falsehood, however qualified by circumstances" (V, 89–90).

Always the realist, Fielding is willing to grant that not even Sophia is perfect, for "we do not pretend to introduce any infallible characters into this history" (III, 125). But in the real world he is trying to describe, the good in any case must acquire some of the craftiness of the bad if they are to survive in that world. The point is, however, that Sophia, in so doing, never really compromises her purity of soul, and she is deceitful, unlike Blifil, Mrs. Fitzpatrick, Mrs. Western, Lady Bellaston, *et al.*, only in self-defense. This is the true prudence which Fielding the realist advocates, and the condition of the good person who lacks Sophia's ability to adapt the weapons of deceit to the defense of virtue is suggested in Mrs. Miller: "This poor creature might, indeed, be called simplicity itself. She was one of that order of mortals who are apt to believe everything which is said to them; to whom nature hath neither indulged the offensive nor defensive weapons of deceit, and who are consequently liable to be imposed upon by any one who will only be at the expense of a little falsehood for that purpose" (V, 283). And dramatically this proposition is proved by the ease with which Mrs. Western gets from the well-intentioned Mrs. Miller all of Sophia's secrets.

The benefits which come to Jones at the end of the novel in the shape of the discovery of his true parentage and thus of his eligibility to marry Sophia are not the consequences of his virtue but rather, as in *Joseph Andrews*, of chance. But his *worthiness* to bear the title of a gentleman, to be the heir of Allworthy, and to be the husband of Sophia has been proved by his actions. "Whatever in the nature of Jones had a tendency to vice," Fielding assures us in the second to the last paragraph, "has been corrected by continual conversation with this good man, and by his union with the lovely and virtuous Sophia. He hath also, by reflection on his past follies, acquired a discretion and prudence very uncommon in one of his lively parts" (V, 373). The ideal goodness Fielding is trying to define in *Tom Jones* is the union, symbolized, perhaps, by the marriage of Jones and Sophia, of the warm liveliness of good nature with the cooler "distinguishing faculty" of prudence, or, to adapt Fielding's own definition of true greatness, "the union of a good heart with a good head."[2] The marriage is intended, presumably, to show not only that these two qualities are not incompatible but that they are in fact complementary. Jones, we are assured, for all his acquisition of prudence, remains a lively young man, and though we may have some difficulty imagining him in this new character we do not, even here, have to take it on faith that such a "very uncommon" phenomenon is possible. For in Sophia we are given a dramatic example of a prudence in action that is as lively as the imprudence of Jones and provides a positive alternative to his reckless and indiscriminate good nature at nearly every turn.

Yet, in spite of Fielding's careful dramatic definition of this key moral term, many readers of *Tom Jones* have found its moral theme offensively shallow. Dr. Johnson was almost certainly thinking of *Tom Jones*—and particularly, perhaps, of Fielding's statement in the Dedication that he has taken the inculcation of prudence for his moral because "it is much easier to make good men wise, than to make bad men good" (III, 12)—when he wrote

---

[2]See above, p. 108, n. 77.

in the *Rambler* for March 31, 1750, that "that observation which is called knowledge of the world," which too many modern writers of fiction seem to have taken for their province, "will be found much more frequently to make men cunning than good." As a result, he explained, these writers have not yet learned "to give the power of counteracting fraud, without the temptation to practice it; to initiate youth by mock encounters in the art of necessary defence, and to increase prudence without impairing virtue."[3] The Rev. Edmund Cartwright introduced his sonnet on "Prudence" early in the next century with the remark that Fielding "and other loose moralists" consider prudence "but as a sneaking virtue at the best," and the philosopher T. H. Green was apparently reflecting a similar view when he wrote in 1862 that Fielding's moral, "if moral it can be called, is simply the importance of . . . prudence."[4]

More recent critics who have tried to come to terms with the prudence theme of *Tom Jones* have usually been more sympathetic, but there is reason to believe that their comprehension of Fielding's use of the word is still incomplete. A. E. Dyson maintains that "the ridicule in *Tom Jones* is used in support of a particular moral theory . . . which prefers 'good nature' to prudential calculation"[5]—a reading which ignores Fielding's insistence on the union of the good heart and the good head and which, looking only at the portrait of Tom Jones, whose goodness Fielding clearly regards as only half-formed, ignores the contrastive study of Sophia as the model of prudential good nature. Ethel Thornbury, guilty of the same oversimplification, declares that "prudential morality, a narrow, unhealthy performing of what is conventional just because it *is* prudent, is made to seem thoroughly absurd and thoroughly bad"[6]—which can be accepted only if one rejects Fielding's positive definition

---

[3]*Rambler*, 6th ed. (London, 1763), 1: 20.
[4]Both cited by Blanchard, pp. 293, 466.
[5]"Satiric and Comic Theory in Relation to Fielding," *Modern Languages Quarterly*, 18 (1957): 237. Another recent critic, Morris Golden, argues along the same lines that Fielding's novels always show prudence to be in conflict with charity: "Morally, spontaneous charity is always admirable, even where it is ignorant or foolish; but prudent actions depend for their status on the motivation of the agent. Whenever prudence conflicts with ideals, it should be summarily abandoned." *Fielding's Moral Psychology*, p. 75.
[6]Ethel Margaret Thornbury, *Henry Fielding's Theory of the Comic Prose Epic*, p. 162.

of prudence and treats his negative definition, the examples of *false* prudence, as representing the true meaning of the word; and this, surely, is the opposite of his intention as a reformer of corrupt language.

Even Eleanor N. Hutchens, whose recent article " 'Prudence' in *Tom Jones"* is by far the most intelligent and thoroughgoing study of this neglected aspect of the novel that has yet appeared,[7] does not seem fully to understand Fielding's purpose. She recognizes, refreshingly, that "the necessity for prudence as a concomitant of goodness is one of the major themes of *Tom Jones,"* and she places her finger squarely on the source of traditional critical confusion when she observes, "Yet . . . the words 'prudence,' 'prudent,' and 'prudential' are used unfavorably three times as often as they are used favorably. Nearly every unadmirable character in the novel is described as prudent or is shown advocating prudence." If the "prudence" of Miss Bridget Allworthy and Mrs. Deborah Wilkins is old-maid prudishness, Partridge's "prudence" is cowardice and timidity. Mrs. Western is "prudent" in the sense of ruthlessly ambitious, and is particularly interested in arranging for Sophia a "prudent" (i.e., materially and socially advantageous) marriage. But as Miss Hutchens points out, it is "the arch-villain of *Tom Jones,* young Blifil, [who] is the most 'prudent' character in the novel." Repeatedly Fielding describes Blifil's cunning, hypocritical concern for appearances as "prudent," and just as Mrs. Fitzpatrick's hypocrisy is played against Sophia's genuine prudence, so is Blifil's calculating attention to the appearance of virtue at the expense of the substance played against Jones's careless disregard for the appearance of his actions even when they are intrinsically good. "It is one of the larger ironies of the novel," as Miss Hutchens says, "that part of the task of the hero is to acquire one of the chief traits of the villain." But Miss Hutchens is mistaken when she implies that this trait is prudence. For the point is that though Jones, to be sure, lacks prudence, Blifil lacks

[7] " 'Prudence' in *Tom Jones*: A Study of Connotative Irony," *Philological Quarterly,* 39 (1960): 496–507. This essay has since been reprinted as Chapter V of Miss Hutchens' *Irony in "Tom Jones"* (University of Alabama, 1965), pp. 101–18. Henry Knight Miller, in his recent article "Some Functions of Rhetoric in *Tom Jones,"* *Philological Quarterly,* 45 (1966): 222–23, also has some brief but excellent remarks on the subject.

it as well. For surely the lesson of Mrs. Fitzpatrick is that cunning without virtue is *false* prudence. What Jones must acquire is Blifil's attention to appearances while retaining, like Sophia, his own basic commitment to virtue, this combination being, in Fielding's view, *true* prudence.

For all her excellent analysis of Fielding's ironic variations on the prudence theme in *Tom Jones*, in fact, Miss Hutchens' explanation of why he uses the word ironically is ultimately unsatisfactory: "While teaching the desirability of prudence, Fielding wishes to say at the same time that it is not all-sufficient and should not be allowed to get in the way of more important qualities. Its desirability he teaches directly, by straightforward exposition and illustration; its dangers . . . he illuminates obliquely through connotative irony." But in fact it is not the dangers of *prudence* that Fielding's irony illuminates. It is the dangers of a hypocritical cunning that in popular usage is *called* prudence. His irony, here as elsewhere, is an attempt to reclaim an important moral term from the corruptions of language.

In a footnote at the end of her article, Miss Hutchens observes that "a few years after Fielding's death, Charles Churchill noted a complete change in the use of the word:

> Prudence, of old a sacred term, implied
> Virtue, with godlike wisdom for her guide,
> But now in general use is known to mean
> The stalking-horse of vice, and folly's screen.
> The sense perverted we retain the name;
> Hypocrisy and Prudence are the same."[8]

But Miss Hutchens misses the point of Fielding's irony and does him an injustice which is itself ironic when she wonders if *Tom Jones* "influenced" this perversion of the word. For of course, as with "greatness" and "virtue" and "love" and "honor," it is the perversion of the word that brings it into his ironic vocabulary. He does not, as Miss Hutchens thinks, take a word with "favorable" connotations and *make* it ironic by putting it in an "unfavorable" context. He rather takes a word which, by virtue of the abusage of "custom," has already a kind of built-in ironic

[8]The Churchill poem is "Night: An Epistle to Robert Lloyd" (1762).

potential, and playing this ironigenic corrupt sense against the "proper and original" meaning of the word that is developed in the definition by action, seeks to restore the word to its rightful dignity of meaning.

For "prudence" (*prudentia*) was in its original sense, like "charity," one of the cardinal virtues, with an honorable genealogy that can be traced back as far as Plato and that comes through Aristotle and the Stoics into Cicero's *De officiis* and thence into St. Ambrose's *De officiis ministrorum* and the mainstream of Christian ethics, where it meant, traditionally, the practical wisdom (as opposed to speculative or theological wisdom) of moral conduct. To the "Divines and moral Writers" whom Fielding regularly takes as his standard of proper usage, "prudence," as a historian of philosophy sums up the traditional meaning, was "involved in moral excellence; for it is required to determine in any particular case that due limitation of feeling and action in which perfect virtue consists, and it cannot be conceived as existing apart from moral excellence—we do not count a man practically wise for such mere intellectual cleverness as a vicious man may exhibit. The man we count wise must be not merely skillful in the selection of means to any ends; his ends must also be rightly chosen."[9] And until the end of the seventeenth century this appears to have been the sense in which the English word was dominantly used. Charles Herle, in 1665, treats "worldly Wisdom" and "Moral Prudence" as entirely distinct categories; Bunyan, in *Pilgrim's Progress* (1678) makes Prudence one of the damsels at the Palace Beautiful (along with her sisters, Piety and Charity) and does not suggest that she has anything in common with Mr. Worldly Wiseman; for Milton, according to Arnold Stein, "wisdom and prudence are not separable"; and Sir John Denham declared near the close of the century,

> He's truly Prudent, who can separate
> Honest from Vile, and still adhere to that.[10]

[9]Henry Sidgwick, *Outlines of the History of Ethics* (London, 1886), p. 65. I am indebted to this work for much of my discussion of the history of "prudence" above.

[10]Charles Herle, *Wisdomes Tripos* (London, 1655); Arnold Stein, *Heroic Knowledge* (Minneapolis: University of Minnesota Press, 1957), p. 204; Sir John Denham, "Of Prudence," *Poems and Translations*, 5th ed. (London, 1709), p. 140.

But Fielding was not alone in sensing that the word was falling into disrepute. In *Humane Prudence* (1680), William de Bretain comes so close to stating what was to be the theme of *Tom Jones*—and in language that is echoed by Fielding—that one is tempted to consider it a possible source of the novel: "Prudence is an Armory, wherein are as well Defensive and Offensive Weapons . . . Policy and Religion, as they do well together, so they do as ill asunder; the one being too cunning to be Good, the other too simple to be Safe; therefore some few Scruples of the Wisdom of the Serpent, mixt with the Innocency of the Dove, will be an excellent Ingredient in all your Actions." But he warned too that "Knavery and Cunning pass sometimes for Prudence, and true Wisdom for Silliness and Simplicity."[11] And Thomas Manningham, in a sermon preached in 1693, declared that "tho' Prudence in the common acceptation of the World passes now for any Cunning Contrivance, for any dextrous Management of an Affair, whatever means are us'd; yet the ancient Moralists never allow'd a wicked Man to be call'd Prudent."[12]

These, of course, are the very distinctions which Fielding, in his contrastive studies of Blifil and Jones, Mrs. Fitzpatrick and Sophia, insists on in *Tom Jones*. But the extent to which the separation of the virtue of prudence from a contaminating confusion with its bordering vices was a preoccupation of the age has not been appreciated. "Since we are fallen into an Age full of Artifice; wherein Words, which were invented to express our Thoughts, seem now to be applyed only to the concealing them with a good Grace," wrote Thomas Fuller in *Introductio ad prudentiam* (1726), "it must be confessed, that Innocence had need of a Mask. . . . Honesty ought to have Wisdom (tho' not ill Craft) for its Guard."[13] Nathaniel Lardner, in *Counsels of Prudence for the Use of Young People* (1735)—taking for his text, like De Bretain before him, the biblical injunction (Matt. 10:16), "Behold, I send you forth as sheep in the midst of wolves: be ye therefore wise as serpents, and harmless as doves"—argues that

[11]Pp. 68, 98–99.
[12]*Of Religious Prudence: A Sermon Preach'd before the Queen, . . . on Sunday, Sept. 17, 1693* (London, 1694), p. 11.
[13]P. 224.

"Good men therefore are obliged to be upon their guard, and make use of some methods of defense and security," but reminds his readers that "Prudence . . . supposes the maintaining of innocence and integrity" and that "we are not out of a pretense of discretion to desert the cause of truth."[14]

Swift, elaborating on the same idea in *A Letter on Mr. McCulla's Project about Halfpence* (1729), both echoes De Bretain and provides a model himself for Fielding's assertion in the Dedication of *Tom Jones* that "it is much easier to make good men wise, than to make bad men good," when he observes that "those who are honest and best intentioned, may be the instruments of as much mischief . . ., for want of cunning, as the greatest knaves; and more, because of the charitable opinion which they are apt to have of others. Therefore, how to join the prudence of the serpent with the innocency of the dove . . . is the most difficult point. It is not so hard to find an honest man, as to make this honest man active, and vigilant, and skilful."[15] Pope, in the same *Peri Bathous* passage which advocates "converting Vices into their bordering Virtues," suggests as one example of this rhetorical art that "Cowardice may be metamorphos'd into Prudence"—a corruption of the word that Fielding registers in his portrait of the "prudent" Partridge—and in *The Dunciad*, where the four Cardinal Virtues in their perverted sense appear as guardians of the throne of Dulness, Prudence has become the cynical expediency "whose glass presents th' approaching jayl."[16] Dr. Johnson, who defined "prudence" in the *Dictionary* as "Wisdom applied to practice" but seems to have believed that the effect of *Tom Jones* would be "to make men cunning [rather] than good," nevertheless recognizes, in *The Vanity of Human Wishes*, published the same year as *Tom Jones* (1749), the same distinction Fielding makes between prudence and cunning and the same possibility of confusion with its bordering vices which informs Fielding's irony. When Virtue is missing, Johnson says, its "guardians yield, by force superior ply'd; / By Int'rest, Prudence; and by Flatt'ry, Pride."[17]

[14]Pp. 7–9.

[15]*Prose Works*, 12: 102.

[16]Bk. I, line 51, Twickenham ed., 5: 274.

[17]Lines 339–40, *The Poems of Samuel Johnson*, ed. David Nichol Smith and Edward L. McAdam (Oxford: Clarendon Press, 1941), p. 47.

But if we want to isolate the most likely immediate source of Fielding's own conviction that the word in his time was becoming corrupt, we need look no further, probably, than the work which also provided, in a more conspicuous way, the corrupt sense of "virtue" to which he addressed himself in *Joseph Andrews*. For next to "virtue" itself, the quality which Richardson's Pamela most often claims for herself is "prudence." Writing to her mother and father in the opening letters of the book, she proudly recounts Mr. B's opinion that she "had a good share of prudence," and, a little later, Mrs. Jervis' declaration that "she was very well pleased to see my prudence and modesty, and that I kept all the fellows at a distance." To which Pamela adds, by way of commentary on her prudence, "I am sure I am not proud, and carry it civilly to every body; but yet, methinks, I cannot bear to be looked at by these men-servants, for they seem as if they would look one through." And when Mr. B asks Mrs. Jervis if Pamela is never molested by these same male servants, Mrs. Jervis replies (as Pamela reports it), "No, indeed, sir, . . . she keeps herself so much to herself, and yet behaves so prudently, that they all esteem her, and *shew her as great respect, as if she was a gentlewoman born*" (my italics).[18]

Richardson, we may be sure, was as sincerely moral, according to his own lights, in his conception of Pamela's "prudence" as he doubtlessly was in his conception of her "virtue." But the recurrent appearance of the word in such compromising contexts—so similar to the *ironic* contexts in which Fielding uses it in *Tom Jones*—is not likely to have escaped Fielding's contemptuous notice when he read the novel. Richardson's use of the word betrays his own, if not his heroine's, association of "prudence" with social rank and its material rewards. "Prudence," like "virtue," is clearly for Richardson primarily a *social* value, a means to a social end, and if *Joseph Andrews* is Fielding's attempt to rescue "virtue" as a moral term from its degradation

---

[18]Samuel Richardson, *Pamela*, Everyman ed. (London: Dent, 1914), 1: 5, 6, 17. See also the effusive response of her young ward Miss Goodwin in Part II to Pamela's cautionary tale of "the amiable PRUDENTIA" who "endeavours to appropriate to herself the domestic virtues, which shall one day make her the crown of some worthy gentleman's earthly happiness: and which, *of course*, . . . will secure and heighten her own." " 'O Madam! Madam!' said the dear creature . . ., 'PRUDENTIA is YOU!—Is YOU indeed! It *can* be nobody else!—Oh teach me, good God! to follow *your* example, and I shall be a SECOND PRUDENTIA!' " 2: 470–71.

in Richardson's popular and influential novel, *Tom Jones* may be regarded as a similar attempt to reclaim the "proper and original" moral sense of "prudence."[19]

[19]There is no evidence, however, that Fielding's efforts in behalf of "prudence" succeeded in practical terms in arresting the degeneracy of the word into the sense of worldly policy that has been its dominant meaning ever since. Only two years, in fact, after the publication of *Tom Jones*, the moralist John Milner, in *Instructions for Youth, Prudential, Moral, and Divine* (1751), was opposing worldly "prudence" to "Moral Wisdom." "The sense perverted," as Churchill put it in 1762, "we retain the name," and when Sheridan has Sir Oliver Surface denounce the scandalmongers in *The School for Scandal* (1777) as "a set of malicious, prating, prudent gossips" it is without any of the ironic reservation that qualifies similar passages in Fielding. Jane Austen, it is true—that last of the Augustans—can still insist on the "original" meaning of the word. "You shall not endeavour to persuade yourself or me," declares Elizabeth in *Pride and Prejudice* (1813), "that selfishness is prudence"; and later she asks rhetorically, "What is the difference in matrimonial affairs between the mercenary and the prudent motive?" But for practical purposes the battle for the restoration of "prudence" to the serious vocabulary of ethics had already been lost, probably, before Fielding joined it in *Tom Jones*.

Chapter VI

"A MIRROUR FOR THE UNDERSTANDING": THE IRONY OF DRAMATIZED AUTHORSHIP

Fielding's use of dramatic technique in the novels is not, then, as has sometimes been suggested, merely a kind of habitual carry-over from his career as a playwright, any more than irony is his "natural speech." Both are conscious and deliberate attempts to approximate in his fiction the conditions of truth in a hypocritical and nominalistic world where it is "the actions of men," as opposed to "their own words" or to "what others say" of them, that are "the justest interpreters of their thoughts and the truest standards by which we may judge them" (XIV, 289–90). Even in his formal definitions, to be sure, Fielding insists on the test of action: Patriotism is not just the love of one's country, but "the Love of one's Country carried into Action."[1] Virtue is "not the bare knowing the right way, but the constant and steady walking in it" (XVI, 97). But dramatic "exemplification" allows the writer to treat moral ideas, which, as precepts, have been rendered all but meaningless by the corruption of language, as Shaftesburian "subjects of Sense . . . presented to our Eye." For as Fielding explains in the Dedication of *Tom Jones*, "an example is a kind of picture, in which virtue becomes, as it were, an object of sight" (III, 12). And in a review in the *Covent-Garden Journal* No. 24 he finds Charlotte Lennox's *The Female Quixote* inferior to Cervantes' original because the story of the former "is conveyed, as it were, through our Ears, and partakes of the Coldness of History or Narration," whereas *Don Quixote* "hath all the force of a Representation; it is in a Manner subjected to the Eyes."

Yet one of the principal objections which has been brought against Fielding's own novels, from his time to the present, has

---

[1] *True Patriot*, Nov. 12, 1745.

been that they depend too much on "precept" and "cold" narration. There is too much which is not "subjected to the Eyes"—too many stylized set speeches and stilted interpolated tales, too much direct moral and esthetic commentary and obvious manipulation of plot and style. Lord Monboddo declared that these stylistic inconsistencies and authorial intrusions destroy "the probability of the narrative,"[2] and Ian Watt, complaining almost two hundred years later of Fielding's inability "to convey . . . larger moral significance through character and action alone," arrives at nearly the same conclusion: the effect, he says, is "to diminish the authenticity of the narrative."[3] Another recent critic, Irma Z. Sherwood, concludes that the result of Fielding's shifting style and of his failure to fuse commentary with action and character is to "focus attention on the mechanism of the work and on the author's attitude toward his material, rather than on the material itself."[4] But an interesting corollary to this traditional view of Fielding's "failure" as a narrative artist is the general concession by those who have held it that this very failure is somehow productive of his finest artistic effects. "His remarks," as Leslie Stephen put it, "are often so admirable that we prefer the interpolations to the main currents of narrative."[5] Even Ian Watt, though he continues stubbornly to regard the authorial intrusions as a sin against "formal realism," allows that "our residual impression of dignity and generosity comes mainly from the passages where Fielding is speaking in his own person."[6]

But who is to say that effects so arrived at are less legitimate or otherwise of a lower order of achievement than the more or less pure realistic illusionism of Defoe and Richardson, or that "the author's attitude toward his material" cannot be a proper part of "the material itself"? Alan D. McKillop, noting how in Richardson's *Pamela* Mr. B intercepts Pamela's letters and later gains access to her journal, and how the information he gleans

---

[2]Cited by Blanchard, p. 227.
[3]*The Rise of the Novel: Studies in Defoe, Richardson, and Fielding* (Berkeley and Los Angeles: University of California Press, 1957), p. 285.
[4]"The Novelists as Commentators," *The Age of Johnson* (New Haven: Yale University Press, 1949), pp. 119, 124.
[5]*Hours in a Library* (London, 1907), 3: 9.
[6]*Rise of the Novel*, p. 287.

often influences his own subsequent behavior, observes that "thus not only the earlier action but the record of the earlier action and the analysis and reception of that record condition the story. The writing of the novel is part of the action of the novel."[7] This is an interesting and useful insight, but it is inaccurately expressed. For surely in *Pamela* it is the writing of the *journal* which is part of the action, not the writing of the *novel*, which is never overtly acknowledged by Richardson at all. It is rather Fielding—in his prefatory chapters and digressions, his self-conscious shifts of style, his mocking chapter headings, his frank manipulations of plot—who truly makes the writing of the novel a part of its action.

If we therefore find that the author, struggling with his materials, is the most dramatic "presence" in the novel, the sharpest objective image, this is not a flaw but a triumph of Fielding's art, a victory over the forces of linguistic corruption which have made precept and narration "cold" and suspect verbal forms. The corrupt medium of truth is purified by verbal irony; the corrupt agent of truth is purified by the irony of dramatized authorship. And in both instances the effect is the illusion of objectivity. The ironic vocabulary and the burlesque diction, always in one way or another at odds with the objective facts the reader is allowed to perceive beyond the words, stand for the falsifying surface of language which the reader must break through if he is to discover the reality of character and event underneath. The pointed rephrasing of ironic passages into direct statement (Captain Blifil "was one of those wise men who regard beauty in the other sex as a very worthless and superficial qualification; or, *to speak more truly*, who rather choose to

---

[7]*Early Masters of English Fiction*, p. 62. McKillop's excellent chapter on Fielding contains what I believe is the first of a series of recent defenses of Fielding's authorial commentary (pp. 108–111). The present essay is indebted, in a general way, to Wayne C. Booth's admirable discussion of the problem in *The Rhetoric of Fiction* (Chicago: University of Chicago Press, 1961), esp. pp. 211–21, and, more particularly, to William B. Coley's stimulating article, "Gide and Fielding," *Comparative Literature*, 11 (1959): 1–15. But see also Booth's "The Self-Conscious Narrator in Comic Fiction before *Tristram Shandy*," *PMLA*, 67 (1952): 163–85; Michael Bliss, "Fielding's Bill of Fare in *Tom Jones*," *ELH*, 30 (1963): 236–43; Martin Price, *To the Palace of Wisdom*, pp.292–304; Sheldon Sacks, *Fiction and the Shape of Belief* (Berkeley and Los Angeles: University of California Press, 1964), pp. 70–109; and Andrew Wright, *Henry Fielding: Mask and Feast*, pp. 1–56.

possess every convenience of life with an ugly woman, than a handsome one without any of these conveniences"), the renderings of polite euphemisms into specific terms ("Sophia, finding all her persuasions had no effect, began now to add irresistible charms to her voice. . . . *In a word*, she promised she would reward him to his utmost expectations"), the translations into "plain English" of heroic similes or other passages of mock-sublime rhetoric ("Twelve times did the iron register of time beat on the sonorous bell-metal, summoning the ghosts to rise and walk their nightly round—*In plainer language*, it was twelve o'clock") (III, 54; IV, 233, 235–36; my italics)—all work to bring the process of verbal purification and the author's struggle with a corrupt medium into the forefront of the reader's awareness and to equate plainness of language with bedrock truth.

Burlesque diction, Fielding argues in the Preface to *Joseph Andrews*, does not debase the characters and sentiments of the comic epic poem in prose any more than clothes, except "in vulgar opinion," make the man (I, 19). On the contrary, to understand the mock-heroic and other ironic passages we must in effect separate style from content, and this creates the illusion that we are independent of the verbal medium, that we have seen through it to the objective truth underneath. But it also conditions us to accept the surrounding language of straightforward narration, in which style and content appear harmonious, as above suspicion. The ironic vocabulary and the burlesque diction are verbal sacrifices offered up to the reader's (and Fielding's) distrust of language so that his "ordinary style" (as he himself calls it after one of the mock-heroic interludes in *Joseph Andrews*) (I, 273) may have by contrast all the force of plain-spoken truth.

The interpolated tales serve a similar function, though here it is not merely the "literary" language that is mocking itself but also the whole conventionalized art of narration. William B. Coley compares Fielding's method to that of Gide, for whom "the ideal work of art must contain within itself a paradigm or parody of itself. Properly devised, such a parody will appear to resolve the rivalry between the real world and the representation art makes of it in favor of the artistic representation. The effect is achieved by heightening the superlative and minute artifice of the parody, so that what surrounds it, the bulk of the work, seems 'real' by comparison."[8] The tales are examples of "cold" narration, conveyed "through our Ears," but the act of narration itself, the *telling* of the tale, is "subjected to the Eyes."

When the lady in the coach in *Joseph Andrews*, after a lively exchange of dialogue between Parson Adams and Mrs. Slipslop which contrasts sharply with the sudden stiffening of style in the tale that follows, launches into her ponderous account of "the unfortunate Leonora, if one can justly call a woman unfortunate whom we must own at the same time guilty and the author of her own calamity," Fielding does not let the world of Leonora displace, even temporarily, the world of Parson Adams and his companions. Not only does he interrupt the tale himself with a chapter in his own most robust narrative style detailing the comic adventures of the company at the inn, but each of the passengers also interrupts the lady at various intervals in a manner which reminds us, even while we are attending to it, that the world of Leonora is at a considerable remove from the more immediate world in which her tale is being told. The tale itself, though not without a certain genteel irony in its own right, is one of romantic pathos; but the reactions of the listeners are broadly comic. Mrs. Grave-airs is priggishly censorious. "I never knew any of these forward sluts come to good," she says of Leonora's quite innocent fondness for Horatio. Mrs. Slipslop is a fountain of malapropistic cynicism. "More fool he," she says of Horatio's timidity in pressing his suit; "it is a sign he knew very little of our sect." Even the loud groans of sympathy with which Adams punctuates each new revelation of Leonora's folly are at comic variance with the elegant pathos of the tale; and his requests for details of dress and other irrelevant particulars, and his pedantic corrections of the lady's account of legal proceedings ("It is not very material," she says, hastening back to her story) and of her pronunciation of classical names, undercut its gravity of tone (I, 117, 119, 120, 124). The interruptions, in fact, are all of them comic variations on the theme of vanity which is also the moral of the cautionary tale, but the counterpoint of comedy and gravity enlarges that theme and frees it from identification with the artificial narrative form in which it is clothed.

Adams' interruptions of Mr. Wilson's story, which provides

[8]"Gide and Fielding," p. 13.

still another variation on the vanity theme, are generally more in harmony, perhaps, with the tone of Wilson's narrative ("the gentleman fetched a deep sigh, which Mr. Adams echoed very loudly"), but even here the informal language of the interruptions contrasts with the formal style of the tale and has the effect of making Adams' remarks more immediate and "real" than the narrative he is commenting on. We do not really listen to the tale so much as we watch Adams listen to it. And Wilson's homiletic observations on vanity ("Vanity is the worst of passions, and more apt to contaminate the mind than any other: for . . . the vain man seeks pre-eminence") are both extended and qualified by Adams' comic reaction:

Adams now began to fumble in his pockets, and soon cried out, "O la! I have it not about me." Upon this, the gentleman asking him what he was searching for, he said he searched after a sermon, which he thought his masterpiece, against vanity. "Fie upon it, fie upon it!" cries he; "why do I ever leave that sermon out of my pocket? I wish it was within five miles; I would willingly fetch it, to read it to you. . . . I am confident you would admire it: indeed I have never been a greater enemy to any passion than that silly one of vanity." The gentleman smiled, and proceeded. (I, 236, 242–43)

We also smile; and in the basic innocence of the kind of vain seeking for pre-eminence that even a Parson Adams can be guilty of we discover the comic corrective to Wilson's moral severity.

Similarly, the Man of the Hill in *Tom Jones*, though his story occupies the better part of six chapters, is not suffered to tell his tale in peace. Partridge's comic interruptions, along with Jones's attempts to silence Partridge (at one point Partridge interrupts the Man of the Hill to tell a story of his own, which is interrupted, in turn, by Jones) disrupt the pessimistic mood of the tale and undermine its misanthropic implications. Like the History of Leonora and Wilson's story, the Man of the Hill's tale is thematically relevant to the novel in which it occurs. His adventures demonstrate the ill effects of imprudence. But our awareness of Jones and Partridge as listeners enables us to be *more* than listeners ourselves. While the story is being conveyed through our ears, the circumstances of its telling are subjected to our eyes, and this gives us an added perspective on the total situation that creates an illusion of objectivity. Our consciousness that the story is being told by a fallible human being and that other points of view are possible, as suggested by the tonal and stylistic variations of the interruptions, encourages us to separate the "objective" elements of the story (those consistent with the more immediate world of Jones and Partridge) from the subjective (those at odds with that world). The moral that the hermit draws from his tale is that human nature is universally corrupt, but the moral the reader discovers is that one of the consequences of imprudence may be a mind so embittered by experience that it sees corruption even where it is not.

The most complex and extended use Fielding makes of this kind of juxtaposition of contrary points of view, however, is in *Amelia*, but here it is not the conflict of comedy and gravity which gives us the illusion of independence from the medium and agent of narration, but rather the conflict of sentiment and cynicism. The greater part of the first three books of the novel is given over to Booth's long and (in the opinion of most readers) tediously formal and undramatic account of his life with Amelia. But Fielding does not lose sight, even here, of the dramatic context in which Booth's story is being told, and it is only by taking this context into account that one can explain and justify Fielding's reliance on the method of "cold" narration. The scene is a London prison, and Booth, who has been arrested and unjustly sentenced for assaulting a watchman, is telling his story to Miss Matthews, an adventuress committed to prison for the murder of her lover. Against this grimly ironic backdrop Booth's sentimental story of his courtship and marriage unfolds. Sandwiched between the sordidly realistic glimpse of prison life in the opening chapters and the scene immediately following the conclusion of Booth's narrative in which he bribes the jailer and retires into a private cell with Miss Matthews and a bowl of rack-punch to pass the evening "in a manner inconsistent with the strict rules of virtue and chastity" (VI, 175), the vision of the saintly Amelia and her world of conjugal love and domestic happiness is not only placed at a decided rhetorical remove from the immediate world represented by the prison but also, because it is so at variance with the cynical tone of that world, seems a falsely sentimental idealization of reality.

Miss Matthews' cynical interruptions of Booth's story, more-over, like the comic interruptions of the grave interpolated tales in the earlier novels, have the effect of subverting this sentimental view of the world even while it is being presented. When Booth praises Amelia's "simplicity," for example, Miss Matthews interrupts to say that "it is highly generous and good in you to impute to honesty what others would perhaps call credulity" (VI, 71). In love with Booth herself and already resolved to seduce him, Miss Matthews' strategy is to flatter the husband and denigrate the wife. But it is rather as a representative of the apparently "realer" world of cynical self-interest that she is a serious rival to Amelia, and since the heroine does not appear herself as an immediate dramatic character until almost the middle of Book IV, we do not know at this point whether Booth's sentimental judgment of Amelia and the world or Miss Matthews' cynical view is the one Fielding wants us to accept.

It is significant, too, that many of Miss Matthews' interjec-tions, like the substitution of "credulity" for "simplicity," take the form of cynical inversions of Booth's sentimental vocabulary. In this novel, in which Fielding largely abandons the devices of verbal irony—probably because he had decided that verbal wit would be inconsistent with the high seriousness of tone that he here essayed for the first time in his fiction—Miss Matthews' corrections and emendations of Booth's words appear to have almost the same function as Fielding's ironic "translations" and definitions in his earlier works. But the difference is that just as he reverses his usual procedure in *Amelia* by making the point of view he wants us eventually to accept (Booth's) less immediate and dramatically "real," at first, than the alternate point of view he wants us to reject (Miss Matthews'), so neither does he follow here his customary method of using a word first in a corrupt sense and then "translating" it into "plain English." Instead, he usually allows Booth to introduce the word in its "proper and original" sense, and then lets Miss Matthews "corrupt" it. When Booth praises "love," for example, as "the best passion which the mind can possess," Miss Matthews ardently agrees—but only, as the subsequent dialogue reveals, because she takes the word in a baser sense. Her own experience, she declares, is proof of the power of "love." "I will join with you, madam, in that," says

Booth. "'Will you join with me?' answered she, looking eagerly at him—'Oh, Mr. Booth! I know not what I was going to say—What—Where did you leave off?—I would not interrupt you'" (VI, 127–28).

But when Amelia does at last appear as an objective presence, the dramatic equal, finally, of Miss Matthews and in the same grim milieu, significantly, of the prison, she instantly becomes a concrete realization of the true values of the words which Fielding had appeared to be trying to undermine. When Amelia rushes into the prison room, Miss Matthews expects from her the insults "of which virtuous women are generally so liberal to a frail sister." But she finds instead that Amelia's "virtue could support itself with its own intrinsic worth, without borrowing any assistance from the vices of other women; and she considered their natural infirmities as the objects of pity, not of contempt or abhorrence" (VI, 182). "Virtue," which under the influence of Miss Matthews we had perhaps been ready to equate with priggish self-righteousness, is here restored, in the person of Amelia, to its proper meaning, and though Miss Matthews and the other corrupt characters in the novel (the noble lord, Colonel and Mrs. James) continue to supply an alternative cynical point of view which sees Amelia as a prude and her values as hypocritical or naive, the sentimental point of view objectified in Amelia (and in Dr. Harrison and Sergeant Atkinson) is never again displaced as the higher standard of truth. Booth's surrender to Miss Matthews immediately after the conclusion of his story may seem at first to give the lie to the sentimental affirmation of true love and virtue of which he has been the spokesman. But the ultimate effect, after we have seen this sentimental view supported by dramatic exemplification, is once again rather to separate the objective truth from its subjective narrative agent. Booth may be personally weak and vacillating, but his sentimental view of life is confirmed by our own objective experience of the world of the novel.

If the happy ending of *Amelia* seems false, as most of Fielding's critics have complained, it is not because it is a sentimental betrayal of a pervasive cynicism in the novel, but rather because the melodramatic machinery of the forged will and the recovered inheritance fails to render in terms of plot Fielding's actual resolution of these conflicting points of view. For all his impatience with the doctrine of Virtue Rewarded as a serious moral principle, he can never resist rewarding his own heroes and heroines, and though the patent artificiality of his happy endings may be his way of dissociating the reward from the virtue (the *worthiness* of Booth and Amelia to enjoy a life of happiness and prosperity is the consequence of their virtue, but the actual *opportunity* is the consequence of the chance discovery of the false will), the effect in *Amelia* is to distract us from the genuine triumph of the sentimental overview that he insists on. For it is not by means of the happy ending that Fielding earns his right to this overview but by means of the dramatic realization of goodness that is Amelia.

But if the interpolated tales and other internal narrations are surrogates of the narrative process, sacrifices to Fielding's distrust of verbal professions, they are not the final surrogates or the final sacrifice. The critics who have complained that Fielding's "intrusive" authorial commentary is more vivid than "the main currents of narrative" have read him correctly in spite of themselves, for just as Parson Adams' commentary on Wilson's story is more immediate, more "real," and, finally, more significant than the narrative it interrupts, so are Fielding's "intrusive" interruptions of his own narration. The author who appears in the novel himself as an overt and "interested" commentator and who is constantly making his presence felt through ostentatious elevations of style, through the self-ridicule or mocking self-congratulation of the chapter headings, and through what Ian Watt calls an "intrusive patterning of plot"[9]—this intrusive author is the final surrogate. "He comes in effect to stand for the 'reality,'" as William B. Coley puts it, "that we always suspected was behind the mystery of artifice."[10] He is the objective representative within the novel of the subjective human agency of truth.

One of the most interesting developments of Fielding's career as a dramatist is his movement away from the conventional realistic comedy of manners toward a hybrid form of satiric burlesque in which an author-character appears as a kind of

[9]*Rise of the Novel*, p. 287.
[10]"Gide and Fielding," p. 14.

chorus to comment on a play within the play.[11] The device, of course, is not original with Fielding, any more than is the apparatus of the dramatized author in the novels. The dramatic burlesques are firmly in the tradition of the *Rehearsal* comedy; and Cervantes, Scarron, Marivaux, and LeSage provide ample precedents for such narrative mannerisms of the intrusive author as the ironic commentary, the conversations with hypothetical readers, the facetious chapter headings, and the burlesque diction, as well as for the use of interpolated tales as narrations within narrations. But Fielding's refinement on these devices reveals a consistency of serious purpose which seems to go beyond the spirit of pure literary burlesque in his predecessors and contemporaries. As early as 1739, before he had even begun his career as a novelist, we find him in the *Champion* already exhibiting a philosophical interest in the problem of authorial self-knowledge and self-objectification, and looking, as always, to Locke for a possible solution:

Writing seems to be understood as arrogating to yourself a Superiority (which of all others will be granted with the greatest Reluctance) of the Understanding. In which, as the Pre-eminence is not so apparent as in Beauty or Riches, Pride is often able in our Minds a long while to maintain the weaker Side of the Argument. *The Understanding, like the Eye,* (says Mr. *Lock*) *whilst it makes us see and perceive all other Things, takes no Notice of itself; and it requires Art and Pains to set it at a Distance and make it its own Object.* This Comparison, fine as it is, is inadequate: For the Eye can contemplate itself in a Glass, but no

[11] In *The Author's Farce*, for example, Luckless, the "Master of the Show," watches a production of "The Pleasures of the Town," his written-to-order farce, and comments cynically from the wings on its moral and esthetic implications. In *Tumble-Down Dick* the author Fustian discusses a performance of his tragedy "Phaeton in the Suds" with the impresario Machine and the critic Sneerwell; and in *Pasquin* Fustian and Sneerwell are joined by the comedian Trapwit to provide a running commentary on Trapwit's comedy "The Election" and Fustian's tragedy "The Life and Death of Common Sense." The burlesque classical tragedy of *Eurydice* is accompanied by the comments of an anonymous Author and Critic, *The Historical Register* has remarks by Medley and Sourwit, and Sourwit appears again as commentator in the afterpiece *Eurydice Hissed.* Fielding's most famous burlesque play, *Tom Thumb*, is not of the Rehearsal type, but in its expanded version as *The Tragedy of Tragedies* the pseudo-editor Scriblerus Secundus performs a similar function in the prefatory matter and notes; and in *The Grub Street Opera* Scriblerus appears in the Introduction scene as "a sort of walking Notes" (p. iii of the original 1731 London edition titled *The Welsh Opera*) similar to the "Author" who appears in the Introduction scene of *Don Quixote in England.*

Narcissus hath hitherto discovered any Mirrour for the Understanding, no Knowledge of which is to be obtained but by the Means Mr. *Lock* prescribes, which as it requires Arts and Pains, or in other Words, a very good Understanding to execute, it generally happens that the Superiority in it, is a Cause tried on very dark and presumptive Evidence, and a Verdict commonly found by self Love for ourselves.[12]

With the exception of the whitewashing biographer of *Jonathan Wild*, whose corrupt values and vocabulary must be regularly inverted by the reader, none of Fielding's narrators is a full-blown satiric *persona*. They are rather projections, part caricature and part idealization, of Fielding's own authorial mind. The intrusive commentary, the digressions, the chats with hypothetical readers, the self-conscious rhetorical flourishes, and other mannerisms are not just comic tricks at the expense of the narrative tradition. They are the "Art and Pains" required to set the author's mind "at a Distance and make it its own Object." They are a "Mirror for the Understanding" in which the thinking mind that assumes responsibility for the artifice and the rhetoric as well as for the ethical norms of the narrative is itself made an objective image, a sharper and more compelling image, often, than any of the characters of the fictional worlds for which he is the agency because he is closer to the reality which we ourselves inhabit. Henry James observes that Tom Jones as a character lacks "reality of mind" but that "his author—*he* handsomely possessed of a mind—has such an amplitude of reflexion for him and round him that we see him through the mellow air of Fielding's fine old moralism, fine old humour, and fine old style, which somehow enlarge, make every one and every thing important."[13] We do not have to take Fielding's superiority of understanding on faith. It is abundantly exhibited in the prefatory chapters and other authorial digressions, and those critics who have complained that these too often lack "any organic connection with the story"[14] have missed the point of Fielding's careful separation of commentary and narrative which, like the

---

[12]*Champion*, Mar. 1, 1739/40. The Locke quotation is from the Introduction to *An Essay Concerning Human Understanding*, Sec. 1.
[13]Preface to *Princess Casamassima, The Art of the Novel*, ed. R. P. Blackmur (New York: Scribner's, 1947), p. 68.
[14]Cross, 2: 103.

division of words and meanings in the ironic vocabulary and of style and content in the burlesque diction, is a separation in the interests of an ultimate and higher reunification. The drama of the author in the act of composition and cogitation, theorizing about his art and about the human nature that is his subject, makes the author and the narrative, the theory and the practice, the precept and the example, the reality and the fiction, the word and the action, parts of a single continuum of truth.

The trouble with "mere narrative," as Fielding says in his defense of the "introductory chapters" of *Tom Jones*, is that it can be imitated more or less successfully by any competent hack, however ignorant or insincere, and that in fact the very success of narration may conceal the author's lack of such basic qualifications of "the true history writer" as "genius" (the union of "invention and judgment" which makes possible "a quick and sagacious penetration into the true essence of all the objects of our contemplation"), learning (which will enable the writer to test his own insights against the standards of "history and . . . belles-lettres"), "conversation" (experiential knowledge of the world at all levels of society), and "a good heart, . . . capable of feeling." But the introduction into the novel of essays and reflective passages where the author must step out from behind the protective illusionism of the narrative and confront the reader direct with his claims to genius, learning, conversation, and good nature may enable the reader "to distinguish what is true and genuine, in this historic kind of writing, from what is false and counterfeit" (IV, 154–60).

The "trite but true observation" at the beginning of *Joseph Andrews* "that examples work more forcibly on the mind than precepts" (I, 25) is not discredited by the author's ironic choice of *Pamela* and Cibber's *Apology* as illustrations. Instead it is given a surprising new vitality which emphasizes the truth of the observation as idea even while Fielding exposes its triteness of language. For his real point is that works like these are dangerous precisely because the bad examples they provide *are* more forcible than the pious precepts their authors profess, or, to put it another way, because the liveliness of the narrations blinds us to the shallowness of their authors. The author of *Joseph Andrews*, on the other hand, though he first appears, in keeping with the parodic purpose of the early chapters, in the familiar *persona* role of the naive innocent, admiring *Pamela* and the *Apology*, deferring to the rank of Lady Booby, and in general mistaking appearance for reality and profession for truth, soon begins to reveal positive qualities of mind and depths of understanding which complement and reinforce the values implicit in the narrative. The narrator, in a sense, grows and develops in moral awareness and understanding of human nature in much the same way that Joseph does. When he tells us at the beginning of Chapter X that "Joseph would not have had an understanding sufficient for the principal subject of such a book as this if he had any longer misunderstood the drift of his mistress," he is not only announcing an important stage of Joseph's development but is also signaling a significant shift in his own point of view; and when he explains to the reader that Joseph did not recognize the truth about Lady Booby sooner because of "an unwillingness in him to discover what he must condemn in her as a fault" (I, 56), we are provided with a rationale for Joseph's earlier naivete that also serves to account for the naive pose of the narrator in the opening chapters and yet is consistent with the more serious function of both hero and narrator in the rest of the novel. For the author as much as the characters is an exemplification of the doctrine of good nature, and his tendency to accept characters at their face value until they condemn themselves by their actions is as objective an instance of the virtue of charity as an author who wants to show that he practices what he preaches can supply. "Upon the whole," he says in *Tom Jones*, explaining why he does not condemn Black George for stealing Jones's purse, "the man of candor and of true understanding is never hasty to condemn" (III, 335). The naivete of his narrators in the face of vice and folly is not Fielding's naivete, but the benevolent disposition of good nature which this pose of naivete at once caricatures and idealizes and so sets "at a Distance" is intended, we may assume, as a reasonably faithful mirror of his understanding.

But Fielding's sense that the implicit authorial claim to "Preeminence" of the understanding may often be merely an expression of "self Love" is reflected in his constant self-mockery and in his readiness to allow for alternate points of view. For authors,

like other men, and like other "professional" users of language
in particular, are prey to bias, interest, insincerity, ignorance,
and the other hazards of agent which contribute to the corruption of language, and especially are they subject to the temptation
of vanity. "The vanity of knowing more than other men," Fielding says in the Preface to the *Voyage to Lisbon*, "is, perhaps,
besides hunger, the only inducement to writing, at least to publishing, at all" (XVI, 183). But if this is so, and if the problem of
the serious writer, then, is to make his commitment to objective
truth transcend his vain desire for "Pre-eminence," the way of
coping with the problem is not to try to efface the author (for
this would be merely to dodge the issue) but to make the truth
independent of the author—not to pretend that he is free of
vanity and the other subjective limitations of agent, but to dis-
arm suspicion by making his subjectivity itself a dramatic fact
which the reader can apprehend objectively as part of the total
truth of human nature that the novel exists to illuminate.

Even in the *Voyage to Lisbon*, which is not a novel but a personal memoir where the narrative voice is surely his own,
Fielding deliberately involves himself in the general vanity of
authorship by declaring that his purpose is "to bring about at
once, like the revolution in the Rehearsal, a perfect reformation
of the laws relating to our maritime affairs" (XVI, 186). But the
allusion to Buckingham's burlesque play (in which a government is toppled by a gentleman usher and a doctor who simply
brandish their swords and then seat themselves in the chairs of
state), and the use of the terms "at once" and "perfect," do not
weaken Fielding's serious criticism of English maritime laws any
more than Gulliver's fatuous expectation of "seeing a full Stop
put to all Abuses and Corruptions" in England within six months
of the publication of his *Travels* weakens the force of Swift's
attacks on those abuses and corruptions. The effect in both cases
is to free the truth of the criticism from too close identification
with the fallible human voice that must deliver it, and though
Fielding's "authors" are not, except in *Jonathan Wild*, fully
developed satiric *personae* like Gulliver, his constant self-
dramatization, self-caricature, and self-mockery, especially in
Joseph Andrews and *Tom Jones*, serve a similar function of
dramatic objectification.

Thus in *Joseph Andrews*, in which vanity as "the common denominator of human kind" is a central theme, Fielding provides one of many narrative exemplifications of this truth in the scene in which the apparent zeal of Barnabas and the surgeon for public justice (in the prosecution of Joseph's assailant) turns out to be really a desire "to display their parts . . . before the justice and the parish." But the author, as Fielding never lets us forget, is a member of "human kind" too, and instead of resting content with the narrative representation of vanity Fielding pursues it beyond the world of the narrative into the more immediate world of the author himself. The narrative illusion of reality is shattered by the sudden intrusion of an invocation to Vanity in which the author not only advertises his presence through the radical elevation of style but carries the personal involvement even further by finally turning the implications of the address to Vanity against himself:

I know thou wilt think that whilst I abuse thee I court thee, and that thy love hath inspired me to write this sarcastic panegyric on thee; but thou art deceived: I value thee not a farthing; nor will it give me any pain if thou shouldst prevail on the reader to censure this digression as arrant nonsense; for know, to thy confusion, that I have introduced thee for no other purpose than to lengthen out a short chapter, and so I return to my history. (I, 82–83)

The spectacle of the author seemingly fleeing before the widening implications of his own theme and absolving himself of guilt only by denying the value of the digression in which the theme is stated is sufficiently diverting and paradoxical that our skepticism in the face of special pleading is effectively disarmed. The responsibility of final judgment as to the truth of his observations on Vanity and as to the validity of the narrative exemplification of the theme is shifted from the author to the reader. It is we who decide whether the digression is "arrant nonsense" or not, and in so doing we free the author from any suspicion on our part or his own that his superiority of understanding is "a Cause tried on very dark and presumptive Evidence, and a Verdict found by self Love" for himself. For even if we decide against him, we discover that our judgment confirms his point. The self-mockery of Fielding's narrators does not negate the moral and esthetic norms they stand for but rather lends them a more objective dimension of reality.

The narrator of *Joseph Andrews*, as we have seen, develops from a naive *persona* into a positive spokesman for Fielding's moral and esthetic norms. The author who in the early chapters labors mightily "to preserve the character" of Lady Booby out of consideration for her social class, is able, by the middle of the novel, to offer a "dissertation concerning high people and low people" (I, 47, 179–82) which is a witty anatomy of social snobbery; and the author who in the prefatory chapter to Book II (the first instance of Fielding's use of the prefatory chapter) defends the practice of chapter divisions with a mixture of pedantry and duncery reminiscent of the hack-*persona* of Swift's *Tale of a Tub*, has become practically indistinguishable in the introductory chapter to Book IV ("Matters Prefatory in Praise of Biography") from the author of the Preface, where Fielding, learned and wise but carrying his erudition and wisdom as lightly as charm, unabashedly speaks *in propria persona*. The verbal irony of the first part of the novel, as when he tells us that "it was by keeping the excellent pattern of his sister's virtues before his eyes, that Mr. Joseph Andrews was chiefly enabled to preserve his purity in the midst of such great temptations," is usually as much at the expense of the narrator as of the characters; but in the later chapters, as when he says of the squire who sets his dogs on Parson Adams that "This gentleman was generally said to be a great lover of humor; but, not to mince the matter, . . . he was a greater hunter of men" (I, 27, 269), it is primarily an irony of corrupt language in which the author's translations into "plain English" become the standard of truth.

The author of *Joseph Andrews* earns his own way, through self-objectification, into our trust and confidence. He earns the right, through the purifications of irony, to speak truth directly and to be taken at his word. But he is mindful to the end of the hazards of authorial vanity and of the dangers of taking himself too seriously. Rarely does he allow any profession or precept, however faithfully it may represent his own belief, to pass without a challenge. Joseph is clearly speaking for Fielding when he delivers an eloquent speech to Parson Adams on charity, articulating not only Fielding's basic moral theme but also his Shaftesburian philosophy of ridicule as the test of truth: "I defy the wisest man in the world to turn a true good action into ridicule." But instead of arousing Adams to applause, Joseph's eloquence (which is also, of course, Fielding's) puts him fast asleep, and anticipating that it may affect some of his readers the same way, the author announces at the end of the preceding chapter that "Joseph made a speech on charity, which the reader, if he is so disposed, may see in the next chapter; for we scorn to betray him into any such reading without first giving him warning" (I, 264–66). Even when he is most anxious that his readers should take him seriously Fielding does not abandon the objective perspective which allows for other points of view, and in so doing, of course, he reinforces our confidence in his own fairness, and hence in his own judgment, even while persuading us that we are independent of it.

The surrogate author of *Tom Jones*, though in general less a caricature than the narrator of *Joseph Andrews* and more of a positive spokesman for Fielding, similarly refuses to take himself too seriously. "I never make my reader laugh heartily," he declares, "but where I have laughed before him; unless it should happen at any time that instead of laughing with me he should be inclined to laugh at me" (IV, 160). The latter possibility is particularly emphasized in the chapter headings, which Fielding uses as a kind of extra-textual commentary not only on the narrative but also on the internal commentary which accompanies it and on the deportment of the author as both narrator and commentator. The author of the chapter heads is coequal with the narrator ("Being Much the Longest of All *Our* Introductory Chapters") (my italics), but he is closer yet to the world of the reader because he is himself operating now as a critical reader of the finished text, providing an extra ironic dimension on the material by offering his own partly detached, partly "interested" afterthoughts. These second thoughts are sometimes vain ("A Short Hint of What We Can Do in the Sublime"), sometimes modest ("Containing Little or Nothing"), but the effect, when the heading is anything more than a neutral description of contents, is nearly always to undercut the seriousness or pretensions of the author as he appears in the text proper and make his human limitations a part of the objective scene we are invited to judge. It is the author himself who assumes responsibility for Squire Allworthy's solemn lecture to Jenny on the virtue of chastity, "Containing Such Grave Matters that the Reader Cannot Laugh Once through the Whole Chapter, Unless Peradventure He Should Laugh at the Author" (III, 36, 105, 145; IV, 58).

Even in *Amelia*, where the narrator would seem for the most part to speak directly for Fielding and where most of the playful mannerisms of self-objectification have disappeared, the chapter headings are still sometimes facetious enough to supply an objective overview which sets both the author and his gravity of tone at an ironic distance: "In Which the Author Appears to be Master of that Profound Learning Called the Knowledge of the Town" (VII, 155). But the author of *Amelia* is most clearly seen in his dialogues with hypothetical readers. For in seeking to objectify the process of narration in his novels Fielding does not forget that the reader is a party to this process as well as the author. Just as the presence of listeners representative of alternate points of view gives us an objective perspective on the interpolated tales which allows us to be more than listeners ourselves, so the dramatic interplay between author and assumed readers of the novels enables us in a sense to be more than mere readers because we seem to stand outside a completed circuit of communication. We read, as it were, over the shoulders of the assumed readers within the novel and so are able to view the whole process of communication as a dramatic action which may be judged, like other actions, objectively. The story, as with the interpolated tales, may be conveyed through our ears, but the telling of it is subjected to our eyes.

As in the other novels, the narrator of *Amelia* addresses a divided audience of "good natured," sentimental readers on the one hand and of cynical, "critical" readers on the other, and is concerned lest the latter should be bored or disgusted by scenes of sentiment or passages of moral seriousness. "This little dialogue," he says of the tender scene in which Amelia instructs her children in the elements of morality, "we are apprehensive, will be read with contempt by many" (VI, 191). But unlike the narrators of the earlier novels, the author of *Amelia* assumes that the majority of his audience (like the "good-natured reader" he addresses in the Dedication, who, "if his heart should be here affected, will be inclined to pardon many faults for the pleasure he will receive from a tender sensation") (VI, 12) are "with" him already and do not need to be persuaded or cajoled into sympathy with his sentimental and moralistic point of view.

The narrator of *Jonathan Wild*, by contrast, is writing primarily for readers who share his own inverted values and vocabulary. He refuses to describe a "scene of tenderness" between Mr. and Mrs. Heartfree because it is "too low and contemptible to be recounted to our great readers." He recognizes that some of his audience belong to "that pitiful order of mortals who are in contempt called good-natured," and in fact it is for the benefit of these "vulgar" readers that he supplies the "plain English" translations of the corrupt language of "greatness": "And, should I speak in the language of a man who estimated human happiness without regard to that greatness which we have so laboriously endeavored to paint in this history, it is probable [Wild] never took (*i.e.* robbed the prisoners of) a shilling which he himself did not pay too dear for" (II, 51, 77, 157). But he clearly regards these good-natured readers as a minority.

In *Amelia* this minority readership has become the majority, and even greatness itself is offered an opportunity to redeem itself by identifying with good nature. When Booth bribes a war office toady whom the author refers to as a "great man," Fielding invites "my good-natured reader" to reflect on the injustice of such abuse of public office and then adds, "And if any such reader as I mention should happen to be in reality a great man, and in power, perhaps the horror of this picture may induce him to put a final end to this abominable practice of touching, as it is called" (VII, 268). Some accommodation, it is true, is still made in *Amelia* for hypothetical readers of other persuasions. When Booth, telling his story to Miss Matthews, begins to describe his parting with Amelia, the narrator interrupts to announce that he will "place this scene in a chapter by itself, which we desire all our readers who do not love, or who perhaps do not know the pleasure of tenderness, to pass over." But the dichotomy of viewpoint between sentimental and "critical" readers is made to parallel that between the sentimental Booth and the cynical Miss

Matthews. Having concluded his account of his departure, Booth apologizes to Miss Matthews for "having obtruded upon you" a scene which may have "been tiresome to you," for "no one is capable of tasting such a scene who hath not a heart full of tenderness, and perhaps not even then, unless he hath been in the same situation" (VI, 111, 117). The alternate point of view is allowed for, but, identified with Miss Matthews, it is discredited.

But if Fielding speaks more directly through his narrator in *Amelia* than in the earlier novels, relying less on both verbal irony and the irony of dramatized authorship, it is also because he is assuming a continuity with the earlier novels that makes any elaborate scheme of verbal purification and self-objectification unnecessary. At the beginning of the second chapter the author interrupts the account of Booth's trial to "premise some things which it may be necessary for thee to know," and this, he says, is *"after our usual manner"* (my italics). When he offers to set the scene of Booth's leavetaking in a separate chapter, he says he will, *"according to our usual custom,* endeavor to accommodate ourselves to every taste" (my italics). And when he invites the "critical reader" who "may have the same doubt with Miss Matthews" about the validity of Booth's sentimental view of human nature, to use the chapter break to consider "Whether we have, in this place, maintained or deviated from that strict adherence to truth which we profess above all other historians" (VI, 15, 75, 111), he is referring not to any profession made in *Amelia* but to the frequent claims by the author of *Joseph Andrews* and *Tom Jones* that he is determined "to guide our pen throughout by the directions of truth" (III, 107). The first Book of *Amelia* establishes a continuity with the "usual manner" by means of a prefatory chapter in the manner of *Tom Jones*, a digression in Chapter II on public magistrates in the familiar ironic style ("I own I have been sometimes inclined to think that this office of a justice of peace requires some knowledge of the law") (VI, 17), and a mock-heroic simile in Chapter VI describing Miss Matthews that is as ludicrous as any in *Joseph Andrews* or *Tom Jones*. But with the principle of continuity of authorship thus established, Fielding is able after Book I to dispense for the most part not only with the burlesque apparatus of self-objectification but also with the ironic rhetoric of the earlier novels, both of which he no doubt felt would be inconsistent with his high seriousness of tone and purpose in *Amelia*.

Many of the same words and locutions that he had habitually used ironically in his previous writings, in fact, appear in *Amelia* as straightforward expressions of truth. When Booth bursts into tears upon describing Amelia's courageous acceptance of the fact that her beauty has been spoiled by a broken nose, the author assures us that his tears were such "as are apt to flow from a truly noble heart at the hearing of anything surprisingly great and glorious" (VI, 67). The natural response of the reader who has come to *Amelia* from *Joseph Andrews* and *Tom Jones* is to read such a passage ironically. But he will soon find that there is no support given for such a reading. When Fielding says that Amelia's courage was "great and glorious" he means precisely and literally that, and he is choosing his words, we may be sure, with deliberation. But at the same time we cannot assume that he was unaware of the reader's temptation, on the basis of the author's previous practice as well as the reader's natural suspicion of hyperbole, to read a mocking intent into such a passage. Perhaps Fielding wants (or at least *expects*) his reader to be misled until such time as Amelia herself is allowed to appear on the scene and reveal the justness of the language applied to her, just as he probably expects us to find Miss Matthews' cynical view of Booth's matrimonial adventures more "realistic" at first than Booth's sentimental version. But when, toward the end of the novel, Booth guiltily tells Amelia, "I can't sup with you to-night" (because he has a secret engagement with Miss Matthews), and Fielding uses a heroic simile to describe Amelia's disappointment—

As in the delightful month of June, when the sky is all serene, and the whole face of nature looks with a pleasing and smiling aspect, suddenly a dark cloud spreads itself over the hemisphere, the sun vanishes from our sight, and every object is obscured by a dark and horrid gloom; so happened it to Amelia, . . . and with a faint trembling voice she repeated her husband's words, "Not sup with me to-night, my dear!" (VII, 284)

—he clearly expects us by this time to be sufficiently committed to the sentimental point of view to accept the sublimity of language at its face value as wholly appropriate to the expression of domestic pathos.

The narrator of *Tom Jones* is also at least partly in earnest in his sublime introduction of Sophia. The elevated passage beginning "Hushed be every ruder breath," while gaily facetious in tone, contains scarcely a single false note of the bathos which Fielding elsewhere employs to puncture his own inflated rhetoric, and the concluding invocation of his beloved first wife, "one whose image never can depart from my breast, and whom, if thou dost remember, thou hast then, my friend, an adequate idea of Sophia," can certainly not have been meant in a mocking vein. Yet the afterthought commentary of the chapter heading—"A Short Hint of What We Can Do in the Sublime"—provides the objective perspective which sets even the most heartfelt and sincere effusions of the author at an ironic distance; and the disquisition on the rhetorical license permitted the writer of a "heroic, historical, prosaic poem" in the preceding prefatory chapter, distinguishing between the "similes, descriptions, and other kind of poetical embellishments" and the "plain matter of fact" of the narrative proper, frankly identifies such "ornamental parts of our work" as expressions of the author's sensibility. He pleads, with some seriousness we may assume, the precedent of "our tragic poets, who seldom fail to prepare their audience for the reception of their principal characters," but then proceeds to undercut his own pretensions by also citing the precedents of theater managers with their kettledrums and troops of scene-shifters, and, finally, of politicians, who, like the lord mayor in his annual procession, recognize the utility of pomp and pageantry. His own intention, he concludes, is thus "to introduce our heroine with the utmost solemnity in our power, with an elevation of style . . . proper to raise the veneration of our reader," for "I must confess that even I myself . . . have yielded not a little to the impressions of much preceding state" (III, 143–47). A similar distinction between the rhetoric of the author and the objective "matter of fact" of the narrative action is implicit in the Preface to *Joseph Andrews* when Fielding declares that though he has admitted burlesque "in our diction, we have carefully excluded it from our sentiments and characters" (I, 19), and even the narrator of *Jonathan Wild* recognizes the sacred obligation of the "historian" to adhere "faithfully to the matter, though he embellishes the diction with some flourishes of his own eloquence" (II, 116). Only in *Amelia* does Fielding treat matter and diction as an inseparable unity. Only in *Amelia* does he permit himself the unqualified luxury of expressing the truths of sincerity in her own "distinct terms."

"Now, it is well known," he says in the prefatory chapter to the last book of *Tom Jones*, comparing the relationship of author and reader to that of travelers who, after a long journey together, are now arriving at the parting of the ways, "that all jokes and raillery are at this time laid aside; whatever characters any of the passengers have for the jest-sake personated on the road are now thrown off, and the conversation is usually plain and serious" (V, 293). The privilege Fielding claims in the last book of *Tom Jones* to lay aside his irony and his mock rhetoric and to throw off the character he has "personated" as narrator, he also claims in his last novel. He does not have to "purify" his medium by irony or erect an elaborate mirror for his understanding because that work has already been done. In *Amelia* he demands nothing less than the right he has earned in his earlier writings to use language directly and literally—to deliver himself at last of the plain-spoken truth that he had made it the business of his life to rescue from the contaminating corruptions of language.

INDEX